Shaping History

Featuring extraordinary personal accounts, this book provides a unique window through which to examine some of the great political changes of our time, and reveals both the potential and the challenge of narrating the political world. Molly Andrews' novel analysis of the relationship between history and biography presents in-depth case studies of four different countries, which offer insights into controversial issues such as the lifelong commitment to fight for social justice in England; the explosion of patriotism in the post-9/11 USA; East Germans' ambivalent reactions to the fall of the Berlin Wall; and the pressures on victims to tell certain kinds of stories while testifying before South Africa's Truth and Reconciliation Commission (TRC). Each of the case studies explores the implicit political worldviews which individuals impart through the stories they tell about their lives, as well as the wider social and political context which makes some stories more 'tell-able' than others.

MOLLY ANDREWS is Reader in the School of Social Sciences, Media and Cultural Studies, and Co-director of the Centre for Narrative Research, at the University of East London.

Shaping History
Narratives of Political Change

MOLLY ANDREWS

CAMBRIDGE
UNIVERSITY PRESS

CAMBRIDGE UNIVERSITY PRESS

Cambridge, New York, Melbourne, Madrid, Cape Town, Singapore, São Paulo

Cambridge University Press
The Edinburgh Building, Cambridge CB2 8RU, UK

Published in the United States of America by Cambridge University Press, New York

www.cambridge.org
Information on this title: www.cambridge.org/9780521604697

© Molly Andrews 2007

First published 2007

Printed in the United Kingdom at the University Press, Cambridge

A catalogue record for this publication is available from the British Library

ISBN 978-0-521-84365-2 hardback
ISBN 978-0-521-60469-7 paperback

For Charlotte and Peter
Long may you ask questions about how the
world works
And continue to care about what is fair

Contents

Acknowledgements

As this book covers the four main studies with which I have been involved over the past two decades, it would be impossible to list all of those who have influenced my thinking, and helped me along the way. There are some, however, who stand out, those without whom the research would not have been as rich, and may not even have happened.

I wish to thank Wolfgang Edelstein, of the Max Planck Institute in Berlin. From the first moment I described to him the project I wished to pursue, he believed in it, and in my ability to carry it out. His kindness and support were so important to me. Birgit Schmidt and Stefan Walter always made me feel welcome in their home in Berlin where I shared a room with their newborn daughter. They acted as friends, translators, and great supports.

The Women's Studies faculty at Dartmouth College were very welcoming to me during my six months' sabbatical there. Jeff and Maureen Doyle define for me 'the kindness of strangers' by offering my family their wonderful home on the riverbanks in the woods just outside Norwich, Vermont.

Ongoing conversations with Cathy Riessman, Mark Freeman, and Jens Brockmeier have always pushed my thinking further. I thank Elliot Mishler for inviting me to present an earlier version of my patriotism paper (chapter 4 in this volume) to the Narratives Group which met at his home. This was a deeply rewarding experience for me; the feedback I received could not have been more critically supportive and, indeed, helped me to find my own voice narrating the fall-out of 9/11. Corinne Squire and Maria Tamboukou are exemplary colleagues and friends, and our work together building the Centre for Narrative Research has been rewarding in many ways. Anna

Constanstas' help in the final stages of copy-editing was much appreciated. Shirin Rai's careful reading of draft chapters of this book illustrates why she will always be my 'connected critic'.

Thank you to my parents, Joan and Peter Andrews, for bringing their six kids with them to the anti-war demonstrations in the 1970s in Washington, DC; this, and other adventures, instilled in all of us a love of political stories.

Charlotte, Peter, and Ted have kept me sane all the while. I will never forget Peter's question to me as we sat watching the events of 9/11 unfold on the television. Barely four years old, he turned to me and asked 'Mommy, do the baddies think they are goodies?' It might be mother's pride, but I have not heard a more pertinent question than this about those fateful events and what followed in their wake. Peter and Charlotte, your inquiring minds help me to think better.

Finally, and most importantly, I acknowledge those women and men who have participated in my research. All of them gave of their time selflessly, and it is because of this that we have the possibility of looking through the window of their lives onto some of the most tumultuous events of our times.

I   History, biography, and political narratives

The year is 1992. I am in East Berlin, in the living room of Wolfgang Templin, the man Erich Honecker, Secretary General of the East German Communist Party from 1971 to 1989, once identified as the 'number one enemy of the state'. Three years have passed since the fall of the Berlin Wall, and life has changed considerably since that time for Templin, and for his country. In 1987 he, along with a handful of other leading anti-state activists, had been exiled from the country. He and his family ended up living in West Berlin. I ask Templin to tell me about his experience of the night of November 9, 1989.

He responds with great warmth: finally, after nearly two years away, he was allowed to 'come home'. Fighting against the crowds pouring into the west, Templin made his way back into East Germany:

> I immediately rang friends and said, if the Wall comes down, then my route back into the GDR [German Democratic Republic, or East Germany] is free, and I was ecstatic … the fall of the Wall for me meant that I could go back into the GDR rather than get out of it. And purely physically I experienced this – everybody pushing past me in the opposite direction and me pushing against the stream the other way. I was overjoyed and it was in that mood that I re-entered the GDR … Two, three weeks later … my family moved back here.

Templin's story is most compelling, for a number of different reasons. At one level, it is a simple tale of a family man who has finally been allowed to return to the land of his birth, a land that he loves and to which he has dedicated his life. He was forced to leave, and he is now allowed to return. He is 'overjoyed'.

But there is much more to this story than Templin's personal happiness: implicitly his account challenges the received wisdom of the meaning of the fall of the Berlin Wall. As Templin expands on his overpowering feelings of that night and the weeks that followed, I am forced to try to understand what lies beneath his reaction to these events. This requires contemplating a political framework which is significantly different from the one most often used to explain the radical changes of 1989. Why wasn't he dancing on the Wall, drinking champagne, with all the other revellers that fateful night? More challenging still, why, having managed to 'escape' from East Germany, did he move back, once circumstances made this possible? Templin's account raises these, and many more, questions.

For the last two decades, I have been talking with, and listening to, people like Wolfgang Templin, trying to understand the broader meaning of the stories they tell me about their lives. For I am convinced that there is a profound sense in which the personal is political, and the political is personal. It is through the minutiae of daily life that human beings access the political ripples, and tidal waves, of their times.

This book is about the relationship between the stories people tell about their lives, and the political frameworks which form the context for those stories. When we relate stories of our lives, we implicitly communicate to others something of our political worldviews, our *Weltanschauung*. But why are some stories selected and others ignored? Facts do not speak for themselves. We choose certain facts, and hope that they will speak for us, through us. But what do we think we will achieve by telling our stories in the way that we do, to the people we do? What is it that makes us interpret the events of our time in one way and not another? Who do we perceive ourselves as being in relation to those events? How actively are we engaged in trying to shape our political environment? What do we identify as being primary forces for change in our lives? To what group or groups do we feel we belong, and how, if at all, does this contribute to our understanding of the political universe?

I have been fascinated with these questions since I was a child. And perhaps it is not surprising that it is so, given my own background.

I first came to political consciousness in the late 1960s, living in Washington, DC. The Watergate Affair which unfolded in the early 1970s was for me local news, and I was utterly transfixed by it. I personally knew the children of some of the key players in this national saga, and I was forever perplexed by how people who seemed good could do things which were so blatantly wrong. For me, it was a simple question with no obvious answer.

I have dedicated myself to exploring the relationship between the personal and the political since that time, in a variety of contexts. This book is about that ongoing investigation, and the places it has taken me. Chapter 2 examines the challenges I have confronted in conducting my research, and explores who I am in relation to the stories I have collected. Stories are never told in a vacuum, and nor do we as researchers simply tabulate information which we gather. Rather, we feed into the process at every level, and our subjectivity is always a part of that which we are documenting. How, then, do we train ourselves to really listen to the stories of others? In this chapter I also consider the relationships I have built with the people who have participated in my research, and how this impacts on the stories they have told me, and my understanding of these stories. I explore, too, what makes some stories more 'tell-able' than others, and question the extent to which it is ever possible to 'read' silence, or the 'not told'.

Each of the next four chapters has as its focus a case study. Chapter 3 discusses a study I conducted with fifteen British lifetime socialist activists who had been politically active for fifty years or longer, from the perspective of twenty years of hindsight. What is it that looking back over that project teaches me now about who I was then? How has this research continued to function in my life, after many of the original participants have died? And what remains with me from our conversations together, where I explored how they had sustained their commitment to work for social change throughout the course of their long lives?

Chapter 4 presents research I conducted in Colorado Springs, Colorado, during the Gulf War of 1992, interviewing anti-war activists. I was fascinated by the American flag they sometimes waved at their 24/7 vigil which they held in the midst of winter in the Rocky Mountains. What did this mean to them? What does this research mean to me now? This chapter examines the way in which national narratives of patriotism and belonging have evolved since the time I conducted my research, including an analysis of the impact of 9/11 on this discourse.

Chapter 5 focuses on the work I conducted in East Germany in 1992, immediately after the opening of the Stasi files. At that time I spoke with forty people who had been leaders in the 'bloodless revolution' of 1989, curious to know what sense they made of the transformation of their country. How did the hopes and dreams which motivated their underground anti-state activism in the years before 1989 compare to the reality in which they found themselves in the early 1990s? How did they make sense of the changes which had occurred? And how did these stories compare with the ones which saturated western media at that time?

Chapter 6 uses some of the testimonies presented before South Africa's Truth and Reconciliation Commission (TRC) to examine the role of national storytelling in the building of the new South Africa. What is the relationship between the tales of the 22,000 people who gave testimony to the TRC and the collective memory of that country? Who and what determines which stories ultimately become woven into the national narrative? Here, also, I discuss the ethical dilemmas faced by researchers who have as their focus traumatised societies to which they, themselves, do not belong.

Finally, chapter 7 makes comparisons across the four case studies, and offers some concluding comments.

The sequence of the chapters in this book mirrors the chronology of when I conducted the research which underpins them. I feel that this is important because, as I will discuss, the projects built upon each other in subtle but important ways; insights which came from earlier experiences were revisited, usually revised, and often endowed with new relevance. This book, then, provides an account not only of the particular case studies, but also of my own intellectual development.

OLD AND NEW STORIES

While I have written and published on each of the four case studies presented in this book, it is my hope that here I am able to offer a new way of looking at these projects, not only individually, but also in relation to each other. I have not tried to encapsulate arguments which I have made elsewhere, though I have indicated these in the references cited in the bibliography. Rather, it has been my intention to explore the new and unfolding meanings that I continue to find in each of these research endeavours.

Previously, I have argued that there is never in any research a final end-point from which one can decipher ultimate meaning (Andrews forthcoming). Rather, even data which appear to stay constant, such as transcripts, change their meaning over time, just as we ourselves come to see new and different aspects of our research. In this way, old stories actually become new stories; quite simply, over time we find new layers of meaning in them. It is not that this new perspective is more adequate than that which we previously held; but it is grounded in a different standpoint, the place from which we presently see the world.

This then is what these pages contain; an exploration of what it means to look back on work I have conducted over the past twenty years, and to take account of the ways in which altered circumstances in my life, combined with altered historical circumstances, have caused me to view things differently than I originally did. Revisiting the political stories I have researched in England, East Germany, the USA and South Africa has brought me to a new understanding of the changes, both within these countries and within myself. There are different, and sometimes overlapping, arguments which can be made for revisiting old data (Andrews forthcoming). While some of these focus on logistical and financial constraints, epistemologically the most powerful of these relates to altered personal and political changes. Writing this book has been an exercise in identifying those changes, and examining their implications for my research.

Revisiting my study on lifetime socialist activists has made me think about all that has changed since the time of the original research. Most of the people who participated in that study have now died, and my own life circumstances have altered considerably. Although I do have ongoing conversations with a small number of the original respondents, the 'new' conversations have mostly come from my re-reading of the transcripts of our interviews and of the many letters sent to me by these women and men. It is clear to me that there were certain stories which I was more receptive to hearing than others. It is only in retrospect, for instance, that I have come to view the accounts of their relationships with their mothers as representing a fundamental challenge to the dominant psychological paradigms which attribute much blame to inadequate mothering (Andrews 2004).

Many people have argued that the USA has been irrevocably changed since the events of September 11, 2001. But the interviews which I collected nearly a decade earlier, in the wake of the first Gulf War, suggest a more complex picture. The debates about what it means to be an American, and the ways which are considered to be appropriate for expressions of a sense of national belonging, have long occupied American political discourse (Huntingdon 2004; Lieven 2003). Still, it is difficult to look at these data and try to remember the world before 9/11. In this chapter, I review not only the data I collected in 1992, but also my own struggles to come to terms with my insider/outsider position *vis-à-vis* the land of my birth. As I have lived outside of the USA for fifteen of the last twenty years, even some people who are close to me have commented that I can't understand the US retreat into uncritical patriotism which marked the post-9/11 world, because I 'wasn't there'. Wasn't it equally possible, I wondered, that 'not being there' had allowed me to see both more and less than those whose lives were more immediately and directly affected by those events? Here I explore the impact of my dual position of belonging and detachment on my research in the USA.

In my work in East Germany, it is a different kind of transformation that strikes me. More than fifteen years after the opening of the Berlin Wall, I now look back with an altered perspective on the time in which I gathered my data, in 1992, when East German society was saturated with debate about how to deal with the past, of both individuals and of the country. I can see in the very design of the project a certain romanticism on my part, a disposition which undoubtedly led me to seek out the exceptional people who had tried to reform the East German state for many years prior to the momentous changes of 1989. Now, in the twenty-first century, there are some who are still trying to make sense of what the forty years of state socialism meant for those who lived under its dictates, but for most people, Germans and non-Germans alike, East Germany is a land of the past; many of the themes addressed in chapter 5, however, suggest its continued importance in the political imagination of the East German people. It is, then, the very dramatically changed circumstances of East Germany in the intervening fifteen years since the time of unification which beckons me to revisit the meanings of the data I collected during the special window of political transformation which immediately followed the opening of the Berlin Wall.

My re-examination of my work with transcripts of South Africa's TRC has been illuminating to me not so much because of the changes in South Africa – though, of course, there have been many – but rather because this journey led me to confront directly some very uncomfortable issues. Over the years I came to view the work that people like myself had been doing as essentially voyeuristic. Because of the open availability of the transcripts of the TRC – published in books and on DVDs, and available on-line – it has been tempting to regard these data as legitimate material for anyone wishing to access it. But working with this material, combined with several trips to South Africa, has caused me to view the situation differently. This chapter outlines a number of overarching themes which I have observed in the material I have read, but avoids citing passages from traumatic testimony of individuals, as I no longer feel comfortable about my role in

replicating these accounts. This chapter represents my attempt to provide an analysis of the key narratives as I see them in the new South
Africa, while extending more respect to the individuals who have
suffered and continue to suffer there.

THE POWER OF POLITICAL NARRATIVES

Chilton and Schaffner (2002) identify two broad strands in their definition of politics:

> On the one hand, politics is viewed as a struggle for power, between
> those who seek to assert and maintain their power and those who seek
> to resist it ... On the other hand, politics is viewed as cooperation,
> as the practices and institutions a society has for resolving clashes
> of interest over money, power, liberty and the like.   *(2002: 4–5)*

What is appealing about this definition is its attempt to bring
together both the conflict and the cooperation which are an integral
part of any society. In this book, I am interested not only in how
people view struggles for power and attempts to resolve such struggles, but also in how they locate themselves within this process.
When I use the term 'political', I am interested in small 'p' politics
and its relationship to power: How do people understand the concept
of power, who do they think has power, over whom, to do what? Is
that power perceived as legitimate – and if so, from where does it
derive its legitimacy? Finally, how do people place themselves
within the political world that they identify? I am, then, interested
in what kinds of stories people tell about how the world works, how
they explain the engines of political change, and the role they see
themselves, and those whom they regard as being part of their group,
as playing in this ongoing struggle.

One of the key reasons I have been drawn to conduct research in
England, the USA, East Germany, and South Africa, was my attraction
to speaking with people as they lived through moments of acute
political change. Talking to lifetime socialists in Britain during the
height of Mrs Thatcher's reign as prime minister, or to American

anti-war activists who were willing to risk their physical safety as they protested the US military engagement in the Gulf War, or to East Germans in the wake of losing their country, or reading the transcripts of South Africans who had testified before the TRC – in each of these settings I was motivated to examine how politicised individuals understood the tumultuous political times in which they were living. What was the wider story which they built around the immediate headlines of their day? Where exactly did they locate themselves in these political narratives?

Yuval-Davis (2006: 201) argues that 'Identities are narratives, stories people tell themselves and others about who they are (and who they are not)'. But identity is something which is always in transition 'always producing itself through the combined processes of being and becoming, belonging and longing to belong. This duality is often reflected in narratives of identity' (2006: 201). These narratives of identity are thus always political, even when they are also personal, as they reflect the positionality of the speaker. Accordingly, the politics of belonging has been described by John Crowley as 'the dirty work of boundary maintenance' (cited in Yuval-Davis 2006: 203), separating the world population into 'us' and 'them' (Yuval-Davis 2006: 203). Each of the four case studies involves some kind of search for political belonging, be it the struggle of connected critics whose dissent stems from a sense of attachment to their still existing country (as in England and the USA), or in the context of their country which is no longer (as in East Germany), or the willingness of citizens to recount their tales of suffering in order to help rebuild their broken nation (as in South Africa). The question of who belongs and who does not – or the politics of belonging – 'has come to occupy the heart of the political agenda almost everywhere on the globe' (Yuval-Davis 2006: 212); this book provides insight into this insider/outsider struggle in four different geographic locations.

The last decade has witnessed an extraordinary explosion of interest in 'the biographical turn' (Bornat, Chamberlayne, and Wengraf 2000: 1), a complete paradigm shift which 'affects not only the orientations of a range of disciplines, but their interrelations with each other' (2000: 1). Part of this biographical turn has been the growth of the interest in, and proliferation of, narrative research, stretching across a vast array of academic disciplines. Narrative research generally, and personal narratives in particular, have been used as an analytic tool for trying to understand wider social phenomena. Stories and storytelling are no longer the province of the playroom, but rather are increasingly regarded as an important arena for serious scholarly investigation.

As noted by Bornat, Chamberlayne, and Wengraf (2000), an important component of this paradigm shift has been a movement towards an increased awareness of the potential of cross-disciplinary and multi-disciplinary research. This is perhaps one of the key reasons I have been drawn to narrative research, as it is sufficiently broad and flexible enough to be able to accommodate the interests represented by my undergraduate degree in political science and my PhD in psychology. What I was really interested in was neither the one discipline nor the other, but rather the shared ground between them. The more my education progressed, the more confident I became that the best way to explore this fertile ground was to listen to stories that people tell about their lives, as these personal stories know no disciplinary boundaries.

Over the past few years, there has been a growing volume of work on political narratives. Dienstag's work on the role of narrative and memory in political theory emphasises the importance of debates over the meaning of history, arguing that 'Human beings fight over history because they conceive their pasts to be an essential part of who they are. And they are right' (1997: 206). The research I conducted in East Germany, for instance, can be seen as an attempt to uncover a different framework of meaning of the events of 1989 from the triumphalist interpretation which was so dominant in the West.

Beginning with Aristotle's *Poetics*, narrative has generally been taken to indicate a temporal sequencing of events, which includes a beginning, middle, and an end (Dienstag 1997: 18). Considerations of time lie at the heart of narrative research (Ricoeur 1984, 1985, 1988), and thus, 'histories that human beings write are not "objective" accounts of events … [but] rather they are, like fictions, creative means of exploring and describing realities' (Andrews *et al.* 2000: 6–7). Clearly, this has profound implications for the political life of any society and its individuals: how are they to write their histories? What parts of the past should be represented in the national narrative? As I will argue in chapter 4, the dominant American narrative of 9/11, which begins on the morning the planes flew into the World Trade Center, has been strategically crafted in such a way as to make some interpretations much more unlikely and less supportable than others. And yet, a different kind of story might emerge were those events placed within a wider temporal framework. Similar questions of the boundaries of political narratives apply to South Africans: who was allowed to testify before the TRC, and what parameters were set around the kinds of stories they could tell? Clear guidelines directed narrators where their stories should begin and end, and thus the project of national remembering was carefully monitored. In analysing the stories gathered by the TRC, I explore the relationship between individual and collective memory, and the ways in which these come together in the grand project of weaving a sustainable new national narrative.

Narratives provide a very rich basis from which to explore political identities; critically, what an individual or a community choose to tell about themselves is intricately tied to how they construct their political identities. But, as Whitebrook (2001) argues, political identity is never a fixed term, and interpretations are always open to re-interpretations. Moreover, different people and different communities do not necessarily hear stories in the same way as the stories' narrators:

> The stories that constitute narrative political identity may be interpreted differently by tellers and listeners, and among

> listeners ... Persons are collectively and individually embedded
> in an ongoing history which in turn requires a process of
> interpretation; but that need for interpretation opens up further
> possibilities for identity narratives.   *(Whitebrook 2001: 40)*

In each of the case studies, I analyse my own interpretive process,
examining the ways in which my particular positioning may have
helped or hindered my ability to listen, a topic which is the focus of
chapter 2.

Polletta (2006: vii) argues that 'narrative's power stems from its
complexity'; the most effective political narratives are those which are
open to an array of interpretation. Narrative, she states:

> demands an effort of interpretation. Following a story means more
> than listening: it means filling in the blanks, both between unfold-
> ing events and between events and the larger point they add up to.
> When listeners or readers reach the story's end, they have the
> experience of loose ends being tied up.   *(2006: viii)*

Polletta focuses on the powerful potential of political narratives for
galvanising political movements, for whom 'Getting the story right ...
is of real political consequence' (2006: 1). Her book opens with a
captivating analysis of the US elections of 2004, attributing the
Republican victory to the party's ability to give voters 'villains and
heroes, new characters in age-old dramas of threat, vengeance, and
salvation' (2006: viii). Stories matter; they do things. In this book,
I shall examine how the narratives of particular individuals help us
to gain a more complex understanding of political turmoil and change.

The political identity of an individual is inextricably tied to
the narratives which are culturally available to that person. Political
identities are 'always, everywhere relational and collective' (Tilly
2002: 61); even when they are articulated by individuals, they are
always socially embedded. As Rice argues, 'The story of an individual
life – and the coherence of individual identity – depends, for its very
intelligibility, on the stories of collective identity that constitute a

culture ... cultures and societies organize individual identity' (2002: 80). Polletta (2002) echoes this, arguing that even in individual story-telling, 'plots are derived from a cultural stock of plots' (2002: 34). Exactly how one positions oneself in relation to dominant cultural narratives may vary from person to person, but all of us create our narratives from the 'toolkit' which is culturally available to us (Bruner 1987: 15). The British lifetime socialist activists, the American anti-war protestors, the East German dissidents, and those South Africans who testified before the TRC, are all individuals whose stories can be understood only within the cultural and political context in which they were produced. For this reason, each of the case studies presented in this book is firmly located within its particular context. While the narratives are produced by individuals, those individuals are social beings who are helping to shape history.

2 Reflections on listening

A good deal of my professional life has been spent gathering stories from people who are living in times of pronounced social and political change. I have long been interested in how people understand the historical moments in which they live, and how this understanding contributes to the ways in which they participate in these upheavals. Mostly, though not always, my research has led me into direct conversations with people whose lives have been marked by acute political change. Among the skills necessary for undertaking research of this kind, none is more important than the ability to listen, with a full recognition of the challenges that lie in such an endeavour.

In this chapter, I would like to reflect on the process of listening. Listening is one of the most vital skills a researcher can develop, and yet our professional training, far from teaching us to be good listeners, focuses our attentions away from those human qualities which might enhance our ability to discern intended meaning in the expression of others. Despite its central importance in our lives (not only in our capacity as researchers) our intellectual training does not include much on listening. Indeed, the skills of critical analysis teach us to engage in a very selective form of listening, one which is sensitised towards ferreting out the inconsistencies in the stories offered us. Yet, as Veena Das (1990) remarks, 'Even the most articulate among us face difficulties when we try to put ambiguous and jumbled thought and images into words. This is even more true of someone who has suffered traumatic loss' (1990: 348–349). Rather than attending to the variability of human emotion, staying with our speakers as they weave in and out of the experiences of their lives, we are trained to keep focused on our research agenda. Invariably this invites a premature dismissal of some topics as 'irrelevant'. As researchers, we forget that 'recounting and listening are serious tasks, worthy of unusual attention' (Greenspan 1998: 16). Semprun comments that that ability to hear requires 'patience, passion, compassion, as well as rigour' (cited in Apfelbaum 2001: 29). Listening is hard work, demanding as it does an abandonment of the self in a quest to enter the world of another; and it takes time.

Researchers do not necessarily become better listeners over time. Indeed, the development may be in the opposite direction: as we develop knowledge in our areas of expertise, we may become increasingly embedded in the arguments we construct and less open to entertaining opposing lenses of interpretation. Here, the important distinction between confidence and certainty becomes blurred. It is right that as we become more practised in our skills, we gain confidence; certainty, in contrast, forecloses on other possible ways of looking at a problem. Indeed, some times certainty and confidence can sit in direct tension, as in that person who is sufficiently confident to say 'I do not know. Can you tell me?'

The Polish poet Wisława Szymborska, in her Nobel Lecture of 1996, wrote eloquently about the importance of this position of engaged ignorance: 'Whatever inspiration is, it's born from a continuous "I don't know"'. She continues:

> This is why I value that little phrase 'I don't know' so highly.
> It's small, but it flies on mighty wings. It expands our lives to
> include the spaces within us as well as those outer expanses in
> which our tiny Earth hangs suspended. If Isaac Newton had never
> said to himself 'I don't know', the apples in his little orchard
> might have dropped to the ground like hailstones and at best he
> would have stooped to pick them up and gobble them with
> gusto.   (Szymborska 1996)

Listening involves risking one's self, exposing oneself to new possibilities and frameworks of meaning. It is psychologically very demanding of us, as it requires a suspension of the aura of certainty that has become our professional trademark. Studs Terkel, one of the most renowned interviewers of recent times, describes the role of the interviewer as one who is 'starting out onto the unknown sea. There are no maps because no one's been there before. You're an explorer, a discoverer. It's exciting – and it's scary, it frightens you' (Parker 1996: 163). Listening requires an openness to the unknown; and at the same time, it requires us as researchers to be not only intellectually but emotionally attentive and engaged.

In this chapter, I would like to explore some of the challenges of listening that I have experienced in the course of my research. The discussion will be organised around four central concerns:

(1) *Audience*   Who are we, and who are we perceived to be, in relation to those whose lives we document? How does this influence what we are told? What is the relationship between what we are told and that which we hear?

(2) *Positioning*   Who are we in relation to the topics that we select for our research? What is our investment in the stories we gather and does this change over time? Can we ever really hear that of which we have no experience?

(3) *Tell-ability*   What constitutes the tell-ability of a story? Are we more sensitised to some kinds of stories rather than others?

(4) *Empowerment*   What do we think we are doing as we ask others to tell us about their lives? What responsibilities, if any, come with the role that we have assumed? We have created for ourselves a powerful, and very flattering, narrative about the strength that others derive from participating in our research. Is the reality so straightforward? If not, what might be complicating factors?

THE CONSTRUCTION OF AUDIENCE

It is an obvious, yet crucially important fact, that most people, most of the time, tell their stories to others, even as they tell their stories to themselves (indeed, here 'oneself' might be constructed as 'other'); who those others are invariably influences the story or stories which are told. In order for us to make sense of the stories which we gather, we have first to identify who the interviewees perceive themselves as addressing. If we are the interviewers, this process will include an interrogation into how our respondents perceive us. Equally, if not more important, are the 'ghostly audiences' (Langellier 2001: 174) – those persons central in the lives of our respondents, for whom or to whom the story may be being told. We as researchers often have little or no knowledge of this imagined audience, yet their presence in our work is significant.

My understanding of the construction of audience has become much more complicated over the years, especially when my own work began to extend to archival research. In three of the four case studies presented in this book, I was the person – and in most cases the only person – who was present when interviewees recounted to me stories about their lives. The contact between us was direct, often intense, and sometimes prolonged. I was clearly accountable to them, and this sense of personal responsibility stayed with me throughout the life of each project and beyond. I felt that I had made, in a sense, a personal promise to take care, to tread cautiously with the material of other people's lives. Does this same level of ethical accountability pertain to the use of data available in the public domain? Was I part of an imagined audience, for instance, in the minds of those who gave testimony before the TRC? A review of the construction of audience across the four case studies reveals some interesting comparisons.

When I arrived in England to pursue my doctoral research, I was a young (mid-twenties), single, American, Jewish, middle-class, white woman. I am certain that each of these aspects of my identity contributed to the way in which respondents viewed me, and coloured much of what they told me. The tendency among those who agreed to be interviewed by me was to identify some area of common ground between us, and to build a bond from this base. One man, for instance, with whom I shared none of these characteristics other than race, explains his trade union activism on the London docks in terms of its similarities with the struggles of Jewish people through the centuries: 'I think when I look back, they [the Jewish people] had a great influence on my life. They taught me to be, I'm going to say it myself, they taught me to be a nice human being … I've been a real mensch'. Elsewhere he develops this theme: 'I'm not cutting the cloth to suit the garment, but I have to use it. Let's use the struggles of the Jewish people … Look what they suffered, but they never gave up'. The strategy here is clearly used to develop a bond, a sense of shared mission, between us. (In fact, he asks nothing of my views on my Jewishness but assumes it to be something from which we can build common ground.)

Being American brought with it a complex set of reactions, undoubtedly influenced by the historical moment in which the research was being carried out: Thatcher's Britain in the mid-1980s was characterised by high levels of political protest against the US military presence in Britain. This included, notably, the Women's Peace Camp at Greenham Common where, beginning in 1981, tens of thousands of women either lived at or visited the US Airbase in protest of its land-based missiles. To be an American interviewing peace activists at this time in the country's history was an interesting position to occupy. One man, who, through written correspondence, had agreed to be part of my study, changed his mind once he heard my American accent over the telephone. 'I don't want to have anything to do with Americans', he told me, and that was the end of the conversation. A woman who was about to commence her first interview with me asked, as I arrived at her home, if I was with the CIA. I told her I could understand her reservations, given the current political environment, but I assured her that my own political inclinations were in a very different direction. She accepted what I said, agreed to be part of the study, and became a close friend of mine for the rest of her life. Ironically, several years later we would go together to RAF Molesworth (another military base in Britain which was the site of much protest). A fence separated me from the US soldiers who were guarding the base, and people made jokes that the soldiers were on the wrong side of the fence. There, the crowds chanted 'US Out'.

There is also evidence throughout my research of respondents' attempts to gauge my views in relation to their comments on gender politics. There were a number of times when this was overtly addressed, with comments which began with phrases such as 'You might not agree with this, but ... '. Feminist consciousness was notably not something which I shared with most of my British socialist respondents, and one of the most instructive challenges for me was to develop an understanding about how we had come to hold such different views in this area, given the extent of agreement elsewhere (Andrews 2002). Although initially I struggled with this difference between us, and did not want to look at it too closely in case it would unravel my construction of this special group of people, I later came to view it as illuminating our respectively different historic locations.

Despite the clear indicators that respondents' perceptions of me and my general life circumstances had a strong influence on the tales I was told, I was undoubtedly not the only person included in their imagined audience. As I discuss in chapter 3, there were moments in this project when I realised that my function in their lives was that of archivist. After they were gone, their stories would live on. I was there recording their lives' experiences for the sake of posterity. In that sense, I was a representative of future generations, and the stories which I heard often had this texture to them. I knew that I was being entrusted with one of the most important responsibilities someone can give you: not only to document the stories of their lives, but to pass them on.

In the project which I carried out on American anti-war activism, I was positioned in a very different way. First, I was the same age as, or older than, most of the people I interviewed. Some of them were students whom I had taught in the past; others were colleagues of mine at the college where I taught; and still others were well-known activists from the local community. Most of the people in the study I had met prior to our interview, an indicator that in some capacity we operated within the same community – and, significantly for my project, we largely shared a political framework through which we interpreted the events unfolding in the Persian Gulf.

There were, however, two exceptions to this shared political identity between myself and my interviewees. Both of these participants had helped to organise the 'One Hour for America' political rally, which I describe in detail in chapter 4. My first contact with these two men was when I telephoned them to enquire whether or not they would be willing to participate in my study. I think that it was significant for them that I was a full-time faculty member at the local college, which had a strong national reputation and which they both held in high positive regard. However, they were also aware that some members of the college (students and faculty alike) had been vocal in the local anti-war movement, whose aims and objectives they actively opposed. I had a surprise at the end of one of these interviews: as I was winding up the session, I began to explain to the participant that I would transcribe the interview, and send him a copy of the transcript for comment. 'There's no need for you to do that', I was told. 'I've been taping us myself', and at this point he directed my attention to a small tape recorder sitting on his desk. This was the first time in my experience as a researcher that I felt my interviewee did not really trust me. His clandestine taping of our session would allow him to review what I said he had said – clearly an adherent to the Russian proverb often quoted by Ronald Reagan: 'Dovery, no proveryay' – 'trust but verify'.

I did, in fact, send a hard copy of the transcript to each of these men. Interestingly, the man who had taped our session offered only minimal feedback. The other man, in contrast, sent back another transcript which had been wholly retyped from the original hard copy. Here, he had altered not only words within sentences, but whole passages. Interestingly, however, he did so without any comment to me on this matter. In fact I have never been a real transcript purist. If, on reflection, a person wishes to express their thoughts or feelings in a modified form, I respect their right to do so. The alteration itself, then, was not problematic for me. Rather what I found intriguing was why he felt he needed to do so without drawing attention to the fact, why someone (not necessarily him) had had to spend probably the better part of a day typing up the conversation he wished we had had.

The research I conducted in East Germany positioned me much more clearly in the role of 'stranger in a strange land'. The political events which had unfolded before us in the previous two years were almost too much to take in. I wanted very much to understand what these changes had really been about, and what they meant to the people for whom they were a part of their daily lives. While I had followed the news very carefully in the English-language press, in fact I did not speak German. For many this might have been reason enough not to pursue this project, but for me it was an obstacle, but not an insurmountable one, to something I felt deeply compelled to do. But how was I seen by those who agreed to talk with me? First of all, I was not alone. Not by a long shot. At this moment in history, oral historians, sociologists, anthropologists, psychologists, and academics of many other persuasions had flooded into East Germany, all there to gather first-hand accounts of what these meteoric changes meant to those who were living through them. There were so many people doing 'this kind of work' over there that it was hard not to see oneself as engaging in some kind of vulture-like activity, the mulling over of a carcass of a once-powerful animal. But, in actual fact, that was not how I experienced the work I was doing.

I was taken aback by how many people agreed to meet with me, despite the intense pressure of daily living in the context of acute political and social upheaval. I believe that one of the reasons for this openness was due to a desire to create a space for telling a different kind of story about the meaning of the changes around us. By 1992, the year of my interviews, the production and consumption of the 'end of history' interpretation of world events had been widespread. I was regarded by virtually all who spoke with me as first and foremost someone from the West. (I would cringe every time I saw the poster, plastered all over Berlin, advertising a cigarette brand called 'West'; its slogan read 'West is Best'.) I was there as some kind of representative of the West, someone who had grown up in Washington, DC but also someone who had devoted considerable effort to documenting the lives of lifetime socialist activists. All of the interviews began with a general conversation between us, in which prospective interviewees wanted to know more about my interest in their worlds. As had been my experience in the past, once one or two people had opened the gate to me, others quickly followed. But clearly had I articulated a 'West is Best' position, my entrance would have been limited if not barred. So I was regarded by and large as a sympathetic, interested, in many ways ignorant, western researcher. The fact that I could not speak German meant that I was always accompanied by an interpreter. For most of the interviews, a West German colleague and friend performed this vital function, but for approximately ten interviews, I employed a professional interpreter from East Germany. Their presence, in different ways, undoubtedly had an influence on the dynamics and content of our interview (Andrews 1995).

I had thought that my communications with those whom I interviewed had proceeded relatively smoothly, and the indicators were that many of them had found the experience sufficiently engaging to recommend that their friends and acquaintances also be interviewed. I was, then, completely taken aback when, at the end of a two-and-a-half-hour interview with Bärbel Bohley, one of the most recognisable faces of *Neus Forum*, the largest of the citizens' groups which developed in the autumn of 1989, I realised that something had gone astray between us.

When I ask her the question which I had used to end all of the previous interviews, sparks fly:

MA: Can you tell us, retrospectively, what would you do the same as you did before? What would you do differently?

BB: How? Where? When?

MA: Well, in your life.

BB: I would do many things differently, wouldn't you? ...
What I suspect is, honestly, this is neither a question nor an

answer ... I suspect somehow, that the people in the West
have not yet comprehended that the Wall is gone. They
have not yet comprehended that half of ... yes, half of the
world ... yes, that an empire has collapsed. It has not fully
penetrated people's awareness what this really means ...
It should really be that, likewise, people in the West are
being asked questions. If you come here and ask me questions for two-and-a-half hours, that is meaningless ...
it is really I who should put the questions, I mean somebody from the West, somebody from the East. It should be
more like a discussion. People from the West come and
want to understand, but they do not want to understand
themselves. They only ask us. Well, an empire has collapsed ... there is something missing, do you understand
what I mean?

Bohley's passionate response to my question provides very useful
information regarding her construction of the 'audience' to whom
she has been speaking for the previous two-and-a-half hours. While
she begins by questioning the lack of specificity of my question ('How?
Where? When?' she asks me), she then maps this critique onto a more
fundamental concern: 'people in the West' – and here she is clearly
referring to me – 'have not comprehended that the Wall is gone'; 'they
want to understand, but they do not want to understand themselves'.
Bohley's comment struck me directly; I felt that I was being positioned
in a way which did not resonate with my own self-perception. It was, I
thought, my commitment to understanding the political and personal
meaning of these momentous changes, not only for others, but for
myself, which had motivated me to pursue this research. And yet her
comment was one I could not ignore. Bohley had correctly placed me
in a category 'people from the West' which produced in me an uncomfortable realisation that others did not necessarily see me in the way I
saw myself. Of course I knew this intellectually, but this was more
visceral. The discrepancies between these two constructions of myself

and the work I was doing were important for me to confront, and ultimately proved very useful in exploring meaning in the data I was collecting.

There were instances in interviews with others which revealed a similar, if less caustic, construction of 'us' and 'them'. For instance, nuclear scientist Sebastian Pflugbeil commented to me:

> Well, it has become quite clear that we are different from you over there … there are issues which we cannot address mutually. The Stasi business is one matter which we cannot discuss with a 'wessi'. A 'wessi' discusses it theoretically and … hmm, well, it practically chopped our legs off. So one can, hmm, at most, chat about it but not seriously discuss it … My apologies for the outburst against the 'wessis'.

Pflugbeil's comment, summarised in the phrase 'we are different from you over there' clearly positions the two of us on different sides of a divide (in this way, it is similar to that of Bohley). However, Bohley's comment, though more caustic in style, is also ultimately more optimistic; she feels that there can be, but isn't, real dialogue between us (or at least she laments the absence of such dialogue). Pflugbeil, however, questions the possibility of serious discussion, as opposed to chat, on issues – such as the Stasi – whose existence have framed lives in the East, but with which a 'wessi' has only a theoretical acquaintance. Pflugbeil locates me explicitly in what he is saying, and finishes by apologising for his 'outburst'.

Clearly the fact that I was from the West could not help but play a part in how people perceived me in our conversations. But equally it would be misleading to think that this was the only lens through which I was viewed. For some, the fact of my being Jewish was important, while for others it was significant that I had spent the previous few years writing and thinking about lifetime commitment to socialism. Throughout my time in East Germany, my encounters were marked by a generosity and openness that never ceased to touch me. I struggled with the question of who people perceived me to be in our conversations, and considered how this influenced what they said or didn't say to me; throughout this time I was guided by the familiarity of human contact, which helped me find my bearings.

All of this changed with my research on South Africa. Here, for the first time in my professional life, research data were not a product of conversations I had had with other people. Rather, my 'presence' in that research was of a wholly different nature; my inquiries rested on reading words which had been spoken to an audience of which I was not a part. One could argue that the painful extracts I spent hours and days mulling over were in fact never intended for my eyes. In chapter 6, I explore a number of possible reasons and incentives which may have contributed to people being willing to 'tell their story' to the TRC, and how their perceptions of the audience(s) of these tellings may have impacted on what they told and how they told it. There are many sound political reasons why the transcripts of the TRC hearings should be publicly available, and indeed most of those who testified before this committee would have been aware that the stories they recounted in that context would have, or could have, a more public afterlife.

However, nothing could have prepared some of those who gave testimony for what was to follow. Yazir Henri, former anti-apartheid activist and officer in Umkhonto we Sizwe (MK), the military wing of the African National Congress (ANC), discusses the painful aftermath which followed from his public testimony:

> At the time of my testimony I had no idea what the consequences
> of 'public' could have meant in the context of public hearings.
> The fact that my testimony could be appropriated, interpreted,
> re-interpreted, re-told and sold was not what I expected … Serious
> thought needs to be given to the ethics of appropriating testimony
> for poetic licence, media freedom, academic commentary and dis-
> course analysis. Arguing these lines and 'It's on the public record'
> are too easy a position to take since they do not address the rights of
> self-authorship and the intention of the speaker, the reclamation of

one's voice and one's agency. This ethical dilemma also needs to be addressed as a meta-analytical and methodological question, by theorising the relationship of the layers of listening and subjective hearing positions (proximity, relationality), mediations, disseminations of testimonies and voices of listeners and readers.

(Henri 2003: 266)

Henri's comment highlights the ethical difficulty for those of us whose research includes the use of archival materials. (While these problems also exist in research where there is direct interaction between interviewer and interviewee, there are clearer mechanisms in place for self-monitoring.) It is disturbing that so many academics and public policy-makers regard personal testimony in the public domain as exempt from the ethical scrutiny required of other research involving human subjects. Henri's description of the pain which followed his public testimony makes clear the intuitively obvious: painful stories which are told either in public or for the public record should be treated with the same level of sensitivity as painful stories which are spoken behind closed doors. Often 'data' in the public domain are the articulations of individuals recalling their personal experiences, which might include traumatic loss and suffering. These stories should be treated with the same level of sensitivity which we would like others to show towards our own private stories which we may share with them, or which they may encounter in whatever context.

Henri's statement refers to the importance of 'theorising the relationship of the layers of listening and subjective hearing positions' a phrase which encapsulates the challenges of ethically accessing and using archival material and/or material which was gathered in another context for another purpose. Every researcher must ask herself 'who am I in relation to this story I am now reading/listening to?'. The answer will never be straightforward; however, the fact that data are 'on the public record' should make the question of researcher accountability more, and not less, complicated.

RESEARCH AND DESIRE

Most often, the questions which guide our research originate from deep within ourselves. We care about the topics we explore – indeed, we care very much. While our projects may be presented with an appearance of professional detachment, most of us most of the time are personally invested in the research we undertake. Our chosen areas of expertise mean something to us; there is a reason we examine the questions we do. Sometimes we might even feel that our questions choose us; they occur to us (sometimes, arriving almost imperceptibly, other times like a thunderbolt) but then will not go away.

This has been my experience with every research project I have ever pursued. Here I would like to examine my relationship to the four case studies recorded in this book. Why did these particular contexts call to me in the way that they did, and how did this impact upon the research I carried out? Was I so intent on exploring one particular kind of story that I closed my eyes to information which might have diverted me from my mission? And how has my relationship to the projects which I have undertaken changed over time? Looking back on the research I have conducted over the past twenty years, why have I chosen those particular topics? What have I wanted these stories to say or do? Did I find what I was looking for? What happened to me as a result of each of these explorations?

My study of British lifetime socialist activists was important to me not only intellectually, but more significantly this research provided me with the means and the opportunity to construct for myself a positive model of aging within the context of a society which devalues individuals on the basis of their age. The project I designed and carried out enabled me to have conversations with old people who instilled in me a blueprint of what meaning in old age might look like, not only in others' lives, but potentially in my own.

The stories which I was looking for, and which I found, had a very profound personal significance for me. The conversations which I had as part of this research were evidence to me that old age, far from representing the disengagement and depression of which we so often hear, could be a time of fulfilment and deep engagement. These women and men, as they spoke of their ongoing commitment to fighting for social justice, argued that their increased age had brought with it the advantage of perspective. Old peace activists were critical to social movements because they were less susceptible to becoming depressed through lack of immediate tangible results.

As one of my respondents, Eileen, explains to me: 'It's the old people who keep going. I think age brings that perspective'. Archbishop Trevor Huddleston, or Father Trevor as he was known to me, was the founder of the International Anti-apartheid Movement and one of the participants in my study. He echoes Eileen's sentiment. Speaking in 1987, he tells me: 'I think I've become more revolutionary every year I've lived. And certainly now, because life is so much shorter. I mean I want to get apartheid dead before I'm dead. There's no time to do that'. That he would indeed outlive apartheid, and return to South Africa as the honoured guest of Nelson Mandela, the new President, was beyond his greatest dreams. And yet fighting apartheid was something to which he had dedicated the whole of his being, for all of his adult life.

Age played an important factor in the relationship which I developed with each of them. I was clearly a daughter, though not yet a mother. Although I was considerably younger than any of their children, it was evident in many of the interviews that they saw their participation in my project as a contribution to future generations, of which I was in some sense a representative. When I originally conducted my research, I was interested in how political commitment to social change was sustained over the course of a lifetime. At the time, I myself was politically active, three thousand miles from my family, single, and without children. In different ways, I think all of these descriptions fed into what I took away from the conversations I had. When, years later, I returned to the transcripts from this study, I was the mother of two. This added dimension to my own life's experience helped me to see things in the personal accounts of my interviewees which before had been side-lined. Returning to the transcripts, I was ready to hear something new, and it was there waiting for me, waiting for that time when I might be prepared to receive it. In my experience, this is often the way in which analysis and interpretation proceed; we are able to see only so far beyond our own horizons, and it is for this reason that return journeys to 'old data' often hold such promise.

It is ironic to me that such a small portion of my work has been conducted in the country of my birth, the USA. I have lived outside of the USA for fifteen of the past twenty years, and throughout this time, I have grappled with what it means to me to be an American. The research I did in Colorado Springs, Colorado, on peace activism as a form of 'loving one's country', can be understood as my attempt to locate myself and my convictions on the political canvas of my own country.

Why was it that I could not see myself, or others with a similar political orientation, in the stories which I encountered about who 'we' were as a people, as a nation? My research helped me to identify myself as part of a significant, but often invisible, portion of the US population who disagreed with the international policy of the country, not from a position of 'anti-Americanism' but rather as patriots of a different kind. Immediately as I saw their US flag at the anti-war vigil which they kept throughout the cold winter months, I knew this was a different kind of story than the one which was widely circulated about who we were and what we were doing.

The Gulf War coincided with my return to the USA after four years of being a PhD student abroad; the research provided me with a vehicle for exploring, in conversation with others, what it meant to me to be an American, even as I disagreed with many things which were being done in the name of the American people. My experience of living outside of the country had confirmed in me a strong feeling of 'critical loyalty' (Staub 1997), and the conversations I had as part of this research helped me to rethink the meaning of patriotism.

The most lasting impression of my first return trip to the USA after the events of 9/11 (several months later) was the predominance of the national flag. Everywhere one looked, there it was, in all shapes and sizes. Everywhere. But what did these flags mean to those who exhibited them? Was there really one national message which they expressed, or did they contain a range of meanings? Reading through the transcripts from the interviews I conducted in the early 1990s in Colorado Springs, I realised that what was new in the post-9/11 world was not the patriotic narrative itself, but rather its revitalisation.

Issues which I had initially identified as salient in the early 1990s were indeed even more in evidence nearly fifteen years later. The more I thought about the story I had tried to tell about the small group of anti-war activists in Colorado Springs during the military operation of Desert Storm – the battle over the meaning of 'good American' – the more I came to question the assumption that everything had been changed on the morning of September 11, 2001. Indeed, revisiting the data I had collected in the early 1990s, I could see traces of the national rhetoric which would come to dominate political discourse in the USA in the post-9/11 world.

My desire to interview East German dissidents after the fall of the Berlin Wall was something which I pursued with passion. Though I applied for a number of different grants to assist me in this project, I was not successful at attracting conventional forms of support. Highly conscious of the urgency of the project, I decided my efforts might be better directed in putting together a 'patchwork quilt' of support; and so it was that I had pockets of money from a range of sources, covering travel, office space, even tapes. This, combined with the flexibility of a job share and the generosity of friends who welcomed me as a semi-permanent fixture in their Berlin flat (I shared a room with their new baby), produced the result I was determined to achieve: I arrived in Berlin in February 1992, weeks after the opening of the Stasi files, ready to begin my new project.

Where did this determination come from? The timing of the collapse of state socialism in East and Central Europe in 1989 coincided precisely with finishing my study on lifetime socialist activists. This not only meant that I had the psychological preparedness to entertain the possibility of a new project, but also that I was presented with an acute challenge to socialist identification on an unprecedented scale. It was difficult to read the papers and not to feel that we were living in historically significant times. But what did the collapse of state socialism in this part of the world really mean? While politically I rejected what I regarded as triumphalist interpretations of the meaning of these events, equally I felt a personal and intellectual obligation to explore the meaning of these events of 1989 in terms of my own political commitments. For me, neither of the two explanations in wide circulation were palatable; I did not accept that this demise was inevitable and revealed socialism for the morally bankrupt system that it was, but neither could I convince myself, as some on the left did at that time, that socialism as it was practised in Eastern and Central Europe was not really socialism at all, and therefore did not represent a challenge to a belief system encompassing socialist principles. I did not see history moving toward, or having arrived at, a definitive ending as was popularly suggested, but I did think that it was essential for those of us living in the West to try to comprehend the enormity of the changes which we were witnessing, and their impact not just on other countries but the important implications of this seismic shift for all of us. Zygmunt Bauman's description of the consequences of the demise of communism, as set forward in *Intimations of Postmodernity* (1992) are most insightful on this point:

> The continuing polarization of well-being and life chances cannot be made less repulsive by pointing to the general impoverishment which had resulted elsewhere from efforts to remedy it ... The world without an alternative needs self-criticism as a condition of survival and decency. *(1992: 185–186)*

The excerpt from my interview with Bärbel Bohley, cited earlier, relates to this important point. Exasperated with me, she exclaims that 'the people in the West have not yet comprehended that the Wall is gone. They have not yet comprehended that half of ... yes, half of the world ... yes, that an empire has collapsed. It has not fully penetrated people's awareness what this really means'. My personal challenge, then, was to explore what this collapse of an empire 'really meant', and that is precisely what had driven me to go to East Germany and to speak with people there, to learn more. The fall of the Eastern Bloc necessitated a reorganisation of our entire way of thinking about the world – politically, economically, socially – and our place within it. It would take me years to fully comprehend all that I saw, heard, and experienced in my six months there.

The motivations which drew me to my research on South Africa were rooted deep in my own developmental biography. In chapter 6, I elaborate on the meaning that South Africa had had for the awakening of political consciousness in those of my generation. This country was for many of us a place that we could not go to (because of the international boycott) and perhaps, not coincidentally, a place that held a great deal of symbolic importance for us. For decades we had been told that we were unrealistic in our hopes and dreams, that the only possibility for change in South Africa would be through civil war. Bloodshed did accompany the changes in South Africa in the 1990s, but it was not on the scale that had been predicted by many.

The national narrative of the new South Africa was a deeply hopeful one, and contrasted dramatically with that which we had been told would come in the wake of the end of apartheid. I was compelled to explore how people came through such deeply traumatic experiences with their integrity intact, and it was this that led me to the transcripts of the TRC.

During the apartheid years, Desmond Tutu's optimism in the face of adversity was the embodiment of hope. But how, I wondered, had people come to terms with such traumatic histories? I wanted very much to believe the TRC narrative of the resilience of the South African people, their ability, against all odds, to rebuild their communities and prepare the grounds for a liveable future together. What had happened in South Africa was an antidote to those who had not believed that change without war would be possible. Not surprisingly, the more I read, and heard, and spoke with others, the more realistic I became about the length of the journey still ahead. But even while much of the country continues to be ravaged by sickness, poverty, and the legacy of apartheid, the most critical change is that people have begun to 'dream their own dreams', as one South African described it to me.

TELLING AND 'TELL-ABILITY'

Many researchers interested in biographical methods have argued for the importance of the cultural location which frames the stories which individuals tell, and don't tell. Denzin, for instance, argues that a story has a 'cultural locus' which lends the account a framework of meaning (1989: 73). Personal narratives assume forms which are particular to the culture which they construct and are constructed by; the stories which our research participants tell, and the stories which we as researchers hear, are heavily influenced by the norms of the community. We are socialised to think of our lives in particular ways, and (mostly) we construct the stories about our lives in relation to those expected tales. In this sense, then, the 'tell-ability' of stories is highly influenced not only by the level of intimacy between speaker and listener, but critically by the larger context in which the narrative is recounted. Here I would like to consider how the 'tell-ability factor' may have featured in the conversations I have had with the women and men who have participated in my research over the years.

My research on lifetime socialist activists can be read as a response to George Bernard Shaw's maxim: 'If you're not a socialist when you're young you've got no heart; if you're still a socialist at forty you've got no head.' Growing up in the highly political environment of Washington, DC in the 1970s, with the events of Vietnam and Watergate as strong formative experiences, I was determined that fighting for the causes you believed in neither was, nor should be, something which was unique to any one age group.

The stories recounted to me by anti-war protestors in the USA derive much of their meaning from the wider context of the discourse of patriotism. Their attempt to reclaim their identity, or to take back the flag, makes sense only in relation to the master narrative of what it means to be a good American; the political strategies they have adopted are constructed as a conscious challenge to this accepted tale. Clearly the events of 9/11 have wielded a powerful influence on the national narrative of responsible citizenship in the USA. As I discuss in chapter 4, legislation such as the Patriot Act enshrine into law sentiments that in former times were open to question. The tale's tell-ability is historically sensitive; the events of September 11 produced a political climate in which it was far more difficult to couple responsible citizenship with anti-war activism. Post-9/11, even those who wish to criticise some component of the US domestic or foreign policy position their critiques within a broader context of support.

The 'un-tellable tale' of East Germany is one which casts doubt on the story which constructs the events of 1989 as an indicator of universal celebration of capitalism's triumph. In the words of Bärbel Bohley, 'it was simply the revolt of the humiliated people. And they did not ask why they revolted, for capitalism or socialism, they were simply fed up to live with this lie … it was not a victory for capitalism'. I went to East Germany to find out more about activists' experiences of living through the revolutionary changes, and to talk with them about the new world in which they then found themselves. What I heard was something rather different, both to what I had heard in the western media, but also to what I myself had expected. Theirs was, in a sense, an unintentional revolution. Bauman (1992) offers an analysis of the demise of communism which resonates deeply with the narratives I heard:

> Dissent the old system could not but generate tended to exceed
> the system's capacity for accommodation and thus pushed the
> crisis to breaking point; but this effect was precisely the result
> of couching demands in the language of the extant system …
> and thus facing the system with output postulates it was unable

to meet ... forces that destroy the *ancient regime* are not consciously interested in the kind of change which would eventually
follow the destruction.   *(1992: 158)*

But this is a very different story to the one which saturated the western
world, which was instead characterised by widespread 'self congrat-
ulating glee' (Bauman 1992: 175): ' "our form of life" has once and for
all proved both its viability and its superiority over any other real or
imaginary form' (1992: 175).

   Post-apartheid South Africa is a country which is dedicated to
creating a new national narrative, one which attempts to acknowledge
the abuses of apartheid and, in so doing, to move beyond them. This
national narrative is one which is peopled by repentant victimisers
and forgiving victims who, through dialogue, come together to form
the new South Africa. In chapter 6 I describe the pressures in South
Africa to tell certain kinds of stories about experiences under apartheid. The TRC was created as a means for assisting South Africans to
move from a position of rupture and trauma to one of rejuvenation, at
the level of both the individual and the nation. Stories which undermined the project of building the new nation were far less tell-able
than those which, however horrific in their detail, could be seen as
vehicles for overcoming the past. Commissioners of the TRC were
effectively more sensitised to stories of forgiveness, and in some cases
may have created the very storyline which they wished to hear.
Personal accounts allowing for the possibility of reconciliation and
even forgiveness were highly tell-able, and as such were not only
individually but culturally produced and reproduced.

   In this section, we have seen that what individuals are able to
tell about their experiences, and what others are able to hear, is very
much influenced by the characteristics of a society. In the forthcoming chapters, we shall see in more detail what aspects of the society of
our four case studies made some stories more tell-able than others, and
will examine my attempts as a researcher, not always successful, to
uncover some of the less told stories.

HEARING THE TOLD AND THE UNTOLD

Clearly, however, what a researcher is able to absorb is not only a function of what she is told but, equally, a function of what she is able to hear; 'narration', Erika Apfelbaum reminds us, 'is tragically bound to the interlocutor's capacity to hear what is said' (Apfelbaum 2002: 12). It is not only those who participate in our research who frame their stories in relation to expected storylines but, critically, we ourselves are more prepared to hear some kinds of stories than others. An important aspect of our socialisation as individuals and as members of communities is the orientation towards, and enthusiasm to receive, particular kinds of stories, and our deafness towards others. Thus not only are some stories more tell-able than others, some stories are also more hear-able than others. As researchers, we need to train ourselves to a high level of awareness of those stories which may fall outside of our habituated cultural sensitivity. That means that we must allow ourselves to entertain truths and cultural norms which may be distant from, or even contradict, those into which we have been socialised.

Erika Apfelbaum tells the story that, on the fiftieth anniversary of her father's deportation to Auschwitz, she published in *Le Monde* a remembrance note about the convoy in which her father had been sent to his death. Following this, she received a letter from a former schoolmate, someone with whom she had shared the same bench at school. In the letter, the woman writes 'I knew nothing of you and of your tragic story ... how has this been possible?' (2002: 14). Much has been written about the inability of Holocaust survivors to speak of their unutterable trauma, and this has been used as an explanation of why so little was communicated about their experiences in the years immediately following the war. However, such explanations put the burden of responsibility for the silence on the shoulders of the survivors. But who would speak of such things if there were no one to listen? Simone Weil writes 'One hears commonly that those who came back from camps preferred to forget ... It may be true for some, but untrue for most. As for me, I always have been willing to speak, to bear witness. But no one was willing to listen' (cited in Apfelbaum 2002). Similarly, Primo Levi, in *Survival in Auschwitz*, describes his recurring nightmare of 'the ever-repeated scene of the un-listened to story' (cited in Laub 1992: 68). Henry Greenspan, who has been engaged in research with Holocaust survivors for more than twenty-five years, comments that survivors were not only silent in the decades following the war, they were also silenced. He describes 'an active process of suppression and stigmatisation' experienced by survivors, who evoked 'a shifting combination of pity, fear, revulsion and guilt ... they were isolated and avoided' (1998: 34). But this phenomenon of socially excluding those who have endured deep rupture in their lives is not unique to the Holocaust.

Paul Fussell writes of what some have described as the 'unspeakable' horrors of the First World War:

> Logically, there is no reason why the English language could not perfectly well render the actuality of ... warfare ... The problem was less one of 'language' than of gentility and optimism ... What listener wants to be torn and shaken when he doesn't have to be? We have made unspeakable mean indescribably: it really means nasty.
>
> *(Cited in Brison 2002: 51)*

Similarly, Susan Brison writes compellingly of the trauma she suffered as one who had survived an attempted murder and rape, saying 'it is so difficult for survivors to recover when others are unwilling to listen to what they endured' (Brison 2002: 50–51). We are, Brison argues, social beings, but in our traumas we are often made to stand alone. Elie Wiesel writes of the reception often meted out to Holocaust survivors: 'People welcomed them with tears and sobs, then turned away' (cited in Greenspan 1998: 34). Others wish not to see the possible connections between trauma survivors and the rest of the world, and so the strategy of particularising the event, or events, is adopted. And yet re-integration of the self into the social world depends on communication; 'No one finds peace in silence, even when it is their choice to remain silent' (Laub cited in Apfelbaum 2001: 16). This refusal to enter into another possible world is epitomised by the word which often greets tales of suffering:

> 'Unimaginable': with this single word of comment the listener brushes aside any further attempts to understand, reduces the teller to silence … and protects himself from the risk of having to cross the boundaries of the familiar safe world into the unknown of a radically different planet … The refusal to hear is also an indication of the fear … of people when their sense of existential and episte-mological safety is being jeopardised. It is as if one opens a window onto a threatening truth which forces them to face a grim reality for which they have no references, and in which they no longer feel safe.
> *(Apfelbaum 2001: 28–29)*

In these passages we see some possible answers to the question which Apfelbaum's former schoolmate posed to her: how is it possible that these stories are left unspoken, unheard? In order for one to speak, there needs to be one who is willing to listen. As Laub writes:

> Being witness to a trauma is, in fact, a process that includes the listener. For the testimonial process to take place, there needs to be a bonding, the intimate and total presence of an other – in the position of one who hears. Testimonies are not monologues; they cannot take place in solitude. The witnesses are talking to somebody: to somebody they have been waiting for for a long time.
> *(Laub 1992: 70–71)*

Without an empathic listener, the unlistened-to receives an evalua-tion of the story they would share; it is an 'ultimate annihilation of a narrative that, fundamentally, cannot be heard and a story that cannot be witnessed' (Laub 1992: 68).

But listening brings with it no promises of comprehension or understanding. Indeed, Apfelbaum suggests that there may be an 'unbridgeable gap' between the world of the speaker and that of the listener. This does not matter. 'Understanding', she writes, 'is irrelevant (the reality always exceeds what the narrative is able to represent and convey). What is important is the willingness to become part of the transmission' (2001: 31). Greenspan reflects on the question 'Why *should* we listen to survivors...?' (emphasis in the original) and lists a number of recognisable possible responses, ranging from educating children to bestowing meaning on suffering, and ensuring that history will not repeat itself. He then reflects on these readily available answers:

> Let me speak frankly. I used to believe some of these assertions;
> I now believe very few of them and those few only with the
> strictest qualifications ... the sufficient reason to listen
> to survivors is to listen to survivors. No other purpose is
> required.   *(1998: 171)*

Greenspan's thoughtful and thought-provoking book closes with the comment that we should be less concerned with what we can 'get out of' personal testimony, and more focused on how we might 'get into' all that survivors have to retell (1998: 172).

In order to bear witness, one must be ready to enter into another, possibly threatening world; this demands courage. Apfelbaum warns that 'It requires a willingness to follow the teller into a world of radical otherness and to accept the frightening implications it carries for our personal lives and society as a whole' (2001: 30). Following a teller into this other world means not only attending to that which is said, but acknowledging the importance of silence. Laub comments:

> The listener must ... listen to and hear the silence, speaking
> mutely both in silence and in speech, both from behind and from
> within the speech. He or she must recognize, acknowledge and
> address that silence, even if this simply means respect – and
> knowing how to wait.   *(1992: 58–59)*

This patience is often challenging for researchers, whose inclination may be to either rush through the silence, or to impose onto this space their own interpretive frameworks of meaning. We must accept that we do not always know the meaning of the unspoken, nor are we the best persons to evaluate what may or may not rest in the unconscious worlds – the hidden or unknown desires – of those with whom we speak. As responsible and responsive researchers, we must accept that some events 'resist simple, straightforward comprehension'; they 'demand witness but defy narrative expression' (Apfelbaum 2001: 1). Our role as researchers is to be there, to accept that there will always be things which lie beyond our knowledge and comprehension, to follow where we are led – through the stories, through the silences – and to allow ourselves, in Wittgenstein's words, to 'feel the pain in the body of the other' (cited in Das 1997: 94). Veena Das builds on this metaphor, contrasting the routes by which we come to know ourselves and the route which characterises how we get to know others:

> My knowledge of myself is something I find, as on a successful quest; my knowledge of others, of their separateness from me, is something that finds me … I might say that I must let it make an impression on me … And it seems reasonable to me, and illuminating, to speak of that reception of impression as my lending my body to the other's experience.   *(Das 1997: 97–98)*

But this process demands that we make ourselves vulnerable to new truths, new joys and pain, that we suspend ourselves in as much as it is possible to do so, and let ourselves, however briefly, consider what the world might look like from another point of view.

THE MYTH OF THE 'EMPOWERMENT NARRATIVE'

Valerie Walkerdine (2003) has used the term 'empowerment narrative' to identify the story which many researchers tell themselves about what they are doing. Over the past two to three decades, many scholars have come to identify in their work not only its scholarly merits, but its emancipatory potential. Many believe that their work 'gives a voice to' others who are disenfranchised and/or socially marginalised. Debates within oral history and feminist methodology have been two key sites in which much of this empowerment project has been pioneered, with some voices more exuberantly, and less critically, embracing this perceived aspect of their work than others.

Patti Lather (1988), for instance, examines 'feminist efforts to create empowering research designs' (1988: 569), while Paul Thompson's now classic *The Voice of the Past* (1978) makes bold claims for the potential of oral history which can 'transform the content and purpose of history ... it can give back to the people who made and experienced history, through their own words, a central place' (1978: 2). Here, Thompson emphasises the importance of the use of individuals' 'own words' in reclaiming 'a central place' in documenting history. Implicit in his statement is a belief that first-hand accounts have a great potential for revealing realities which might otherwise be hidden within the tombs of history. Verbatim quotations often assume a sense of authenticity which elude other forms of data. However, sometimes the appearance of having been 'given a voice' may in fact work to undermine the very empowerment project with which researchers credit themselves (Bhavnani 1990: 146). The use of decontextualised, first-person data is a strategy which may be used to mask inequalities rather than redress them, as research participants may appear as if they are 'speaking for themselves', rather than as people whose words are spoken in response to specific questions, and who have little input into how their thoughts are represented in the write-up of the research.

Typing the phrase 'give a voice to' into Google yields more than 850,000 hits. It seems that everyone is trying to give someone else a voice. According to Google, the 'recipients' of this 'gift' include the following: 'cognitively impaired children', 'palliative patients', 'black women', 'street children', 'Muslim women', 'gaming people', 'lesbian parents', 'the deaf', 'mourners', 'older disabled people', 'the unsung', 'the voiceless'. But who is asking to have voice given to them – and, indeed, what would this mean? From whose point of view is someone, or a community, voiceless? Most probably from a position which identifies itself as distinct from the group which it seeks to empower – the verb 'to give' requires two parties, one to give and one to receive. Far better to see oneself as a giver, than as a taker, a label which might equally well be applied to some researchers.

Although this empowerment narrative has come under considerable critique since its emergence in the 1970s, it has managed to survive in different, and perhaps less severe forms. Currently, the 'biographical turn' much touted in the social sciences has become a favourite venue for giving a voice to a hidden, suppressed or simply marginalised self or community. Much narrative research is based on the idea that we are 'storied selves'; our identity, it is argued, is constructed through our self-narration. We create stories about our pasts, and in so doing we establish who we are and who we are in the process of becoming. We as narrative researchers often see our jobs as assisting others to articulate their narrative identities. We listen to the stories they tell, and from this try to make sense of them and the worlds they inhabit. We privilege our own ability to know the meaning of someone else's life, and rarely question the harmful effects that our work may inadvertently cause.

Considering these questions in light of my research, I must ask myself about the long-term effects of the conversations I have had in such a wide range of settings. Here I wonder not only about the overall beneficial or harmful impact that the research has made but, at a more intimate level, what has been the effect of my entering and leaving (and sometimes re-entering) people's lives?

Of course it is difficult to respond with any certainty to these probing questions, primarily because I am not necessarily the best judge of the effect of my intervention in the lives of others. Moreover, oftentimes it is not our presence but our absence which causes concern, and we are no longer there to observe the fall-out we may have left in our wake. I remember once, following a life history which I had conducted over several years, the research participant wrote to me a postcard, simply asking 'Are you through with me now?'. Her words meant quite literally: were we done with one another? My response was quick and reassuring, communicating something to the effect of 'yes, this phase of our relationship is now complete, but there is no reason we cannot continue with our conversations'. But having completed that research, I then moved to another country, and we never saw one another again (she died before I returned). Had the intensity and duration of our contact, in the context of my research, set her up for an abandonment, however unintentional, once my work was completed? It is difficult to conclude otherwise.

We don't often have a way of evaluating the effect of the work we do on the people who participate in it. One situation, however, does stand out in my memory as unusual in this regard. I had accepted an invitation to deliver a paper in a seminar series at a British university which is located within a few miles of the home of someone who had participated in my research on lifetime activists nearly fifteen years earlier. We had kept in touch during the intervening years, through letters and occasional visits. When I realised that I would be relatively nearby, I informed her of my engagement, and asked her if she would like to meet. Yes, she assured me, not only did she want to see me, but she also wanted to attend the talk. (At eighty-eight, she was not bothered about taking two public transport buses to the university.) Having made these arrangements, I then realised that the paper I had intended to deliver was one in which she featured quite prominently. How would she feel being present while I publicly discussed the physical abuse she suffered as a child at the hands of her frustrated mother? Should I instead deliver a different paper? I decided to consult her directly on this. Her reaction was immediate and clear: if others might benefit from hearing about these experiences and her (and my) interpretations of them, then she was comfortable with me using it. Thus, I delivered the paper as originally planned, in the presence of my long-time friend who sat anonymously among the audience. On the bus leaving the university, we travelled together and she began to tell me many more early memories relating to her relationship with her mother, including their final moments together as her mother lay dying. The exchange meant a lot to me for two reasons: first, and most important, was the mere fact of its existence. Here we were, fifteen years later, still deeply engaged in conversation with one another. However, our bus-ride conversation also reassured me that she did not reject the interpretive framework which I had offered to make sense of the early experiences she had recounted to me years ago. On the contrary, it seemed that it had fitted not only what she had originally told me, but indeed had prompted her to elaborate further.

Does this anecdote reveal anything about the potentially harmful – or, indeed, the emancipatory – potential of my work, or work of this nature more broadly? Perhaps not. But this encounter did leave me with a gentle assurance that at least sometimes we can, and do, hear stories which extend beyond our own experiences. And when people feel that they are being listened to, they are quite likely to continue sharing their stories with us.

And so then it is left to us to ask ourselves the hard questions about what we are doing and why we are doing it. What do we think it means to listen to others who are in pain (or who are overcome with joy, or in the throes of a life transition) and what is the ongoing nature of the responsibility we have towards those who have made our research possible? If we do not feel ourselves to be personally at risk when we interrogate the lives of others, then we are not doing our jobs. For listening must be just that: a risk of one's self, taking the journey to enter into the life experiences of someone else, lowering the resistances that so often keep us at a safe distance from those who we consider 'other', knowing all the while that our capacity to understand fully is inevitably impaired.

3　England: stories of inspiration

The first time I moved to England was in 1979, little more than a month after Mrs Thatcher had been voted into office as the first woman Prime Minister of Britain. I was nineteen, and lived there for one year. Six years later, in 1985, I returned to England, to begin work on a project which would fully occupy my heart and mind for the next four years. I was interested in what sustains lifelong political commitment to social change – a question which was both personally and intellectually compelling for me. My reasons for selecting England as the site for my research were trivial, based on circumstances more than on anything intrinsic about the political culture of England. No sooner had I moved there, however, than I realised that I had no possibility of accessing the stories that I hoped to collect without an understanding of the broader history in which those biographies had been lived. And so it was that I spent the first year of my doctoral work in England buried in books on the twentieth-century social history of England.

The project I designed entailed fifteen life histories of women and men between the ages of seventy-five and ninety who had been active on the left in Britain for fifty years or longer. I found these people through a number of ways: trawling through newspapers; consulting archives of the Trades Union Congress (TUC), the Marx Memorial Library, and the Mass-Observation Archive; reading social history; and talking to people. Eventually, respondents recommended other people who I might interview – the 'snowball effect' – but I was wary about limiting my sample to a group of people who were overly similar and travelled in the same circles. I wanted variation in my sample in terms of class, sex, focus of political work, and geographic location. Unfortunately, the sample I ended up with, as rich as it was, was limited in terms of ethnic diversity. All of the fifteen respondents were white. At the time, I felt that this was due to the chronology of waves of immigration into Britain; the number of non-white octogenarians in Britain was not large, and finding among them people who had been politically active on the left for fifty years or longer would have been very challenging. Still, I think now that that was a challenge I should have pursued further. If in the end I had not been able to identify old non-white lifetime socialists who had been born in Britain, but rather had immigrated here, this would not have compromised the design of my study, but would have added another layer of interest. I feel that as a PhD student I did not have the confidence to be flexible, and I therefore missed an important opportunity.

Of the four case studies reported in this book, this is the only one which takes the whole of an individual's life course as its focus. This project adopted a far more intensive approach, with countless conversations, including but not limited to tape-recorded interviews, over several years. The character of the interactions which took place in this time was such that once the research had concluded, many of the relationships were well established and continued into the present time. I stayed in people's homes, socialised with their families, and over the years we became integrated into each others' lives. One of them accompanied my newborn daughter on her first protest; less than two years later I would speak at her memorial service. At some point, imperceptibly, the boundaries of research had faded, replaced by a genuine intimacy.

IN SEARCH OF STORIES OF INSPIRATION

For the first nine years of my life we lived in the city where both my parents had been born and raised, and where their parents still lived. In my early childhood years, my grandparents were a very active presence in my life. When I was six, our house burned down in the middle of the night. By the next morning, my family had moved in with my paternal grandfather, and we lived there for the six months that it took to repair our house. All of that changed when I was nine. My father, a newspaperman, was posted to Washington, DC, and as a result my family moved to a city 500 miles away. At the time that we moved I had only one grandparent remaining, my maternal grandmother, who I used to telephone daily, just to chat, during my lunch break from school. Within little more than a year after we left, she had died, and I felt her absence acutely.

If anyone had ever asked me how I chose the topic for my doctoral dissertation, I probably would not have connected my decision with this biographical information about myself. However, looking back on my life it now seems to me that in constructing for myself the project which I did I was effectively building back into my life the generation of my absent grandparents.

And so this project had deep personal significance for me, as through the conversations I had with these inspirational women and men I could envision for myself the kind of old person I hoped I would be some day. It gave me a sort of blueprint for my future. As for those who agreed to participate in my research, there were indications that part of their motivation for doing so was that they saw me as somehow an ambassador for my generation – not that I was in any way representative of any particular group of young people but simply that I was young, and curious. As they considered my request to partake in my study, some of the potential respondents were rather explicit in what I later came to call 'interviewing me for the job of interviewer'. Those who accepted the invitation to be part of my research realised the significance of the task I was asking them to undertake, and part of their deliberations of whether or not to accept this challenge was an appraisal of who they would be telling their stories to. In all cases, I spent a considerable amount of time talking with people very candidly about my project and what I hoped to achieve by it. This warming-up period ranged from minutes, to hours, to days.

CONTEXT OF THE RESEARCH

The England in which I conducted this research was one in which the effects of Thatcherism were in evidence all around. It had been the vision of Mrs Thatcher to eradicate all traces of the socialist left in the country, which she held accountable for the ills which had befallen the nation in the 1970s. It is important to consider this environment and the impact it had on the research I was conducting. The women and men who participated in my project were people who not only had been active all their long lives but who, at the time of our encounters, continued to be fully engaged in daily political struggles. On the international scene, this was the period of the 'special relationship' between Margaret Thatcher and Ronald Reagan, whose shared ideals combined into a formidable coordinated foreign policy. With the Falklands War, not to mention the proliferation of nuclear weapons, the peace movement was faced with a range of challenges. On the domestic front, Greenham Common was established during this time, and some of the adult children of my respondents were regular visitors to this peace camp. Trade unions across the country were a particular target for Mrs Thatcher's reforms, and they suffered significantly during this period. In brief, there was much work to be done for anyone who considered themselves to be a socialist activist. At the time of writing this, it is the twenty-fifth anniversary of Mrs Thatcher's election into office. The socialist basis of the Labour Party in Britain appears to be a thing of the past, as Blair's New Labour champions many of the causes traditionally associated with the Tories. The clarity of the struggles which occupied my participants in the 1980s has diminished.

The interviews themselves can be understood only in this political context. One example of this can be seen in the following passage in which Father Trevor Huddleston, speaking in 1987, describes for me his morning of that day. I ask him 'Do you ever have moments where you just feel discouraged?' to which he replies:

> Oh more than moments. I had one this morning ... We delivered a letter to the Prime Minister on, you know today is Human Rights Day in the United Nations, and we're appealing for the immediate release of detainees in South Africa. Thatcher wouldn't see me, but she asked me to see her minister at the foreign office, Lynda Chalker

> ... I've been saying for the last, well thirty years anyhow, you cannot reform apartheid, you've got to abolish it ... The only instrument that you can use apart from armed force is an effective sanctions policy ... Thatcher has been prepared to divide the Commonwealth on that issue twice already, and of course Reagan has been so supportive by his policy of 'Constructive Engagement'.

At this point I ask him 'What keeps you going at those moments, when you feel down?' to which he responds:

> What keeps me going is that I know that the African people will win, I mean there's no question, they're going to win alright ... All I'm here for is to try and keep the conscience of the world alive on this thing. There are plenty of areas on which I've still got a lot of work to do, if I'm allowed to, if I'm still alive, in that direction.

This statement is clearly embedded in the Britain of the 1980s. Three years later, in 1990, we returned to the topic of his 'life's work' still left to be done. The political tides in South Africa had begun to turn, and in this context he told me 'I've often said in the last two years "I'm determined that apartheid will be dead before I am"; as I'm seventy-seven this year, they'd better get a move on'. Before the end of his life, he would return to South Africa, the first time since attending the notorious Treason Trials more than thirty years earlier. This time, he was to be the guest of the newly elected President, Nelson Mandela. Father Trevor died shortly thereafter, his life's work done. It is not possible to disentangle his life from the times in which he lived.

Between August and December 1989, the 'Iron Curtain' was dismantled in many Central and Eastern European countries. During this time, I was engaged in rewriting my doctoral dissertation into a book (Andrews 1991). I knew I could not reasonably write about my respondents' lifetime commitment to socialism without incorporating their reactions to these momentous changes. I wrote to each of them, inquiring about how they read the situation as it was then unfolding. The responses which I received were rather varied, ranging from a full-hearted embrace of the overthrow of communist regimes, to bewilderment, to disgust at the triumphalism characteristic of the media portrayal of the events.

Some time later, the news that my next project would focus on East German dissidents prompted many of the British respondents to recount to me (by this time, via letters) experiences they had had either there or in other Eastern Bloc countries. Thus it was that the historical changes which formed the context for our interviews had changed considerably, and our ongoing communications reflected these changed circumstances.

WHY LIFE HISTORIES?

As mentioned earlier, this is the only study of the four reported in this book in which the focus of my data was on the whole of the life course. In my interviews with these old women and men I was not interested in a particular event or period of time in their lives. Rather, what I wanted to learn about was how and why these people had sustained their political commitments for so many years. How was it that they had not 'outgrown' their idealism, as conventional wisdom might have it?

It was evident to me from the very earliest stages of the project that what I needed to do was to talk with people, at length, about their lives. In my first attempt to write up a report on my intended methodology, I received very critical feedback from an academic who was renowned in the area of social science methodology. Though she had personal sympathy with the topic of the project I wished to pursue, she was very sceptical about my methodology. While it was the inspiring stories of individuals which had originally attracted me to my subject, 'real' research in the area would involve large numbers of respondents yielding vast amounts of data which could be objectively and quantifiably analysed. Intuitively, I knew that what she was proposing was not compatible with my vision of the project I wanted to pursue. The stories which had originally attracted me were not the hook into the research, they (and stories like them) were the heart of what I wanted to explore.

Ken Plummer makes a distinction between 'long' and 'short' life histories. Long life histories are 'the full-length book account of one person's life in his or her own words' (2001: 19) while short life histories are more focused, and typically involve interviews lasting between one half-hour and three hours. The life histories which I conducted for this study did not clearly fall into either category but incorporated elements of each. There were at minimum three interviews with the ten 'core' respondents of the study, with each interview lasting about two hours. But the interviews were not my only source of 'data'; rather this material was supplemented with other rich sources of information such as formal and informal archives, photographs, journals, and an abundance of written correspondence. Short life histories, Plummer notes, are 'more likely to appear as one in a series' (2001: 24). Clearly each of my respondents was only one of a larger group of people whose stories I was collecting. Yet, each story had a distinctive, and very individual character. The lives as they were recounted to me were both unique and had much common ground between them.

In the course of conducting my interviews, I was often asked by respondents to what extent the experiences which they recounted to me were shared by others in my study. Not surprisingly, there was much overlap in the themes which emerged in our long conversa tions together. But the stories were, at the same time, unique. Personal narratives thus reveal not only much about the narrating self but provide a small window into the engines of history and historical change, as we both shape and are shaped by the events of our day.

It is interesting for me to note that the opening lines of my book on this study read: 'This book tells the story of fifteen people; who, for at least half a century, have dedicated themselves to working for progressive social change' (Andrews 1991: 1). The phrase 'the story' is used twice again in this first paragraph. Is that what I was writing? A singular story? What was the relationship between the fifteen life stories which I collected? Did they, together, make a homogeneous whole, or were there important differences, hidden beneath the blanket of the singular story? Although the life stories were clearly distinct, taken together there was, at the same time, a sense in which they constituted one collective story. This story was one which, implicitly, challenged notions of what it means to grow old, and provided by example an alternative vision of human developmental potential. While I did identify and analyse important differences between the stories, my discussion of the material I gathered tended to focus on this counter-story which I felt that they embodied.

Plummer has encouraged life history researchers to regard life stories as 'topics to be investigated in their own right' and here he raises a number of pertinent questions:

> Just why do people tell the stories of their lives? What makes
> them tell their stories in particular kinds of ways? Would they tell
> them differently – or not at all – in different times and places? And
> are some stories simply not able to be told: the so-called silenced
> voices? *(2001: 41)*

These questions are not only important theoretically but they are central to questions of interpretation. How do we as researchers make sense of the stories which are told to us, which we have requested be told to us? What is the agenda of the people who are obliging us in our research?

Although I have of course had to confront these questions in all of the research I have conducted, nowhere were they more central than in my work in England. Perhaps this is so because the project itself demanded ongoing and intensive conversations between myself and my respondents over a number of years. As the participants in this study were in the later stages of life, one could argue that they were well positioned to reflect back on their lives. In psychological theory, this relates to Butler's concept of life review (1963) and its prevalence in old age. There is some evidence in my data that the positioning of my respondents in the life course assisted them, and me, in their efforts to articulate a broad framework of meaning for their lives. In one of our conversations, Elizabeth, seventy-eight at the time of our conversation, makes a comment to this effect:

> When you look back you see the path or the paths that you've taken. The path would obviously not be so clear when you're groping up and finding it, would it? I mean it's rather like going up a mountain, you're sort of looking that way and that track and it looks too steep and you're going round another one. Whereas when you're high up you can look back and see and it sort of stands out much more clearly, things you didn't realise at the time.

The 'path' that one sees at any one time is dependent upon one's perspective, and in some sense the coherence that our life stories sometimes take on in later life is a function of distance from the events we relate – that is to say, a function of age. As we live our daily lives, many of us experience high levels of chaos, discontinuity, a lack of integration. Yet, even this sense of chaos can be woven into a more coherent narrative which becomes more available to us as we stand back from the immediacy of our engagements and responsibilities.

Regardless of when in the life course a life story is told, the story itself is invariably a cultural product. We understand, live, and recount our lives to others in ways which are culturally accessible not only to others, but to ourselves. Even while we may resist certain frameworks of meaning as we spin the tales we tell, we cannot help but weave our stories in relation to those very frameworks. In life history research, particularly the intensive kind which this project entailed, there is an underlying assumption that there is an individual story to tell. Even while we, as researchers, may believe that narratives are essentially social (that is to say that they take on meaning only in social contexts, to be communicated, even if that communication is intra-individual) the life history method focuses on the individual, conforming to dominant western psychological models which emphasise the private nature of self-knowledge, with the effect that 'we remember our past as if it were a drama in which the protagonist is the focus of the plot and determines the storylines' (Wang and Brockmeir 2002: 47).

Thus it appears that not only the content of the life story, but its very structure, is a cultural product. As Wang and Brockmeir (2002) comment: 'It appears to be common sense in Western cultures that when individuals tell their personal life stories, they talk about their selves ... about what has made them who they are and what they have become and are becoming' (2002: 46). This contrasts with an essentially social understanding of autobiographical memory, in which

> autobiographical memory is an active construction embedded in
> a social weave of dialogues that are negotiated not only between
> an individual and his or her immediate social environment ...
> but also, equally important, between the individual and the larger
> cultural milieu. *(2002: 47)*

The cultural context in which a life story is rendered cannot be separated from the way in which that process occurs. However, while some cultures orient more towards an individuated 'I' than others, the self of the 'I' is always complicated, no matter where it may be situated. That is to say that we are never isolated beings whose life trajectories proceed untouched by others, and by the communities in which we live. No one is an island, and talking to people about their lives reveals just how intertwined our life stories are with the life stories of others.

The implications of this argument for my research with lifetime socialist activists are strong. Throughout the months and years that I spent in one-to-one conversations with these men and women, I was implicitly asking them to accommodate to a model which did not necessarily fit the way they understood their lives. One of the most striking characteristics across all of the respondents was the very marked social nature of their identity. This is hardly surprising given that the basis for our original contact was the high level of their sustained social action.

Years later, I now ask myself what was the effect of this structure of storytelling on the interviews I conducted. Even while the stories themselves retained a very social orientation, the research was set up in such a way that they were recounted in a highly indivi-dualised form. Comments made by some of the respondents revealed a slight discomfort with the medium. Eileen, for instance, describes her reaction upon reading the transcript of our first interview:

> I found it rather shocking because I felt it was very self-indulgent. I think that's what hit me and I think after our discussion I had felt the same … my reactions were 'Oh dear, we do try to get away from our egos – how do you break out of the circle of your ego – and here I am locked into it'.

Dorothy, in her mid-eighties at the time of our interviews, told me that this was the first time in her life that she had ever looked back on the things she had done, and accomplished, in her many years of social service. In a letter to me, she wrote 'It had never occurred to me to look at what I had been doing with my life, so the self-examination has made me evaluate'. At our next meeting, I was curious to hear more about her reactions to engaging in such a review; my assumption here was that she would feel very satisfied with her life's work. However, she describes her reactions instead as:

> a dead feeling really. It's gone and it's still going and it's successful [i.e. various organisations she helped to establish] and that's all that matters. Quite honestly I don't have any feelings about any of these things and if it hadn't been for the interview I wouldn't have looked back and made an assessment.

In fact, it was rare that I ever interviewed Dorothy on her own, as her husband Joe often sat in on our sessions, mostly observing but occa-sionally contributing to our conversation. I was aware at the time that this was not methodologically conventional, yet neither did I feel in a position to discourage it, as clearly both Dorothy and her husband preferred this combination. Also significant here is that one of the most fundamental bonds between them was their shared political activity; her story of her lifetime's commitment was intricately bound to his, just as his was to hers.

In an interview with Mary, I pose a question about her identity, which clearly does not sit comfortably with her. She tells me 'I don't really think of myself as having an identity'. She later expands on this:

> It's a funny word [identity] isn't it? … I mean if I do something that I wished I hadn't, I think about it, [but I] certainly don't bother to think about an identity … I suppose I would only think of myself in terms of … what I like and … what I do … Perhaps you as the younger generation think more in that kind of way. I wouldn't think many people go on consciously thinking about themselves really.

While life history research does not entail explicitly asking someone to discuss their identity, if one believes that the self is constituted by the stories in which it is encased, then it does by implication involve aspects of the kind of identity work to which Mary refers here. I, as a researcher, am asking those who participate in my project to 'consciously think about themselves'. In this sense, looking back on the work which I conducted with this small group of lifetime socialist activists, I wonder to what extent I designed a project which was against the grain of my chosen topic. Still, it is interesting that nearly one-third of the respondents have now written some form of their memoirs. Indeed, I have been honoured to comment upon draft copies of chapters which I have been sent. What role their involvement with my own project played in motivating them to put pen to paper is not possible to say, and nor is it important. I interpret this willingness to write autobiographically, for a public audience, for those who have done it, as a way of 'bottling' some of their life's work, so others may benefit from it. They knew that the journey they had taken in their lives had been worthwhile, and that it had meaning and purpose, not only to themselves individually but to a wider world. They modelled for successive generations a possible alternative to the decline and emptiness so often associated with old age, a blueprint to help others visualise what kind of people they would like to be in old age.

As time passed and I grew increasingly familiar with my respondents, they began to ask me more and more questions about the other participants. Although some of the questions were practical (How did they react to being tape recorded? What did they feel about using their real names in my future publications?) more often they were interested in the substance of other stories I was gathering. While most of the respondents did not know one another, there were exceptions to this. Two had been close friends since childhood, and a few others were passing acquaintances. Several people mentioned to me how much they would like to meet the others who had been involved in my project – indeed, the suggestion was even made that perhaps I should interview them all together – and so I organised a gathering for all of us after completing my research. This meeting, attended by more than half of the respondents, was a day that I will long remember. The day ended with them expressing a desire to meet again soon, if not in this life then in the next. At that time I did not think about how many painful goodbyes were in store for me as a by-product of this research. Never again did we meet as a group as we had on that one day.

STORIES OF RADICALISATION

The people who participated in my study found in their early lives an outlook on life which was both sufficiently broad and flexible to be able to guide them in their actions for a very long time. How did this happen?

Mannheim's (1952) work on generations suggests that the life stage of youth yields a particular force of influence on subsequent political development. For Mannheim, generations are the engines of social change, but critically he argues that times of social upheaval are most likely to politicise a generation. For him, there is a symbiotic relationship between the generation and historical epochs. Mannheim's work is not unusual in positing youth as a time of politicisation; indeed most of the work in political psychology which emerged in the mid-twentieth century adopted a similar approach. What is more interesting here is that Mannheim implicitly suggests that there are lifespan implications for the politics which one adopts in youth. As someone whose primary interest was in epistemology, Mannheim argued strongly that all knowledge is based on perspective, or 'positionally determined':

> That a view of history is 'positionally determined' means that it is formed by a subject occupying a distinct position in the 'historical stream', all parts of which – those occupied by us as well as those occupied by the object we examine – are constantly in transition and motion.
>
> *(1952: 120)*

Mannheim's interest in generations stemmed from his belief that the time when individuals are born wields a powerful influence on their perspective of history. 'Individuals who belong to the same generation, who share the same year of birth, are endowed, to that extent, with a common location in the historical dimension of the social process' (1952: 290). Obviously he did not think that all persons born at the same time shared a political outlook – they may 'work up the material of their common experiences in different and specific ways' (1952: 304). But members of a generation have been exposed to the same historical events at the same time in their life courses. This is important for Mannheim, because of his belief in a fundamental connection between knowledge and socio-historical structure.

   Critically, for Mannheim, the life course of any individual is strongly influenced by the historical moments in which they are born but, equally, that history is made by individuals, particularly when they act as part of a group. One is reminded here of Marx's statement that 'men make history, but they do not make it in circumstances of their own choosing'. Mannheim distinguishes between generation as location, and generation as actuality. The first of these is akin to a cohort; however, cohorts become transformed into generations only when 'many of its members become aware that they are bound together by a shared group consciousness and mobilise as an active force for political change' (Braungart and Braungart 1986: 217). In Mannheim's words, a generation realises its potential – i.e. becomes a generation as actuality – through 'participation in the common destiny of this historical and social unit' (1952: 303). Thus, Mannheim's discussion of the critical role of generational consciousness in creating political change mirrors that of class consciousness, as outlined by Marx.

The importance of generational consciousness was pronounced in my study of lifetime socialists. All the respondents became politicised in Britain during the inter-war years (1918–39). Although there was an age-span of approximately fifteen years, broadly speaking they were part of the same generational cohort. Ralph Miliband summarises Britain during this time, and the attraction to the newly formed Communist Party:

> Unemployment and the Depression; the blandly reactionary
> face of Conservatism and the tarnished reality of British imperi-
> alism, the blatant inadequacies of Labourism; the rise of
> Fascism; Spain appeasement; the attractive certitudes of
> 'Marxist–Leninism'; the promise of a new world to be gained
> by striving and strife; the immensely strong will to believe that
> the new world was already being built in the Soviet Union and
> that it must be defended from the permanent threat of the old
> world … What is remarkable is not that many young men
> and women felt the pull to the left, but that there were not
> more of them.   *(Miliband 1979: 16–17)*

In our interview together, Christopher echoes this perspective, but he is speaking from his personal experience. With passion, he tells me:

> You can see it, can't you, how unemployment, fascism, war
> preparations, political reaction … one knew that all the right
> wing conservatives were really anti-Semitic and pro-Hitler in their
> heart of hearts, and they really wanted Hitler to attack Russia …
> one saw in Russia this wonderful, creative, just, egalitarian society
> with infinite potential, and everything seemed to add up and
> everything seemed to cut the same way.

The environment was ripe for radical political awakening. All the respondents spoke to me in detail about what it was like growing up in these circumstances. Still, not everyone who was unemployed participated in political protest, such as the Jarrow Hunger Marchers; shared historical circumstances do not, in themselves, determine shared political outlook.

Despite the many differences between the respondents in the study, all of them were exposed to a 'political education' which provided for them an explanatory framework which they felt was sufficient as a means for understanding, and ultimately acting upon, the political issues of their time. They received their political education through a range of sources. Though all of the participants in the project mentioned the importance of particular individuals, many also spoke of the indelible impact made on them through books, movies, and religion.

When participants described the process by which they had arrived at their political understanding, they often identified a moment when their radicalisation crystallised, but this moment was itself a culmination of life experiences and exposure to political explanations which somehow seemed to 'fit'. Eileen tells me of a 'sudden illumination' of political awareness, but then goes on to say 'Mind you, if it hadn't been there, it would have been somewhere else, and it would have happened in another way. There isn't just one way. So I'm not romantic.' She explains the process of radicalisation, saying:

> ideas don't just appear, do they? It's an accumulation. It's the old Engels [saying] isn't it? ... he's explaining ... qualitative changes, and how the kettle is boiling and suddenly the water turns to steam. It becomes something else. Now it's taken that water a long time to boil.

Christopher was very influenced by his older brother John, who from a young age was a Communist and who died on his twenty-first birthday on the battlefields of Spain. Christopher describes the effect of this relationship on the development of his political perspective:

> It never occurred to me that he could be wrong about anything, so I felt sure he was right. On the other hand, I didn't feel that it applied

to me ... until one day ... he said 'You could be a communist too' and it was rather like St Paul on the road to Damascus. Bang. Flash. Wallop ... I began reading the Third International pamphlets he had with him.

This very intimate encounter was supplemented by endless reading, and watching movies, all of which contributed to his political understanding, and made him evaluate the very privileged conditions of his own life from a Marxist, class-conscious perspective. He describes how he experienced the environment in which he grew up:

> The world of these three quarters of an acre of land became very complete, because you didn't have to go outside it for anything. Everything was provided for and the environment was lovely to play in .... one went into the fields and occasionally one went into the town, but one lived in a very sort of protected, isolated, cosseted environment. And later on ... when I became politicised and a communist ... I felt that working-class kids don't have this same fantastic amount of privilege and protection and ease and security.

Jack's radicalisation came in quite a different form. He was born into a very poor family; his father became an alcoholic after suffering a work-related accident, after which he was laid off, and his mother died when Jack was seven. As a young child, his family were evicted from their home, and sought refuge in the theatre, sleeping in the stalls after audiences had gone home. Jack describes himself as 'a gut Communist. I've been hungry ... I mean these things are unforgettable.' Still, of the four children in the family, he was the only one who became a socialist. He says his earliest education came from a socialist pacifist who he met when he was a hod-carrier, working on a building site in London's East End. The old socialist recommended that Jack read certain books, which Jack did, and together they would discuss them. 'That was laying, not overnight, but it laid the foundations that made me enquire more and read more ... The soil was being fertilised.' He describes the effect of reading these books, and the conversations they would have:

> I aligned myself with what was being written in the books. And Jack London, he had the greatest impact on me of all … All those fitted into my brain and then it was clear, and I knew something, I've got to become a political person, I've got to take part in the struggle. In other words, I became class conscious.

In another interview, he returns to this theme:

> It laid the foundations, helped me to understand it, you see by reading it fiction-wise, it's much easier to understand. Where the characters are working class people, you know, and their struggles, and you identify yourself, although you live here and not in America [as in Jack London's books] but you know the problems that are facing them, because you're facing it or been through it.

The power of these stories for Jack cannot be overestimated, as they helped him to 'lay the foundations' for his political understanding, and thus provided him with a framework for making sense of the very harsh living conditions which surrounded him. Whitebrook (2001) argues that understanding political narrative identity requires us to go beyond existing theory, and that close reading of novels provides a particularly useful tool for doing this, as it facilitates our ability to examine individual lives 'extra-politically and across time' (2001: 15). In Jack's case, we can see a poignant example of art informing an individual's understanding of their life, and their location within it.

Jack's words cited in the passage above reveal a clear determination to embark on a particular path in his life: 'I've got to become a political person, I've got to take part in the struggle.' Jack, along with Christopher and Eileen, remembers thinking consciously about the kind of life he wished to lead. (It's possible that this clarity of purpose was retroactively attributed – but it is not possible for me to tell.) The high measure of personal agency in pursuing the life of a political activist is also echoed in other interviews. Frida, for instance, recalls the impact of the Spanish Civil War, which began in 1936, on her politics. In the early 1930s, Frida had already become involved in left-wing groups, having really 'woken up', as she describes it, with the persecution of Jews in Germany in 1933. She was involved in street theatre and worked with the renowned left-wing director and founder of the Theatre Workshop, Joan Littlewood, with groups of the unemployed in northern England, and even travelled to the Moscow Theatre Festival in 1935. However, it was the Spanish Civil War which she describes as a real 'turning point' for her: 'The Spanish war brought me right over to the left'. She was given the opportunity to drive an ambulance to Spain. 'One feels "I must make this decision and do it" ... you just have to take that decision.' While she had been politically sympathetic to the left prior to this time, in taking 'that decision' she committed herself to a life of activism.

Another example comes from Elizabeth, who relates to me a dream she had in which it became clear to her how her life would be different from that of many people. She tells me:

> I was in a little boat, just a little lugsail, it was a tiny little boat and it had only got one sail ... I was setting sail across the sea on my own. On my right ... there was a huge steamer ... and everybody on board, they were dancing and laughing ... it was setting off, it knew exactly where it was going, they were all going together and they were having a merry time. I didn't want to go on that steamer, it didn't belong to my type of thinking at all, but I was really quite terrified of setting out in this little lugsail. I realised that that's what I was doing and what sort of person I was, and you couldn't be other than that.

Elizabeth's dream, as she conveys it, is both rather simple and multilayered in its complexity. On the surface, it is a dream about independence, about staking one's position in relation to other people, from who one invariably sees oneself as being different. In the terminology of lifespan psychologist Erik Erikson, this is a dream about identity formation, and indeed Elizabeth does have this dream in her early adulthood. In this dream, the people on the other boat are both enjoying themselves ('dancing and laughing') and there is a certainty about their destination (the boat was just setting off, and 'it knew exactly where it was going'). Although Elizabeth is clear in her dream that 'I didn't want to go on that steamer, it didn't belong to my type of thinking', at the same time, being alone in the lugsail does not bring her relief, but terror. The message of the dream appears to be about self-knowledge and acceptance ('that's … what sort of person I was, and you couldn't be other than that'). Elizabeth's account of the roots of her activism focuses on her coming to accept that being located on the margins was simply who she was. Elizabeth does not see herself as a passenger on a ship steered by someone else but rather as someone who takes control of her own destiny, even while that passage may be full of risks and uncertainty.

KEEPING THE FAITH

The stories which the participants in my study related to me of how they came to their activism varied in their particulars, but shared a sense of a consciousness of the intersection of their own biography with the historical process. Supporting Mannheim's hypothesis, the acute social upheaval in which they entered early adulthood had a powerful influence on the way in which they perceived the social world and their potential role within it. The political outlook which they adopted at that moment in their lives was one which was to stay with them for all of their years. But how is it, exactly, that they have managed to sustain their commitment while, for so many, political engagement is more transitory?

There are two key factors which feature in the long-term commitment of the respondents in my study: a fundamental identification with a group and a long-term sense of history. Each of these provides a sense of collective identity which mitigates against potential despondency which might set in when the struggles to which activists dedicate themselves suffer setbacks. The sense of sharing a common cause with others, in both the present time and in the historical process more widely, provides activists with an enduring sense of purpose.

In contrast to much of the literature on political engagement, particularly that published in the second half of the twentieth century, all of the respondents regard their life's work as essentially social; that is to say implicitly they reject individualistic explanations of political behaviour (e.g. Kenniston 1968; Rokeach 1960). They do what they do, and what they have done, as social beings, in conjunction with other people, as members of groups and institutions. This social basis is not incidental to, but rather a core component of, who they are, and it lies at the heart of their sustained activism. Edward addresses this when he tells me that without organisations 'We'd be lost. You couldn't do anything.' He then elaborates on this:

> if you took any individual in the peace movement, any of the thousands who go on demos and so on, and said to them what difference have you made, none of us individually, separately could say 'I've made much of a difference'. Even though we have made a difference together.

From this group orientation, the respondents derive a sense of being part of something which is larger than themselves. The sense of accomplishment, then, is not as an individual but as part of a collaborative effort.

Beyond this wider group, respondents share an emphasis on the long-term movement of history itself. Eileen explains her attitude to me: 'If you take a long-term view of history ... then you know things come back'. She speaks to me of her 'certitude about the political process and the march forward of humanity' which she says 'is not a linear progression ... it's full of pitfalls, and ups and downs, but it works round in the spiral we've talked of so often'.

This echoes the view of Edward, who explains that long-term commitment demands 'a very big perspective'. 'The history of the movement has been built as much on defeats as successes … but it's been the way forward, it's the struggle that people have learned'. Jack emphasises the importance of continuing one's efforts, even when short-term results are not encouraging:

> You must not give up, you must keep pegging away … it's just like the farmer who sows the seeds, and one year you get a bad crop, or he might not get a crop at all, but he doesn't give up his farmland, he doesn't give up being a farmer. He still continues to sow the seeds and the next year he probably gets a much more bountiful harvest. So it's the same in the world of politics. You're sowing a seed, you're germinating socialist philosophy.

Critically, activists see themselves as participating in shaping history, and this is sustained by a collective solidarity with others both in the present and across time. They have a wide historical perspective; setbacks can be tolerated as they are seen, in Edward's words, as 'temporary hiccups'.

All of the respondents feel that the political outlook which has formed the basis of their worldview has been sufficiently flexible and comprehensive to allow for personal development and growth, while at the same time being sensitive to environmental change. It is, then, an enduring commitment based on a political–psychological model of consistency within change. Respondents' engagement with the social and political issues of their times has not resulted in an alteration of their fundamental political beliefs. However, through their long-term political involvement, the beliefs themselves have become, in most cases, more complex, accommodating to information acquired by the activists as they encounter new situations. Thus, through their experiences, individuals grow into their ideas. Beliefs branch out in depth and complexity with time and experience. Eileen describes this process, again employing the imagery of a spiral:

> You don't come back, it isn't the wheel has come full circle. You come in a spiral. This is the Marxist theory of progress … Life

doesn't go back to where it began, it comes up a bit further, and that's where you see progress.

When the respondents speak about their sustained commitment, it is clear that after more than fifty years of political struggle activism has become a core component of who they are. For so many years, they have fought for their ideals. To stop doing so now would be to eradicate a primary source of meaning in their lives. As Eileen puts it: 'It gives you a motive for going on living. It is very strong, It's survival'. Activism is as vital to their existence as oxygen.

OUR LETTERS

Throughout the time that I have known these women and men, they have sent me many letters, some of which share common themes. In the letters from the earlier years of our acquaintance there are often references to our most recent meeting, and talk about plans for our next session. These range in tone from rather intimate to more logistical discussion of trains and platforms, and most combine these elements. Eileen, for instance, sends a brightly coloured postcard, telling 'I look forward to seeing you next Monday. Have started to look at the transcript and will find time to do a bit of quiet thinking over the next few days', which she then signs with love.

Some of the letters elaborate on or clarify topics which we covered in our interviews. They were, in this sense, an enhanced source of 'data', which I always made clear were welcomed, though not expected. Walter writes to me:

> I am sorry that a number of your questions left me floundering. One of these ... was on the lines of what was my yardstick to measure and decide what was moral or what was immoral. How did I decide as each issue came up in the course of my life? I completely failed to produce any clear answer and yet it should have been reasonably easy to state what benefits the majority in life is moral and that which only benefits an individual or a class in the minority – at the expense of the

majority – must be immoral and to be resisted. Examples are easy to come by.

The remainder of this long letter is dedicated to examples which support this description of his moral yardstick. I found letters like this very useful and interesting, for two key reasons. First, they provided me with an insight into the respondent's experience of the interview. Walter, in this passage, describes himself as 'floundering'. Yet this is not a word I would have chosen to describe him. To me, he always appeared very thoughtful and articulate. As I read his letter, I am curious why he experiences himself in this way, and wonder how I might have contributed to this self-impression. Second, the letter provides me with more information to help me understand how Walter sees and evaluates the social world.

Another example of this can be found with Dorothy. Both Dorothy and her husband Joe wrote to me regularly between our meetings, with thoughts that occurred to them only after my departure. It was clear to me that they took 'our task' very seriously, and saw themselves as having taken on my political education. I was most fortunate in having these particular teachers; in 1963, when E. P. Thompson published what would become a classic of English social history, *The Making of the English Working Class*, he dedicated it to none other than 'To Dorothy and Joseph Greenald'. Perhaps they saw in me someone who was curious and young, and they felt it worthwhile to try to ensure that the next generation was sufficiently equipped with the necessary tools for understanding the ills of society, and how best to address them. Moreover, because I was a foreigner, any ignorance on my part could be both assumed and forgiven. On my very first visit to their homes, they gave me a complete set of *The Left Review*, the precursor of *The New Left Review*; an acquaintance who is an antique book dealer told me that these were indeed collectors' items. But they gave them to me for one purpose only: if I wanted to understand the history of the labour movement in post-war Britain, I must read these from start to finish. Both of them cared very much that I got the story 'right', and they dedicated themselves tirelessly to providing me with stories from their own lives as well as materials they had collected over the years to ensure that my education was as complete as it could be.

Invariably I received a letter from one, or the other, or sometimes both following the reading of a transcript I had sent them. After reading one of these transcripts, for instance, Dorothy is worried about an impression she may have given inadvertently. She writes a very long letter to me, expanding on her thoughts about this:

> Working at the Dentists looks as though I was happy moving out of my social class, not at all, but interesting looking at those people and hearing their views, but more important was the educative side ... I read every day ... we never had a book or a newspaper in our house ... Working at the Dentists opened my eyes to many enriching experiences.

I am perplexed by the fact that many researchers would consider such feedback 'out of bounds'. They would feel that as the tape recorder had not captured these sentiments, they should not be considered 'data'. As a life historian, I am interested in how we assess the adequacy of the interpretations that we as researchers give to the words of others. What makes one interpretation better than another is the extent to which it can accommodate the complexity and variety of experience of others as they relate it to me. The more supplemental material I have, the better opportunity I have to create such an explanatory framework.

However, spending as much time with research participants as I did, invariably I became aware of aspects of their lives which they may not have wanted me to bring into the story I constructed. I decided that I need not write everything I knew, but that I could not write something which did not fit with the rest of my knowledge about this person. Thus, conversations with friends and family members about the life of 'my participant' were brought into my interpretation of the stories which I heard, but only as one of a number of filtering lenses. The long-term nature of the project, and thus my ongoing and ever-developing relationships with my participants, might have contributed to a particularly enhanced sense of personal accountability to those who had opened their lives to me.

As I sent transcripts to respondents as soon after our interviews as possible – and these formed the first thread to be picked up at our next meeting – some of the letters comment in detail on the actual transcript. Christopher, for instance, writes 'When I read it through it seems authentic and as close to the truth as I could get' – a contrast to Dorothy's feedback that the written form of her spoken word describing to me the process by which she became class conscious did not resonate with her feelings about that transformation.

There is also a scattering of letters in which I am being lightly reprimanded for not being in more contact. One example of this is in the opening line in a letter from Frida. (Despite the fact that she lived around the corner from me, the letter was stamped and posted.) She writes: 'Sorry not to have seen you for so long. I hoped you might have 'phoned, as I've mislaid your new number and can't reach you so easily.' This, of course, had the desired effect of raising me from my books. A letter from Edward begins 'Many thanks for the letter. No, I didn't think you had gone out of business.' Clearly, I must have worried that I had fallen out of touch, and written as much to him. The natural fondness I felt towards those who were participating in my study was mixed with a sense of responsibility, and this theme reappears in a myriad of ways throughout our communications.

Some of the envelopes are stuffed with supporting material, articles which they have written themselves or clipped from the newspaper which they feel are relevant to our ongoing discussions. Many of the letters report the respondents' reactions to receiving a copy of the book which was the culmination of this piece of research. Walter writes to me:

> It is a splendid book and I am proud to be associated with it even in a minor way. I think you know I left school at fourteen and in spite of trying to learn all my life, I can never truthfully claim to have

caught up with what was sadly lacking in my education – to put it briefly, large parts of your book … leave me struggling … for which I feel sure you will understand and sympathise.

Walter's comment, both candid and non-judgemental, addressed an issue which had already caused me some concern. If I work the material into a form which meets academic standards, will it not lose some of its integrity? This, I believe, is the dilemma of many academics who do research of this kind. If the material that we produce is not comprehensible to the very people who have participated in our research, is our work in some way compromised? Yet, on the other hand, Christopher writes to me that he finds 'the theory section excellent in its handling of the observer/observed problem'. In the examples cited here, the class identity, and corresponding educational background, of my research participants is apparent. Walter in particular refers to the long-term impact of having finished his schooling at an early age; but while abstract theory leaves him 'struggling', for Christopher, the son of a Cambridge Professor of Ancient Philosophy and himself later the Dean of the Royal Academy of Art, the theory was invigorating. The difference of class and educational background between Christopher and Dorothy might also help to explain the contrast of their reactions to transcripts of our interviews, as described above, although this pattern would need to be explored. While I made concerted efforts to conduct my research in an accessible and inclusive manner, ultimately the fact that it was being undertaken for a doctoral degree from one of the most elite universities in the world did enter into what I wrote and who I wrote for, and this in turn made the work attractive to some of my interviewees while it excluded others.

Many of the letters also comment upon the choice I had made for my next major project: a study of dissident activists in East Germany. Some of the respondents had been very active in East–West dialogues, and were enthusiastic about this proposed work. This encouraged me, as it not only gave me some sense of continuity between these projects but in some sense it helped to avoid having to say 'goodbye' to the project in which my life had been so immersed for several years. I felt from these letters, and conversations, that one theme had given birth to another, and that my work with these socialist activists would provide a strong starting point for me as I began my investigations of an entirely different political culture.

Two written pieces, both from Christopher, deserve special mention here. The first was written in response to my letter to him asking if there were any additional comments he would like to make about his commitment to socialism in light of the changes of 1989. His response, dated March 1990, is sixteen pages of A4 paper, and is penned in his remarkable handwriting, not a smudge anywhere. His account is so thoughtful and complex, and when viewed from the distance of more than fifteen years, startlingly prescient. Indeed, it is a piece which merits its own publication, written with passion, humour, and care. In this letter, Christopher describes himself as one who is 'by temperament addicted to seeing human affairs in terms of grand evolutionary sweeps and transformations which … underlie normal everyday "reality" '. He then offers his own view on the key evolutionary phenomena of our times, ranging from the advent of feminism – which he sees as 'a new emergence as impor- tant as any our species has so far experienced, comparable with the advents of speech, of writing, of philosophy, of science … half of humanity is re-inventing itself' – to the global village, to concepts of inter-subjectivity, among others. I look at this document and am honoured that he took the time to write this to me.

The second document is slightly longer than the first, again written in a hand which attests to the fact that he is an artist. This piece, written for more general consumption (I believe it was sent to his sons, as well as to me), has a title 'The Foundations of Bogology' and begins:

> Heaven forbid that any of us should perish without first having founded some new branch of learning with a title ending in-ology. My own contribution shall be Bogology, by which I mean the study

of the bogus, of bogusness or bogisty wherever in human affairs it declares itself.

Here Christopher, great-grandson of Charles Darwin, reveals his intellectual playfulness and utter lack of pretension, which is combined with his natural warmth and humour. This treatise ends with the comment:

> For my part, when I look back on my life I seem to recall a number of contexts in which I either was bogus or tried to be. Nowadays, by contrast, I seem to myself solidly authentic from toe to top. So there must be something wrong somewhere.

Re-reading these materials I am filled with an appreciation for the opportunity I had to get to know such people. The letters serve as a window into our relationships. In contrast to the interview transcripts, which are for the most part rather impersonal in terms of our interaction, what comes through in these pages and pages of writing is the deep affection between us. (Where else am I known as 'Molly Angel', as Christopher often addressed me in his letters?) I am touched to see how cared for I was by this small group of people.

ENTERING AND EXITING LIVES

Earlier in the chapter I mentioned that the history of my relationship with my grandparents might have had an influence on my decision to pursue research in this area. This thought has occurred to me over the years, as I came to appreciate the unanticipated consequences of my relationships with some of the women and men who participated in my study.

In chapter 2, I described a letter from one of my participants, asking me 'Are you through with me now?' . This question caught me off guard. Of course I wasn't finished with her. You can't walk into somebody's life, engage in such intimacy, and then walk out again. I was sure that I had told her that I would be in contact again, but that for several months I would be looking at our transcripts and trying to figure out 'what it all meant'. Did she not hear me say that? Or did I mean to say that, but failed to do so as I worried about how that would sound, and how she might take it? Worse still, was I in fact finished with her, but simply unable to admit to as much?

In fact the boundaries of my relationships with those who had participated in my research became increasingly opaque, as the story above illustrates. I shall never forget the day when one respondent, holding copies of the transcripts of all of our interviews, turned to me and said: 'These are the answers to the questions my daughter never asked me.' At the time, I heard that comment not only as a researcher, but as a daughter. Now I hear it as a mother, as well. Another respondent wrote to me, stating that she hoped she had fulfilled the expectations of the person who had originally suggested that I interview her, adding then 'but he does not know me half as well as you do, nor does anyone else'. It is not perhaps so surprising, given this level of intimacy, that many of these relationships have continued into the present day.

In the nearly twenty years that we have known each other, much has come to pass in all of our lives – marriages, births, and deaths. The intensity of the bonds between us, in some of the relationships, extends beyond anything I could have imagined when I first embarked on this work. How could I know that they would continue to be part of my life when I first became a mother, that they would indulge my children in their early years, and take them to their first protest? And why had I not anticipated that such an enduring contact would also entail very painful times for them, as spouses and others close to them died? (In Dorothy's letter to me informing me of Joe's recent death, she told me they had just received a copy of *Lifetimes of Commitment*, the book I eventually published based on this study in which they had played such an important part. On their last night together, Joe sat reading this book, in his rocking chair which I knew so well. Dorothy even told me what page he had got to before he went to bed. I found myself asking a childish question: What had Joe thought of my work? Had I, his student, been worthy of all his efforts?) And, lastly, wasn't it obvious, given the age of the respondents when I began this work, that I would probably survive them all, indeed that I had created a situation for myself which entailed a very painful series of goodbyes? None of this ever really occurred to me in the early years, and by the time it did, I experienced these losses very personally. I have spoken at several memorial services, including Dorothy's; my challenge here, I felt, was to communicate the sense of totality of these inspirational lives, as they had been conveyed to me.

Spending so much time with this group of very special people as they review the meaning of their lives has caused me to ask myself what kind of life I will want to look back on in future years. What kinds of stories will I want to be able to tell myself about who I have been, based on what I have done? What can I do now that will make me feel fulfilled then? Since conducting this research more than two decades ago, I have had several occasions to return to the original transcripts. Each time I have done so, I have found in them something new; I have changed, times have changed, and the stories I gathered, like all stories, are forever transforming.

I continue to grow and learn as a result of my encounter with these remarkable people. For me, they will always represent a special place in my professional identity, something akin to the first time one falls in love. I feel that I am still growing into the conversations – some of which happened almost twenty years ago, others only last month – with my old friends. Though most of the participants in this study have died, their narratives, and their changing meaning for me, are an ongoing gift in my life.

4 The USA: narratives of patriotism

One of the most powerful and pervasive political narratives which organises personal and public stories is that of the relationship between the individual and the nation. And it is well documented that individuals tend to express strong affiliative ties with their country when they feel that their country is under attack. Ernest Renan, in his famous essay 'What is a Nation', written at the end of the nineteenth century, surmises: 'Suffering in common unifies more than joy does. Where national memories are concerned, griefs are of more value than triumphs, for they impose duties, and require a common effort' (1882/1990: 19). This comment offers much insight into the phenomenon of the explosion of patriotism in the USA in the post-9/11 era. Americans of all stripes have been compelled to rethink their relationship to their country, and how they can best support those aspects of the nation which they feel are under fire and are worth trying to preserve. This chapter explores narratives of patriotism in the USA, before and after the events of September 11th, 2001.

'MY' COUNTRY: THE COMPLEXITY OF THE PERSONAL PRONOUN

In 2001, I had been living outside of the USA for the previous five years. I feel that being born and raised in the USA, and indeed spending much of my childhood in Washington, DC, had instilled in me a strong sense of national identity. As a young girl, I loved the story of Betsy Ross as she sewed the first American flag, and I even visited her home in Philadelphia, a trip which also included seeing the Liberty Bell and the cramped accommodation where Thomas Jefferson drafted the Declaration of Independence. I loved the Fourth of July. But the socialisation into the meaning of my national identity also included being brought to anti-Vietnam War demonstrations in Washington, and participating with my parents in the candlelight vigils, with singers like Peter, Paul, and Mary on the stage nearby. My parents spent much effort to explain to my siblings and me why all these people were gathered, but mostly, as quite a young child, what I took away from this was a deep and lasting impression of a call for peace in a time of war.

My father, a newspaperman, had covered the Democratic Convention in Chicago in 1968, and we sat at home watching the violence unfold on our television sets, and wondering if our father was okay. Mayor Daley had committed over 12,000 police officers, and had called in the National Guard, to combat the anti-war activists who had gathered. Violence erupted, and there were hundreds of casualties. All of this was captured on film, and relayed to the nation live. In the paper the next morning, a column of my father's appeared, in which he wrote with great compassion about spending the night with the protestors who had been so violently attacked. Not many years later, the Watergate affair dominated not only national news but local affairs – and, indeed, was played out as a micro-drama in the classrooms of my high school as fathers of my classmates were involved in a wide range of roles relating to the scandal. Thus, part of the process of our coming of age as adolescents was being plunged into the heart of the unfolding impeachment process of our President, a time which was characterised by Nixon's successor, Gerald Ford, as 'our long national nightmare'. We passionately cared about national politics, and I experienced the day Nixon resigned as one of an inexpressible triumph of good over evil. All of these threads, and many more, had been woven together to create my own story of what it meant to me to be an American.

Oftentimes, one is so immersed in one's own culture and day-to-day life that it is difficult to discern the pull of this national narrative, unless and until one steps outside of one's home environment. This is what happened to me when I went to England in the mid-1980s to study for my doctorate. My understanding of what my nationality means to me, personally and politically, has changed over time, and doubtless will continue to do so. I remember how surprised I was on 16 April 1986, to be greeted at my front door by a friend who was clearly angry with me. The previous day the USA had launched a major air raid against Libya in which thirty-seven people, mostly civilians, had died. 'You ought to be ashamed of yourself' he blurted out, before I had even fully opened the front door. Was I, I asked him, to be held personally responsible for all of the military actions of my government, regardless of my political views? My retort, somewhat feeble, was to condemn him, as a British person, for allowing 'us' to use not only British air space, but the F16s as well, thereby enabling us to accomplish our mission. Here we were, my friend and I, speaking as the embodiment of one nation to another, and each of us ashamed of the actions which had been committed in our names.

Yet even while I rejected his implication that I was personally responsible for these senseless killings, at the same time I knew that my identity as an American positioned me in a different way to these events than a non-American, regardless of my personal feelings. This complication is ongoing, and is an important part of my experience of my national identity. It is not surprising that one's sense of belonging to a group, a community, or a nation is altered when one is no longer physically there. But it also true that a sense of connection is not only, and maybe not even primarily, determined by geographical factors. So though one moves from one locale to another, the bond which existed moves too, though in its journey it is transformed.

When we speak of a sense of belonging, or being a member of a particular community, what is it that we mean? In the case of national identity, it is the more intangible aspects of group identity which are perhaps its strongest base. Homi Bhabha refers to the narratives and discourses that signify a sense of 'nationness':

> the *Heimlich* pleasures of the hearth, the *unheimlich* terror
> of the space or race of the Other; the comfort of social belonging,
> the hidden injuries of class; the customs of taste, the powers of

> political affiliation; the sense of social insight of institutions; the
> quality of justice, the common sense of injustice; the *langue* of the
> law and the *parole* of the people. (Bhabha 1990: 2)

It is in its finer detail that this 'sense of nationness' exercises its
greatest lure. What does it mean to be a member of this community,
or a citizen of that country? I confronted these questions anew, personally and politically, in 1990, when I first moved back to the USA. Only
months after I arrived in Colorado Springs, the Gulf War broke out.
What did it mean to be a US citizen, living on US soil, when that
country was at war? What were the effects of the political situation,
combined with my own geographic location, on the sense of attachment I felt for my country?

Before discussing the project I conducted in Colorado Springs, I
would like to explore questions of my own positioning in the project
I carried out on anti-war activism there.

When I moved to Colorado Springs, not only had I not lived in
the USA for the previous five years but I had only ever experienced 'my
country' at war when I was a child. My new home was to be a fertile
ground for me to explore the meaning I attached to my national
identity. The 'findings' of my project cannot, of course, be disassoci-
ated from my own political perspective, both at the time, and now, as I
try to make sense of my emotional and intellectual reactions to finding myself living in such a highly militarised community. It meant
something to me personally to explore the sentiments of the anti-
war protestors, because I felt intuitively that these were Americans
with whom I could politically identify myself. I do not think that I am
unusual in using my position as a researcher to locate 'speaking subjects' who will articulate viewpoints which I also share. I hope that I
can remain open to hearing the unexpected in my research travels, but
it would be disingenuous to posture myself as one without an investment in my object of inquiry. I was personally and politically deeply
troubled by the country I returned to. By doing this research, I was
provided with a mechanism to process and make sense of my

own complex set of feelings for 'my country'. My discussion of this research cannot be reasonably separated from the journey which it represented for me at this time.

The city of Colorado Springs, with five military establishments in the general vicinity, is one of the most densely militarised locations in the USA, with 55 per cent of its total economy involved in the defence industry. The North American Aerospace Defense Command (NORAD) was built into the mountains which dominated the view from my apartment. The daughter of the then-Defense Secretary, Dick Cheney, was graduating from the college where I was teaching in my first year there, and he was the commencement speaker at the graduation. The speech he gave directly addressed a topic close to my own; what it meant to be an American, and the responsibilities that came with this. In this speech, he quoted the words of a song written exactly one hundred years earlier, composed by a faculty member of the college, Katherine Lee Bates, as she ascended Pike's Peak, the mountain that forms the backdrop of Colorado Springs: 'America, the Beautiful, God shed his grace on thee'.

I have always loved this song, but with a sense of unease because of the way in which it has been used to represent an America with which I feel no connection. My 'America, the Beautiful' was not Cheney's, but rather the one conjured up in Ray Charles' rendition of this song:

> And you know when I was in school,
> We used to sing it something like this, listen here:
>
> Oh beautiful, for spacious skies,
> For amber waves of grain,
> For purple mountain majesties,
> Above the fruited plain,
>
> But now wait a minute, I'm talking about
> America, sweet America,

You know, God done shed his grace on thee,
He crowned thy good, yes he did, in a brotherhood,
From sea to shining sea.

You know, I wish I had somebody to help me sing this
(America, America, God shed his grace on thee)
America, I love you America, you see,
My God he done shed his grace on thee.   *(Charles 1972)*

In the reworking of this song's lyrics, Charles delivers nothing short of a love song for his country. Jimi Hendrix's playing of the Star Spangled Banner at Woodstock in 1969, amidst the anti-Vietnam fervour, can be read in a similar vein. Although this rendition of the national anthem was accompanied by simulated sounds of war (machine guns, bombs, and screams), Hendrix himself, who had served for two years as a trainee paratrooper in the 101st Airborne division of the army, protested that the song was not intended to be 'anti-American' but rather that to him, it was 'beautiful' (Hendrix 2006). This overt expression of love for the nation is, perhaps, something which is particular to America, a country which is characterised by an 'exceptional nationalism' (Lieven 2004). While citizens of other countries might identify specific aspects of their homeland which they find appealing, Americans often talk about loving the country itself. As Max Lerner once commented: 'The cult of the nation as social myth has run as a thread through the whole of American history' (cited in Lieven 2004: 21).

Ray Charles and Jimi Hendrix both came from families which had experienced intensive hardship; Charles was born in the 1930s to poor African American share croppers living in the Deep South, and began to go blind at five years of age. 'Talk about poor', he had once said, 'We were on the bottom of the ladder' (Charles 2006). Hendrix's mother was an alcoholic, his father an Irish Cherokee. Both Hendrix and Charles lost their mothers when they were fifteen, and for each of them this had a profound and long-lasting influence. While both men, through their music, attempt to reclaim the songs of the nation, their efforts might also be read as attempts by persons belonging to margin-alised groups to protect themselves, by an overt display of national loyalty, from being targets of discrimination. Clearly, there are many reasons why people do or do not feel and express sentiments of patrio-tism, and these expressions are always more than simple individual preferences.

When Charles sings 'America, sweet America' he is directly addressing the country, which seems transformed into an embodied loved one; he then follows this with his own very personal rewriting of the words, making the song really his, and ours: 'America, I love you America, you see, /My God he done shed his grace on thee.' Like Cheney, I was occupied by what it meant to be a good American, and what my special responsibilities were at that particular moment in history. But I felt offended by the implication, which had been widespread in both the national and local media, that one set of answers was correct and the other was misled. Was one American, or group of Americans, more qualified than another to determine the meaning of the phrase 'good American'? Who, I wondered, was he, to tell me what it meant to love my country? Was there not room for me both to love it, passionately, and to be critical of it? What kind of America had I returned to? I developed a research design that would allow me to explore questions which would not leave me alone.

Michael Walzer (1987) has provided an important philosophical account of the role of the 'connected social critic' – one who, by definition, feels him- or herself to be an insider to the group s/he is criticising. The connected critic, Walzer writes,

> earns his authority, or fails to do so, by arguing with his
> fellows – who, angrily and insistently, sometimes at considerable
> personal risk ... objects, protests, and remonstrates. This critic
> is one of us ... Nor is he emotionally detached; he does not
> wish the natives well, he seeks the success of their common
> enterprise.
> *(1987: 39)*

While Walzer makes a powerful and eloquent defence of the role of the critic, the emphasis he places on their 'common enterprise' risks homogenising all critical politics. What exactly is that common enterprise, and to whom does it belong? Who is included in the construction of 'us' and who remains outside? For Walzer, the connected critics are constituted as a group, yet one can argue that those who occupy this marginal space might well be working towards a range of different political agendas, and this contested space between them is of vital importance. Still, with this caveat, Walzer's argument is philosophically and politically compelling. He describes social criticism as 'one of the more important by-products of ... the activity of cultural elaboration and affirmation' (1987: 40). Social criticism is part of the life blood of a culture, and yet, as Walzer comments 'good social criticism is as rare as good poetry or good philosophy' (1987: 48). Social critics care very much about the fate of the group they criticise; it is their group, and their fate, for which they are fighting. But where exactly is the position of the social critic within the society that they critique?

> A little to the side, but not outside; critical distance is measured
> in inches ... He is not a detached observer, even when he
> looks at the society he inhabits with a fresh and sceptical eye.
> He is not an enemy, even when he is fiercely opposed to this
> or that prevailing practice or institutional arrangement. His
> criticism does not require either detachment or enmity, because
> he finds a warrant for critical engagement in the idealism, even
> if it is a hypocritical idealism, of the actual existing moral
> world.   (1987: 60–61)

Walzer's words, written almost fifteen years before 9/11, identify the difficult space which social critics tried to articulate in the weeks and months following September 11, 2001. Robert Scheer, a syndicated columnist, wrote, for instance, at the time of the attacks:

> War sceptics ... should be congratulated, not vilified, for daring to
> demur ... from government propaganda. Right or wrong, they have

> acted as free people in a free society who understand that if our
> course is correct, it can survive criticism. And if it is not, it is all
> the more important that we gather the courage to state that
> criticism clearly and in a timely fashion ... Dissent is not a luxury
> to be indulged in the best of times but rather an obligation of
> free people, particularly when the very notion of dissent is
> unpopular.
>
> *(Scheer 2001)*

Those Americans, like Scheer, who were courageous enough to voice their criticism of the government openly saw their actions as being motivated by a love for their country. In the words of Edward Murrow, a journalist who fought against the censorship imposed by McCarthyism in the 1950s: 'We must not confuse dissent with disloyalty. When the loyal opposition dies, I think the soul of America dies with it' (Murrow 1953). The basis for the critical dissent is one of belief in the 'idealism, even if it is a hypocritical idealism, of the actual existing moral world' described by Walzer. The right to dissent is the key founding principle of the USA – it is the soul of the country, and worth fighting for.

Walzer comments that 'When our country behaves badly, it is still ours, and we are, perhaps, especially obligated to criticise its policies. And yet the possessive pronoun is a problem' (1987: 36). The problem of the possessive pronoun highlights the importance of the connection for the critics: they belong to that which they criticise, and their criticisms are offered from this inside, albeit somewhat marginalised, position.

The position of the connected critic is epitomised in the letters which Albert Camus wrote to a German friend in the early years of the Second World War. He begins the first of these letters by recalling a conversation between them:

> You said to me 'The greatness of my country is beyond price.
> Anything is good that contributes to its greatness ...'. 'No', I told
> you, 'I cannot believe that everything must be subordinated to a
> single end ... I should like to be able to love my country and still

love justice. I don't want any greatness for it, particularly a greatness born of blood and falsehood. I want to keep it alive by keeping
justice alive.' You retorted: 'Well, you don't love your country.' ...
No, I didn't love my country, if pointing out what is unjust in
what we love amounts to not loving, if insisting that what we
love should measure up to the finest image we have of her
amounts to not loving.   *(Camus 1960: 3–4)*

Camus is passionate about his country, and his criticism is, for him,
an important expression of these deep feelings.

Walzer argues against the radical detachment which is conven-
tionally associated with role of the critic, insisting on the distinction
between marginality and detachment which, he says, are often confused. 'Marginality', he suggests,

has often been a condition that motivates criticism and determines
the critic's characteristic tone and appearance. It is not, however, a
condition that makes for disinterest, dispassion, open-mindedness
or objectivity. Nor is it an external condition. Marginal men and
women are ... in but not wholly of their society. The difficulties
they experience are not the difficulties of detachment but of
ambiguous connection.   *(1987: 37)*

This description of the connected critic wholly resonates with my
own feelings about my relationship to 'my country'. I have grappled
with the problem of the possessive pronoun, and continue to do so.
This chapter can be read, in part, as an exploration into the complexities of criticising, not from a position of detachment, but from one of
ambiguous connection.

ONE TOWN'S EXPERIENCE OF PATRIOTISM DURING
THE GULF WAR

I moved to Colorado Springs, Colorado, in August 1990, days after
Saddam Hussein's army had invaded Kuwait. From the first day that
the Gulf War broke out in January 1991, anti-war activists living in
Colorado Springs established a 24/7 vigil, located on a central

reservation between two lanes of traffic in the centre of the city, which they kept until the cease fire, six weeks later. One of the more intriguing features of this vigil was that sometimes, though not always, people living there had a small American flag staked into the ground. Why did they have this flag? More than a year later, I interviewed about ten people in Colorado Springs, most of whom had been involved in the establishment of the vigil, about their political beliefs and actions during the Gulf War. Specifically, I was interested to learn about why they flew the American flag. What did this symbol mean to them, and what message were they trying to communicate by planting it in what some might consider to be a rather unlikely site?

Historically, and up to the present day, American popular culture has been permeated with the symbols and language of nationalism (Lieven 2004), unusual for a country of such global dominance. Overt expressions of nationalism and enthusiasm for national symbols has tended to be characteristic of developing countries, or countries with a national insecurity, such as Mexico or the Philippines, or of Europe at the turn of the nineteenth century (Lieven 2004: 20). Despite its clear economic superiority in the world, America is a nation which celebrates itself regularly, and in a myriad of ways, ranging from the recitation of the Pledge of Allegiance by most school children across the nation every morning to the fanfare of activity which saturates the country every Fourth of July. This outpouring of national pride is often noted by those who visit the USA – de Tocqueville, writing in the 1830s, called it a 'troublesome and garrulous patriotism' (cited in Lieven 2004: 21) – as well as by some Americans. Herbert Croly, first editor of the *New Republic*, commented in 1909 that 'The faith of Americans in their country … pervades the air we breathe' (cited in Levien 2004: 22). The American flag – or 'Old Glory', as it is commonly called – holds a particular pride of place among the symbols of American national identity.

Although my original remit for this project was to interview only anti-war activists, I decided later that my analysis would benefit from conversations with leading members of the Colorado Springs community whose views were more representative of the city as a whole; I was very fortunate that two such individuals obliged me with an interview. There were ten interviewees altogether who, though holding a range of different political viewpoints, all came across as people who deeply cared for their country. I wanted to learn more about what the fact of their nationality meant to them, and what role, if any, they felt that it played in their actions. The responses I collected were very illuminating.

Arwen, one of the original organisers of the anti-war vigil, is exceptionally articulate and passionate. She is smart, and she is very committed. Other people find her a source of inspiration, and when she speaks, she exudes a confidence that belies her twenty-one years:

> I do love my country … People use this 'love it or leave it' ideal a lot. In some ways I would agree with that, but I define loving more broadly than they do. Most people who say that mean accept it or leave it and that's very different from what I think … it means to love. To love is not to accept it as it is but to consider it worth while to work on.

For Arwen, the country is 'worth while to work on'. She is a '*femme engagée*', and she knows that to love some thing or some one demands hard work.

The question 'Would you say that you love your country?' produces a very elaborate response from Bruce, a cleric and activist from Colorado Springs:

> Oh, I absolutely would … If I didn't care … why would I even bother … I mean why wouldn't I go home at night and forget about this stuff … I don't do it because I like it. I don't do it because it's fun … Why would I bang my head against the Wall in these causes that seem often to be losing causes if I didn't have some sense of what's the larger good there … Love for me is a different kind of an activity and … action than most people think of it as, and for me,

there's lots of commitment and endurance and tough hanging in
there that goes with the notion of love, and doing things that don't
feel comfortable that are important to do for some larger good.

Both Arwen and Bruce make a distinction between their own concep-
tions of 'loving one's country' and what they believe 'most people
think'. The critical tension revolves around competing interpretations
of love. Is love unconditional acceptance, or is it of a more robust
nature, enduring and benefiting from criticism? Jill says 'you can
love something without loving everything about it ... a large part of
love is seeing faults and seeing problems and being willing to face
those and to change those'. For these activists, an action or course of
action must be evaluated, not on merits of convenience and self-
interest, but according to higher principles of morality. Such principles must be upheld, even if this means that one must come into
conflict with one's own group; moreover, this conflict can itself be
read as an expression of love for the group.

The central reservation on which the anti-war vigil was located
soon became a site for a contest over who could, and who could not,
legitimately lay claim to Old Glory. The fact that protestors at the
vigil occasionally waved the flag appeared to have the effect of infuri-
ating those passers-by who supported the war.

Whether or not to have the flag present at the vigil was a topic
debated among the protestors; ultimately it was decided that whatever
group of people were present at the vigil at a particular moment could
decide this among themselves. It was also questioned to what extent the
flag actually offered protection, in that it emphasised that the protestors
were American, and to what extent it fuelled a response of rage against
them. Arwen summarises the arguments in favour of having the flag:

> Some of the people wanted it there to prove that we were American,
> to ... not let other people take over that symbol, you know, this
> 'good American' 'bad American' thing. The good Americans can
> have the flag, the bad Americans can't ... we weren't going to let
> them do that ... [we were going to] simply take that back.

This attempt by the protestors to re-appropriate the country's most emotive symbol was not without risks. Their effort to lay claim to their 'American-ness' – as symbolised by the American flag – served to anger those Colorado Springs residents who felt that these protestors, who from their point of view were supporting the enemy, had no right to exhibit the flag. Arwen elaborates:

> We were clearly 'un-American', right? And our attempts to prove that that wasn't the case, having an American flag there for instance, served to make them, if anything, more angry ... How could we hold up the American flag? We were 'bad Americans'.

In fact, debates about national belonging are prototypically American, as some commentators have observed:

> America is a nation that invites anxiety about what it means to belong, because the national boundary is ideological, hence disputable and porous. Part of what it has meant to be American has been to participate in a debate about what it means to be American.
> *(Gitlin 2003: 116)*

In the winter of 1991, Colorado Springs was the site of a physical enactment of that ideological conflict. The presence of the protestors, and their use of the American flag, clearly did provoke antipathy in many people. Pat, who stayed at the vigil for most of its duration, describes the atmosphere as one of 'continual anger from the Colorado Springs community. At one point a student having a bottle thrown at her head in the middle of the day, and constantly people driving around us honking horns, throwing things, screaming'. Justin's description echoes this:

> the people in Colorado Springs ... pelted us with snow balls, bottles, beer cans, tennis balls, you name it ... [they] just treated us in a really nasty way, [they] spat on us ... tried to run us over, tried to drive up on the median strip [central reservation] where we were sitting ... the whole concept of trying to cause us bodily harm to signal that they disagreed with what we were doing really bothered me.

The American flag featured in some of the violence directed against the protestors. Justin continues:

> There were a couple of times in which people with huge American flags tried to hit us over the head with the actual flag poles and sort of drape the flags over our heads ... there was another time when this pickup truck with some rednecks stopped next to the vigil and they harassed us for a while and then they ran around us with their flag in a circle a few times.

At the heart of these violent episodes was a heated dispute over the meaning of the flag: Whose flag was it? What did it represent? Who was it meant to protect? Those who reacted physically to the presence of the flag at the vigil felt that a most cherished symbol was being misused, even violated. Had the anti-war protestors only burned the flag, the case against them, and their lack of loyalty, would have been easier to make. For their part, the participants of the vigil felt strongly that the flag represented ideals with which they identified their cause. Both sides felt threatened – one physically, the other symbolically.

Jill, who was raised in Colorado Springs, explains how her feelings about the flag changed as a result of her participation in the vigil:

> I'd see it on the Fourth of July. It was a symbol of the country, and it was a symbol that I thought you could be relatively proud of ... [but] during the vigil the flag was used as a weapon against me ... I'd have people waving the flag at me, insinuating or suggesting that I was not a proper American or that I was not an American ... this flag became a symbol more of the war and militarism than it did of my country ... when it was used as a weapon against me that was a very difficult thing.

The students at the vigil made a strong effort to discriminate between 'the present leadership of the country ... and the ideals upon which the country was based'. Although there was never a clear and lasting consensus among the protestors which of these the flag actually represented, Pat says there was at least 'a good argument for the fact that the flag did not stand for George Bush [Senior] leading people into a war, but stood for justice and peace and freedom'.

As a response to the anti-war vigil, some people who supported the war decided that on Friday and Saturday evenings they would hold their own 'counter-vigil' to protest the protestors, as it were. Arwen tells the story of an exchange between participants of the two opposing vigils, provoked by the presence of the flag at both of their camps:

> A lot of times they'd just give us really nasty looks, but ... every now and then we had people who would come and talk and one guy did come and talk ... he wanted to know what we were really all about and why we were there and how come we had an American flag ... he didn't get it, the American flag on our side? ... why did we both have American flags ... he thought we were the un-American ones, and he just didn't understand what was going on ... the more he talked the more interested he became ... And he came back and stayed with us ... He brought his friend over too.

The point is not that the young man had changed his mind about the war; he hadn't. (Arwen explains that even though he stayed at the anti-war vigil 'he would say things about "well, I'm not really against this war"'). His presence there must have been about something else; if nothing more, one can safely assume that he felt there was room at the vigil for dissenting opinions, and that all of these opinions were equally 'American'.

One of the events which was described by virtually all anti-war protestors with whom I spoke was a rally, called 'One Hour for America'. Here, between 12,000 and 25,000 residents of Colorado Springs gathered to show support for the 45,000 service men and women in the community, many of whom were involved directly in the conflict. Knowing that the gathering would attract much media attention, anti-war activists decided that this would be a good venue in which to stage a counter-demonstration. They were not prepared, however, for the strength of reaction their presence would provoke.

Charles, whose idea it was to have the rally, described to me its origin:

> There were some pretty dire forecasts regarding what might be in
> store for them [the soldiers going to the Gulf]. These were indivi-
> duals who are very important to Colorado Springs in a variety of
> ways, and it just seemed our community should convey to them
> that whatever might happen, we would be behind them 100% …
> many of us felt that if we could make not only the individual
> soldiers, but also their families, feel better about what they were
> being asked to do, through an outpouring of support, then let's do it.

Charles contrasts what he hoped would be the support showed by the
American people towards their military in the Persian Gulf with the
treatment that Vietnam veterans received. When I ask him about
the possible effects of the experience of Vietnam on the Gulf War
conflict, he comments:

> There's no question that my experiences during the sixties played a
> role. I think we all now realize we made a mistake in how we treated
> those who were called upon to serve our country. It has nothing to
> do with whether Vietnam was the right place or the right war, or the
> wrong war, or the immoral war. Whatever context you put it in,
> those were still fellow country-men and -women who served because
> their government asked them to. I think the same thing is true here.

Charles was determined that in the Gulf War conflict, unlike in
Vietnam, the troops would know that they had the unequivocal support of their country. One Hour for America was an effort to ensure
that the 'mistake' of Vietnam would not be repeated. Tom, another
key organiser of One Hour for America, tells me of the early planning
days of the event. In the first meeting,

> We told them what our thoughts were about this [proposed event] and
> that we in this community should not, ever again, let happen to those
> who were out there placing their lives on the line, serving this coun-
> try, because, you know, you are ordered to do so. We should never
> again let them feel like the Vietnam veterans felt for all those years.

The Gulf War would not be another Vietnam. Mistakes had been made, lessons had been learned. When the active combat concluded forty-five days later, Bush proclaimed 'We promised this would not be another Vietnam. And we kept that promise' (Craige 1996: 110–111).

I ask Charles about the name of the event: what does it mean to him to be 'for America'? In his response, he outlines three possibilities. First, one can be 'wholeheartedly for this country'. Second, one can query the actions of one's country, but from a broadly supportive framework. Finally, the third approach involves 'people who are opposed to anything the United States does'. When I ask Charles to characterise the actions of the anti-war protestors, he says they follow the second approach: 'They evaluated the situation and thought it was wrong'. Later in the interview, he comments 'Just because people say things I don't like ... I hardly feel we should limit their freedom of expression. I spoke with the Chief of Police about it, and told him that we needed to make sure that all the demonstrators were adequately protected, wherever they were.' Charles' perception of loyalty to the country, thus, encompasses a broad spectrum, which clearly includes the activities of the anti-war protestors, and he emphasises this point several times in our interview. In this respect, he differs from Tom, who concludes his interview with me by stating: 'So that's what patriotism means, that you're patriotic about your support.'

When I ask Tom to tell me what being 'for America' means, he explains:

> Let's celebrate what has happened ... let's try to feel good about ourselves, let's don't be negative for what we've done, let's try to understand what has really happened and why we did it, and give one hour for our country and for the people that fought for us.

One Hour for America was for Tom, quite simply, 'a show of patriotism and Americanism' and 'a euphoria of those of us who have served in the military'. At this event, wherever one looked there were American flags, in all shapes and sizes; some people even dressed up as Old Glory, others as Uncle Sam. When Tom speaks of the rally, it is with great pride and enthusiasm. He describes the 'huge flags, 50' × 50', hanging off of buildings … what that means to you is freedom … There's no symbol as strong as that American flag.' Tom himself 'took three flags down, I had them in both hands and I was just one of the crowd'. The Air Force Academy Choir sang, and there were many speakers; generally speaking, it was a very successful 'feel good' event.

While Charles states that 'as a way to provide some support to military families in a time of uncertainty and deep concern, I think "One Hour for America" was a success', he also recalls seeing the protestors there: 'There were demonstrators at the actual rally loca-tion and I was out there with them part of the time. I saw people protesting, I saw them get some dirty looks, but that's all.' However, the stories of this day which anti-war protestors told me revealed a far greater level of intensity than this comment would suggest.

Mary, a long-time member of Colorado Springs' Peace and Justice Community, describes her experience of the 'Love America rally' as she terms it, which occurred on 'bad Friday' (the event was on a Friday):

> There was so much intense hostility it was incredible … you could just cut it with a knife … after the rally itself was over [people] lined up and you could see that they wanted to attack us and the police were there and they were kind of forming this barricade between us and the people at the parade … It was one of the most depressing moments I've had in a long time … they just wanted to sing louder and wave their flags faster every time they would look at us and spit … but I think that's patriotism. Where is this diversity, this melting pot? … Everybody gets melted into one mould, there is nothing about tolerance for peers.

When Bill speaks of the rally, it is in very similar terms, emphasising the frightening 'power of blind patriotism to wipe out dissent and … rational disagreement … immediately equating opposition with unpat-riotism'. He then adds: 'And all those flags, I mean, why do people have to flaunt something that strongly? You know it's really shallow.'

During the Gulf War, the local newspaper in Colorado Springs, the *Gazette Telegraph*, carried numerous letters to the editor, commenting on the presence of the anti-war vigil. One letter, dated February 5, called the group 'anti-American protestors' and closes with the challenge 'to put your body where your mouth is – any other country anywhere. If you don't like it here, you are free to leave'. This is a viewpoint often encountered by the anti-war protestors. As Mary comments:

> Back in the days of people being worried about the Soviet Union, it was like 'Why don't you go protest in Russia?' and it was like 'Well, because I'm from this country, what do you think?!' ... I mean, do you do that with your children? Love them or leave them?

The very suggestion that Mary should move to another country because she disagrees with some policies of her government implies that love does not allow room for criticism. To illustrate her point, Mary introduces the example of affiliative ties with children. Society expects parents to 'love' their children in a way which is more actively engaged than blind acceptance, which entails staying and working with them through trying times. Children who are the objects of uncritical positive regard are often thought to be over-indulged and spoiled. States which cannot tolerate criticism from its citizens are often thought to be wanting in democracy.

The *Gazette Telegraph* published a response, written by one of the protestors, to the invitation to leave in the next day's paper:

> I have been harassed, threatened, cursed at, pelted from passing vehicles and excoriated by the local media. How is it that people cheer for the demonstrators of Eastern Europe and then call us bums and traitors? How is it that people presume that one must love the government to love one's country? The truth is that I, too, am fighting to keep this country free ... Those who would intimidate me into giving up those rights [to freedom of speech and assembly] are the ones who threaten democracy.

Another section of the same day's paper ran a piece by syndicated columnist and former Reagan White House aide Mona Charen, whose article personifies the inconsistency noted by the protestor above. She begins: 'This time, they carry American instead of enemy flags, and they carry them right side up instead of inverted.' As Charen correctly observes, anti-war protestors in Colorado Springs were not unusual in their decision to fly the American flag. However, the reception that this provoked was perhaps more dramatic than else-where, due to the military make-up of Colorado Springs. For Charen, as for others, the fact that the anti-war protestors carried the flag 'right side up' was problematic: easier to dismiss one who is burning a flag as unpatriotic than one who not only carries a flag while protesting, but proclaims that their actions are motivated by principles enshrined in that symbol. Throughout her article, Charen trivialises the demon-strations as fashion events, describing the protestors as they 'sprang for the guitars and tie-dyed T-shirts the minute the shooting started'. 'We keep hearing that the freedom to dissent is what America is all about', she declares:

> That's true as far as it goes, but let's not confuse the act of dissent with the dissenters. Of course they are free to say whatever they like, but it is quite obvious – and I'll say it if no one else will – that a large segment of the alienated protestors are less patriotic than other Americans ... We Americans guarantee the rights to protest. But we don't guarantee the right to be called a patriot.

In a reversal of the biblical 'Hate the sin but love the sinner', Charen accepts the dissent but rejects the dissenter. The central issue in her letter is that of who should be considered 'patriotic' and who should not. She cites the *American Heritage Dictionary*'s definition of a patriot as 'someone who loves, supports and defends his country'. But a country is larger than any particular policy which is enacted in its name. Loving (a country) and criticising (a policy) are not mutu-ally exclusive. When Charen proclaims 'We Americans ... don't guarantee the right to be called a patriot', her use of pronouns is both emphatic and ambiguous. Are the protestors included in her construction of 'we' or do their activities somehow render them less American? Moreover, by what right can one citizen or group of citizens sit in judgement over the patriotism of another?

'GOOD CITIZENS'

Tom's patriotism is based on a polarisation between 'us' and 'them'. He feels that being an American means 'you have a country and a system that will defend you against barbaric actions of other nations' as well as securing you certain inalienable rights. But with rights come duties. 'To be a good citizen it means that you defend your country as much as you possibly can, and what it's doing; that you support your country, that you try very hard to understand the overall picture of what's taking place; [and] that you are not a taker but a giver.'

Tom spontaneously uses the language of rights and citizenship, and clearly identifies himself as a good and patriotic American. This kind of discourse, while traditionally associated with conservative politics, is both used and challenged by some of the anti-war activists whom I interviewed. Bruce, for instance, says that while citizenship language is 'not language I necessarily would have chosen', for him 'a good citizen is somebody who tries to enrich the public life of the nation ... and does it in a way that lets everybody into the process but still can be very passionate about your own sets of commitments and beliefs'. Justin has similar thoughts: 'it means working for change towards the things that I believe in'. In the context of the Gulf War this translated itself into

> demonstrating during the war, showing the community and the country that we disagree and explaining why ... talking about things that were not talked about by pro-war supporters and political leaders in the country at the time ... that's what ... most people at the vigil thought was their duty as good citizens of this country.

Bill believes that being a good citizen means

> getting behind policies that you think are good … oppos[ing] those
> that you think are not, and constantly try[ing] to be better informed
> about those that you don't know for sure … and [to] re-examine
> positions when it's not really clear what's right or what's wrong.

The theme of a globalised citizenry is one which appears across many
of the interviews. Bill, in particular, has thought a lot about the issue
of world citizenship. His global consciousness is evident in his activism, much of which focuses on the de-militarisation of space, not
even a supranational but a supraglobal issue. It is not that Bill does not
have a particular feeling about being an American; indeed he does. 'I'm
really tied into being an American', he explains. 'I have close ties with
my family, I'm a nut about baseball.' Although Bill enjoys certain
aspects of life in the USA, being 'really tied into being an American'
does not mean limiting himself and his work to concerns within its
borders:

> I think that the concept of world citizenship … has to take center
> stage increasingly, because just the necessity of an interconnecting
> world, and that pluralism is going to be very important … it leads to
> an awful lot of diversity and that's a strength, but we as citizens,
> increasingly have to see ourselves as world citizens first, and then
> work the patriotism and love of a particular region or country or
> tradition second.

Bill spent four years in the army in the early 1960s, mostly in Europe
but also briefly in East Africa. 'I tell people that's where I really lost my
sense of patriotism [in the limited sense], of just seeing the world
through American eyes … a major step in world citizenship.'

Although respondents may feel that their allegiance extends
beyond their country, they do at the same time experience a heightened sense of responsibility for actions perpetrated by their country.
Bruce's consciousness of being an American has been heightened by
taking groups of people to Latin America to do community service

there. He explains 'in some ways that experience defines my role of who I feel I am as an American citizen … I feel I have a real sense of responsibility for what our nation does'. Mary uses somewhat similar language, saying that for her, being a citizen of the USA means 'I feel more responsibility toward what this country does than towards any other country'. Walzer's 'problem of the possessive pronoun' rears its head once again.

PATRIOTISM AND ITS DISCONTENTS

The debates surrounding the meaning of patriotism in Colorado Springs can be read as a local mirroring of a larger national debate. The attempt to legislate patriotism was a theme which ran throughout the presidency of George Bush Senior. From his presidential campaign, which contained on its platform the attempt to mandate recitation of the Pledge of Allegiance to the Flag, to his thwarted efforts to undermine the Supreme Court ruling which failed to ban flag-burning, to the rhetoric he employed throughout the Gulf War conflict, Bush Senior claimed for himself the special role of the protector of Old Glory. This political strategy has a long history, and its effectiveness in silencing oppositional viewpoints is well established. As Craige (1996) comments 'This maneuver … is as old as politics itself. It consists basically in the state leader's identifying himself or herself with the state and identifying any opposition to his or her policies as opposition to the state, rendering personal political opponents apparent opponents of the state' (1996: 108). It was a strategy that Bush would use throughout his Presidency, and that his son, George W. Bush, would later come to use with particular effectiveness.

On 21 June 1989, the US Supreme Court passed its 5–4 judgement in the case of *Texas* v. *Johnson*, proclaiming that the right to burn the flag is protected by the First Amendment, securing freedom of expression. Its ruling stated that 'The Government may not prohibit the verbal or nonverbal expression of an idea merely because society finds the idea offensive or disagreeable, even where our flag is involved ... Moreover, this court will not create an exception to these principles protected by the First Amendment for the American flag alone' (cited in Craige 1996: 106). The next day, the US Senate 'passed a resolution expressing "profound disappointment" and promised "to seek ways to restore sanctions against such reprehensible conduct" ' (Craige 1996: 107). Six days after the Supreme Court ruling, President Bush proposed an amendment to the Bill of Rights, stating that 'the Congress and the States shall have the power to prohibit the physical desecration of the Flag of the USA' (Craige 1996: 107).

President Bush defended himself against claims of partisanship, stating: 'I think respect for the flag transcends political party, and I think what I've said here is American. It isn't Republican or Democrat. It isn't liberal or conservative. And I just feel very strongly about it' (cited in Craige 1996: 107). Eventually, the proposal for an addition to the Bill of Rights died for lack of two-thirds majority support. However, the House and Senate, while not approving the Constitutional Amendment, did pass legislation outlawing physical desecration of the flag, on the grounds that it proscribed behaviour, rather than intention. 'Members of Congress from both parties competed to show the depth of their affection for the flag, arguing less over the wisdom of prohibiting "desecration of the flag" than over the way in which to prohibit it' (Craige 1996: 107). In other words, Bush had lost the battle but won the war. The stage was clearly set for the mustering of patriotism, as defined by Bush, required for the military conflict in the Gulf which was soon to follow. In July 2006, yet another attempt to create a Constitutional Amendment allowing Congress to ban flag desecration failed, but this time by only the one vote which it needed in the Senate to reach the two-thirds majority approval required before taking the proposed legislation to the states for ratification. The debate surrounding the desecration of the flag is almost wholly symbolic, as flag-burning is a relatively rare occurrence in the USA; nevertheless, the proposed legislation is vehemently opposed by many who regard such efforts as an affront to their freedom of speech.

KICKING THE 'VIETNAM SYNDROME'

The attempt to legislate the against the burning of the flag can be read as an effort to correct what were perceived to be imbalances which had emerged from the overly indulgent 1960s and 1970s, in which flag-burning was not uncommon at demonstrations protesting the US engagement in Vietnam. It is not altogether surprising, then, that when Saddam Hussein's forces entered Kuwait in August 1990, Bush regarded this as an opportunity for the USA to 'kick the Vietnam Syndrome', as he called it. Prior to this time, American popular culture – particularly the film industry – was saturated with stories of soldiers returning home, unfulfilled, disillusioned, psychologically frail if not destroyed. Vietnam, followed by Watergate, had left very little of traditional patriotism in the diet of American popular culture. Bush was determined that this national self-flagellation should cease.

On 16 January 1991, when the allied forces commenced attacks against the Iraqi military in the Persian Gulf, Bush announced: 'I've told the American people before that this will not be another Vietnam, and I repeat this here tonight. Our troops will have the best possible support in the entire world and they will not be asked to fight with one hand tied behind their back' (quoted in Craige 1996: 110). Bush continued throughout the war to make the analogy between the then-present conflict in the Gulf and that in Southeast Asia. From the statement above it is clear that, to him, the lesson of Vietnam was that soldiers were 'asked to fight with one hand tied behind their back'. That is to say, they were not given the support that they required to be able to win the war. His proclamation that 'this will not be another Vietnam' is a promise of victory. But for many Americans, the lesson of Vietnam was not that we did not win, but that we had no grounds for being there.

One month later, the conflict still ongoing, he reassured the American people:

It is my hope that when this is over we will have kicked, for once and for all, the so-called Vietnam Syndrome. And the country's

> pulling together, unlike any time – in this kind of situation –
> any time since World War II. And that's a good thing for our
> country. And that sends a strong signal for the future –
> that we're credible, we're committed to peace, we're
> committed to justice, and we are determined to fulfil our
> obligations in trying to bring about a more peaceful world
> order.
> *(cited in Craige 1996: 110)*

Again, in Bush's rhetoric, it is clear that the ghost of Vietnam looms large. His intended goal is rather ambitious: the un-making of history. From Bush's perspective, the Persian Gulf conflict presented the USA with an opportunity to return to a moment in history and emerge with a different, more desirable ending. He comments on 'the country's pulling together, unlike any time … since World War II'. Bush celebrates what he sees as the rebirth of national unity, traditional patriotism, reminiscent of a bygone era. Bush's connection between this patriotism and militarism is also clearly outlined. In language reminiscent of Newspeak in Orwell's *1984*, the USA would have its credibility restored as a country which would meet its (military) obligations to secure world peace.

On 2 March, in his radio address announcing Iraq's defeat, Bush proclaimed: 'The specter of Vietnam has been buried forever in the desert sands of the Arabian Peninsula' (Craige 1996: 110–111). Burying Vietnam, and all the national self-scrutiny that that chapter of history had brought with it, had long been on Bush's agenda. However, the national unity which Bush so longed for, and had partially succeeded in manufacturing, was not sufficient to secure for him a second term in office only one year later.

When the Republican Party's campaign was faltering in the early autumn of 1992, Bush once again returned to the strategy of claiming for himself an exclusive patriotism, while portraying his opponent, Bill Clinton, as 'anti-American'. George Bush argued that by participating in a demonstration in 1969 against the Vietnam War – a demonstration which had occurred 'on foreign soil', as was repeatedly emphasised, at the US embassy in London – his opponent had exhibited fundamental disloyalty to the country he was now asking to lead. Clinton vociferously declared that his protest was an expression, rather than a negation of, his deep concern for the actions of his country. In Bush's acceptance speech for the Republican nomination, he characterised Clinton as someone who says ' "America is a nation in decline" … Well, don't let anyone tell you that America is second-rate, especially someone running for president' (*New York Times*, August 21, 1992). Despite Bush's failure to become re-elected in November 1992, he had managed during his Presidency to reconstruct the national narrative in a significant way. Craige comments that he was 'able to wage a popular, all-out war against Iraq by controlling the viewpoint from which the story was told' (1996: 117). Seeds which were sown during this time were ripe for harvesting after the attacks of 9/11.

THE FROZEN FRAME OF 9/11

The Russian poet, Yevgeny Yevtushenko, wrote in September 2001 of the attacks that had occurred earlier that month: 'These planes were exploded inside us, and their fragments forever will wander under our skin … Something inside us has become ruined forever' (Yevtushenko 2002: 222). September 11, 2001 is considered by many to be one of those rare, transformative events, a memory fault-line, an historical rupture, 'the day the frame froze' (Willis 2002: 219). For many Americans, not only those living near to the scenes of devastation in New York, Washington, and Pennsylvania, their sense of national identity was fundamentally altered.

Between Tuesday, September 11 and Thursday, September 13, Wal-mart alone had sold 450,000 American flags, and Kmart had sold another 200,000 (Stoddard and Cornwell 2002: 179). Stores across the USA sold out of American flags in the days following the attacks. The country was awash in what Princeton International Law Professor Richard Falk describes as an 'unprecedented display of flag-waving patriotism' (Falk 2003: 131). What this flag meant to those who displayed it, most particularly after 9/11, is less clear. Todd Gitlin, left-wing social critic and former president of Students for a Democratic Society (SDS) in the 1960s, hung a flag from his house in New York. 'The flag was a plain affirmation of membership ... it was not meant as support for the policies of George W. Bush but as an affirmation of fellowship with an injured and resolute people' (Gitlin 2003: 110), he would later explain. The White House website, post-9/11, had a special section called 'Standing for the flag' which opened with President Bush stating 'Now, as the country stares down a new peril, Americans are flying the banner proudly, heeding its call for unity' (cited in Stoddard and Cornwell 2002: 180). Is the 'affirmation of fellowship' which Gitlin describes the same as the 'unity' referred to on the White House web page?

But not all Americans were waving flags; indeed, a review of newspapers across the country in the weeks and months after 9/11 reveal that a small but significant number of writers were openly critical of this national activity (see Cockburn and St Clair 2001). Arne Flones, for instance, in an article 'Empty Patriotism: Ideologues at the Gate', posed the question:

> what good is a flag if everything for which it stands is gone ...
> The name of the country is The United States of America. The
> motto of the USA is *E plurbus* [sic] *unum*, one out of many.
> The USA is the summation of many ethnic, religious and
> political backgrounds. To be united in the United States of
> America is not to be all of one race, religion, gender, or political
> opinion.
> *(Flones 2001)*

Barbara Kingsolver, too, argued. 'Outsiders can destroy airplanes and buildings, but it is only we, the people, who have the power to demolish our own ideals', a comment which she then followed with a plea for 'a new iconography of patriotism' – a new symbolism for the red, white, and blue stars and stripes:

> I propose we rip stripes of cloth from the uniforms of public servants
> who rescued the injured and panic-stricken, remaining at the post

until it fell down on them. The red glare of candles held in vigils
everywhere as peace-loving people pray for the bereaved, and
plead for compassion and restraint. The blood donated to the
Red Cross. The stars of films and theatre and music who are
using their influence to raise money for recovery. The small
hands of schoolchildren collecting pennies, toothpaste, teddy
bears, anything they think might help the kids who've lost their
moms and dads.   *(Kingsolver 2001)*

But those who questioned the flag waving were in a small minority.
The events of 9/11 produced a frenzy of unquestioning patriotism that
seemed out of place for the historical conditions which immediately
preceded it. The late twentieth century was a time of relative pros-
perity for many Americans and a time of growing internationalism.
With the rise of multiculturalism, there was an enhanced appreciation
of other cultures, including the many differences contained within
American culture itself. Many questioned the homogeneity of the
'melting pot' and instead embraced identity politics. Globalisation
and the widespread use of and access to the internet had produced
in many an international consciousness which undermined the tendency toward American isolationism. All in all, the foundations of
old-fashioned patriotism had been crumbling for about four decades.
As Gitlin states: 'Even those who had entered the 60s in diapers came
to maturity thinking patriotism a threat or a bad joke. It did nothing
for them' (2003: 122).

On September 11 the 'decline of traditional nation-centerd
patriotism' (Falk 2003: 130) came to an abrupt end:

> The trauma of the attacks, and the penetration of domestic space,
> presented an intense emotional occasion for the reaffirmation of
> their values for those conservative forces still attached to the
> territorial trappings of modernity, and they were joined by many
> who as late as September 10 had conceived of themselves as
> 'globalists' of various stripes with only the vaguest of patriotic
> sentiments.   *(2003: 130)*

As Renan's statement, quoted at the opening of this chapter, reminds us, 'Suffering in common unifies more than joy does'. September 11 was sheer trauma, and the way in which it was processed by the American political leadership and mainstream media encouraged a retreat into an 'unconditional celebration of American life, values and institutions, without a scintilla of willingness to listen to the anti-American grievances so prevalent in the Arab world ... an intense and highly nationalistic patriotism with dangerous implications for ourselves and others' (Falk 2003: 131).

According to Renan, shared griefs impose duties and require a common effort. The duty to avenge the deaths of September 11 was perceived by many as a moral imperative. In Bush's speech on September 20, he declared his intentions as Commander-in-Chief of the armed forces: 'Tonight we are a country awakened to danger and called to defend freedom. Our grief has turned to anger, and anger to resolution. Whether we bring our enemies to justice, or bring justice to our enemies, justice will be done' (cited in Falk 2003: 130).

By October 2001, Bush had pushed through Congress a major piece of sweeping legislation called the USA Patriot Act. It was symbolic that many of the nineteen terrorists who had hijacked the planes on September 11 had been harboured within the safety of the USA. The war against terrorism would be fought at home as well as abroad. It was not only bin Laden who would be 'smoked out', but anyone who challenged US policy, at home or abroad. 'Either you are with us, or you are with the terrorists' Bush had told the world community. But who is 'us'? By creating a new crime of 'domestic terrorism', the Patriot Act 'threatens to criminalize protest activities and stifle dissent' (Chang 2002: 13). Thus, the political narrative of 9/11 offered by the Bush administration, and accepted largely by the American people, was cast in the genre of an old-fashioned morality play and had vast political implications, domestically and internationally.

The irony is that the 'war on terrorism' being launched in the name of freedom has meant for many Americans a loss of freedom in the national pursuit of unity. Dissent has effectively been silenced as being unpatriotic, the now-realised ambition of the efforts to legislate patriotism in the late 1980s and early 1990s. What is new, and different, is that these previous efforts to criminalise dissent were hotly contested; in the climate which was born on September 11, 2001, they have been virtually unchallenged.

REVITALISING THE NATIONAL NARRATIVE

If the rhetoric surrounding the first Gulf War was that of 'kicking the Vietnam Syndrome', the attacks of 9/11 brought with them an opportunity to breathe new life into the story which we Americans tell ourselves about the kind of people we are. This was made possible by restricting the narrative of 9/11 to a very limited and particular plot, with one sunny September morning in 2001 as the opening scene.

However, for some, the attacks were not unanticipated. Only in the previous year, Chalmers Johnson published his book, *Blowback: The Costs and Consequences of American Empire*, in which he warned:

> 'Blowback' is shorthand for saying that a nation reaps what it
> sows, even if it does not fully know or understand what it has sown.
> Given its wealth and power, the United States will be a prime
> recipient in the foreseeable future of all of the more expectable
> forms of blowback, particularly terrorist attacks against Americans
> in and out of the armed forces anywhere on earth, including within
> the United States.   *(2000: 223)*

Such a statement foreshadows with chilling accuracy the events of September 11. But one of the real accomplishments of the Bush administration was to derail versions of the story of 9/11 which had such a broad narrative boundary. According to this version of events, the attacks had no provocation and belonged in no particular context. Rather, they were motivated by a desire to dismantle abstract principles: if Americans were being 'paid back' for anything, it was for our love of freedom and democracy. In this sense, the events of 9/11 were ahistorical – a narrative which is most hospitable to uncritical patriotism.

The official response to 9/11 by the American leadership was characterised by two key components: (1) a refusal to consider the grounds on which any resentment towards the USA might have been based; and (2) a celebration of America – its values, its way of life, the goodness of its people. The primary means through which this was achieved was in the construction of the events as a morality play, old-fashioned style, in which there were clear goodies and baddies. In Bush's address to the Joint Session of Congress on September 20, nine days after the attacks, he commented:

> Americans are asking, 'Why do they hate us?' They hate what we see right here in this chamber – a democratically elected government. Their leaders are self-appointed. They hate our freedoms – our freedom of religion, our freedom of speech, our freedom to vote and assemble and disagree with each other.   (*Quoted in Falk 2003: 57*)

This explanation for the assault on America is entirely devoid of any self-reflection. As Richard Falk remarks: 'Such an attempted deflection of Islamic resentment is profoundly misleading, entirely exempting the United States from self-scrutiny, and acknowledgement of past policy errors' (2003: 57). How one understands what happened on the morning of September 11, 2001, depends critically upon where one begins that story. Oral histories of that day typically begin the chronicle with accounts of bystanders observing the planes travelling unusually low in Manhattan as they made their way towards the towers. This is one kind of story, and it focuses on the terrible human tragedy of that day.

As devastating as the horror of that day was, this story still leaves unanswered the question 'why?'. But the extreme drama which was played out on television sets across the globe demanded an explanation. The one which Bush offered – a simple tale of good and evil – not only appealed to the wounded American people but it also gave permission to react in a particular way. It required no soul-searching, but rather provided a framework for a celebration of national identity. Those who massacred American citizens did so because they resented freedom. In the same address to the Joint Session of Congress on September 20, Bush described the confrontation as 'the world's fight ... civilization's fight. The civilized world is rallying to America's side' (Stoddard and Cornwall 2002: 185).

Falk describes the 'self-glorifying American epic narrative' as being based on

> the supposed reluctance of the United States as a country to engage in warfare, but, once engaged, to view the conflict as one between its forces of good and the enemy's forces of evil ... No dose of historical objectivity has been able to weaken this self-redeeming and seemingly endlessly self-renewing sense of American moral exceptionalism and innocence.   *(Falk 2003: 137)*

This 'self-glorifying' narrative provides a comprehensive framework that both explains the past and delivers a justification for future retributive actions.

The search for the meaning behind the attacks on September 11 was conducted almost wholly independently of any historical context which might have provided insight into the motivation of the terrorists for their actions. At the same time, however, collective historical memory played a significant role in the way that the attacks were psychologically processed by the American people. Even as the events were unfolding, the analogy was made between these attacks and that on Pearl Harbor on December 7, 1941. On September 11, and in the months that followed, the historical memory of 'the day of infamy', as Franklin Roosevelt famously described it, was used as a vehicle for coming to terms with the injustice which had been perpetrated against an innocent people.

The analogy is an interesting one, because of both what it illuminates and what it obscures. While the American people were surprised by both attacks, the same is not necessarily so for the American leadership. In the six decades since Pearl Harbor, a substantial body of evidence has been gathered that 'has raised serious doubts among respected historians about the surprise nature of the attack, suggesting that the pro-war forces gathered around Roosevelt had convincing advance knowledge that a Japanese attack on Pearl Harbor was in the offing, but chose to ignore such warnings' (Falk 2003: 1–2). The 9/11 Commission also found sufficient evidence to suggest that the Bush administration had less reason to be surprised by the attacks of 9/11 than did the American public, having received in the previous months intelligence indicating that al-Qaeda was planning an event on American soil which might involve a hijacking.

However, another analogy, and one with more fundamental long-term implications, is that the attack on Pearl Harbor, and those of September 11, nearly sixty years later, resulted in the issue of 'a blank check … to the White House to wage unlimited war' (Falk 2003: 1). The choice of Pearl Harbor as the key memory referent for the processing of the events of 9/11 meant that the patriotism and heroism associated with the Second World War were immediately galvanised as part of the national artillery, and helped significantly in preparing the country for war. That those who waged the 'war on terrorism' would later be accused of creating 'another Vietnam', thus swapping one national narrative for another, remains a gross irony. Five years after the attacks of 9/11, the national narrative which many Americans are reliving is not that of Pearl Harbor, but rather McCarthyism, which silenced the voice of dissent on the grounds that it was 'un-American' more than half a century ago.

LOOKING BACK TO THE TIME BEFORE THE FRAME FROZE

In March 2003 I was asked, at very short notice, to give a talk on the relationship between politics and narratives. For the basis of the talk, I returned to the data I had collected more than ten years earlier in Colorado Springs, and found in them a number of issues whose relevance had, if anything, grown in the interim period of time. In 2003, I was no longer living in the USA, and the post-9/11 world was in many ways quite a different place to the one which formed the context for my research in 1992. To accompany my talk, I showed a video, given to me by Tom, documenting the 'One Hour for America' which he had helped to organise. On the very day I delivered the paper, the second war with Iraq commenced – a painful illustration that 'data' are never constant, but are themselves changed by history. That video could never be viewed again as simply a documentary about one hour in 1991 – rather, it produced an eerie *déjà vu* effect. We have been told time and again that 9/11 changed everything. The discourse of a narrative rupture set in immediately after the attacks. Patricia Williams, for instance, writing only one week after the attacks, referred to the pre-9/11 world as the 'old world, in the other time zone' (2002: 145). Yet, listening to these interviews and watching the video of 'One Hour for America' eighteen months after the attacks made me realise that not everything really had changed. The data I collected for this project served for me as a small reminder that the struggle over what it means to love one's country was not so very new:

> as compelling as it is to focus on the rhetoric of disjuncture, the continuities between the nation before and after September 11 remain profound ... the imagery of discontinuity implicit in claims such as 'September 11 shattered the world we knew' has a suspiciously functionalist character. Marking off a special time by suspending our sense of ordinary life, such declarations help bind us in a shared mission, forge an expansive sense of community ... [but] such metaphors may not best illuminate empirical reality.
> *(Rieder 2003: 263)*

A case, perhaps, of *'la plus ça change, la plus c'est la même chose'*?

At the time that I conducted this research, I was concerned with documenting the position of the 'connected critic' within the context of the Persian Gulf crisis. Those who criticised our country, my country, did so from an 'insider' standpoint. Their critique of the military engagement, which was also my critique, came from a sense of belonging to that which was being criticised. The USA was, and is, mine and ours to criticise. This criticism may come from the margins, but the margins are still part of the whole.

It is, however, the fragility of the marginal space that seems to have been most dramatically affected by the events of 9/11. Whereas in the past the debate of who was and who was not be considered a 'good American' was open, and even contested, in the post-9/11 era there has been little space to tell stories in which these terms do not have absolute and incontrovertible definitions. The contours of 'us' and 'them' have been so tightly drawn, the national narrative so restrictively controlled, that those connected critics, once securely attached to their positions on the margins, are fighting for survival. Walzer writes:

> Social criticism is a social activity ... No doubt, societies do not criticise themselves; social critics are individuals, but they are also, most of the time, members, speaking in public to other members who join the speaking and whose speech constitutes a collective reflection upon the conditions of collective life.
>
> *(1987: 35)*

We need our connected critics to help provide us with alternative narratives – 'a collective reflection upon the conditions of collective life' – for comprehending the events of our age.

When I look back on the research I conducted in Colorado Springs, I feel that it contains far more than I could ever have realised at the time. Now, when I read the transcripts of my interviews as well as reviewing the materials written by others and myself at the time regarding the issues addressed in the interviews, I am overcome by a seemingly contradictory set of reactions. On the one hand, the project is marked by the absence of 9/11, an innocence of events and their fall-out which were still to happen; on the other hand, the arguments made at the anti-war vigil and at the anti-anti-war vigil mirror those which would dominate our post-9/11 world. America is now a more polarised society than it has ever been in recent history; what it means to be an American, and what duties and responsibilities are attached to being citizens of the sole superpower in the world, are hotly contested issues among Americans. Although Erik Erikson commented that

THE USA: NARRATIVES OF PATRIOTISM 113

'every national character is constructed out of polarities' (cited in Lieven 2004: 5), the USA at the beginning of the third millennium embodies 'both the most modern and the most traditionalist society in the developed world' (Lieven 2004: 5). The importance of this political struggle is immense, not only for America but for the whole world. In the words of Harlem Renaissance poet Langston Hughes:

> O, let my land be a land where Liberty
> Is crowned with no false patriotic wreath,
> But opportunity is real, and life is free,
> Equality is in the air we breathe.
>
> . . .
>
> O, Let America be America again . . .
> The land that never has been yet . . .
> And yet must be . . .   *(Hughes 1938)*

5   East Germany: the contested story

The fact that in the one and only democratic election in the existence of the German Democratic Republic (GDR), citizens voted to dissolve their country is the stuff of classic tragedy. The revolution eats its children, we are told, and so it happened in East Germany in 1989. Sebastian Pflugbeil, a leading East German opposition activist, voiced the fallen hopes of many which followed in the wake of his country's revolution: 'We have helped give birth to a child that quickly turned into a rather ugly creature' (Philipsen 1993: 161). East Germany has been the subject of countless publications since its demise more than fifteen years ago; yet still there is no consensus on the meaning of the changes which occurred there in its 'spring in winter' (Reich 1990).

In March 1990 I heard Jens Reich give a lecture at Cambridge University on the upcoming elections in East Germany. The research questions which I pursued over the following few years directly stemmed from what I heard on that day. In the months preceding his talk, Reich had become a familiar face to many. He was one of the founding members of the East German political group *Neus Forum* (New Forum) which had spearheaded many of the changes of that momentous autumn. Reich was a microbiologist with an international reputation, and a well-known public figure in East Germany. With unusually eloquent English, and a long history of political struggle in his country, for western media he embodied the voice of 'the bloodless revolution'.

It was clear as Reich spoke that for him, the events of autumn 1989 were substantially already over. This was a new phase of the East German political struggle. He described in detail the level of financial backing which was available to political groups such as *Neus Forum*, and for me the image which has endured most is that of the old-fashioned mimeograph machine which leaves traces of purple-blue ink on one's hands as the lever is turned around to make copies. Was this machinery sufficient to combat the resources being galvanised by the Christian-Democratic Union (CDU) in the then-upcoming March elections?

Reich predicted that the first time the East Germans would take to the polls they would do so to vote for the dissolution of their country. He described the glossy, western-style campaign of the CDU, and compared it to the inexperienced – and, most importantly, impoverished – campaign of Alliance '90, the umbrella organisation which groups like *Neus Forum* had banded together to create. Though the outcome of the elections had seemed predictable, when the results came out the margin of difference was staggering, nevertheless. The CDU alone captured 40.8 per cent of the vote, and the Alliance for Germany (of which the CDU was but one part) had 48 per cent of the votes. In comparison, only 2.9 per cent of the votes cast on 18 March 1990 were in support of Alliance '90. How could this be? What had changed in the six months since East Germans had taken to the streets with their emancipating cry 'We are the people'? The tidal wave of support for critical reform dissipated as quickly as it had swelled.

The story of the unfolding fate of East Germany that Reich related to the mesmerised audience in Cambridge was utterly compelling. What intrigued me most was the lingering question: how did those who were living through these changes make sense of them? It was clear to me that the story of East Germany as it was told in the western media was mostly a simple tale of liberation, and the images with which we were bombarded at that time seemed to lend credence to this position. In the academic world, this viewpoint was championed by people like political economist Frances Fukuyama in the USA, who wrote unapologetically about 'the triumph of the West, of the western idea' (1992: 3), and in Germany by Joachim Fest and other conservative historians involved in the *Historikerstreit*. For them, the fact of the growth of western capitalism was itself proof of its evolutionary superiority. The present situation was one to be celebrated. How different it was to the tragic tale that Reich described in such detail. I knew instantly that I wanted to go to East Germany, almost needed to go there, to learn more.

It was just under two years after this encounter that I arrived in Berlin to begin my research. By this time, the GDR no longer existed. Rather, the project on East Germany which I had designed would be carried out in the newly unified, or reunified (depending on your political perspective) Germany. Weeks before I arrived, the files of the *Ministerium für Staatssicherheit* – the 'MfS' or 'Stasi'– had become open to the public. The Stasi, officially designated as the 'sword and shield of the Communist Party', kept files on approximately one-quarter of all East Germans, but their eventual goal was to realise their internal slogan 'We Are Everywhere' (Andrews 1998). The opening of the files, an historically unprecedented act, had a very powerful effect across the population. The political atmosphere had changed immeasurably since the time of the 1990 elections, and the questions which I originally wished to explore now carried different meaning.

BACKGROUND TO THE ORIGINAL PROJECT

While my research in the years preceding 1989 had focused on sustained political commitment, what drew me to East Germany was the challenge to explore deeply held convictions at a time of acute social and political transition. The socialist activists who had held my interest for so long in England were exceptional because of the duration of their activism. The focus in that research was upon retrospective meaning-making; I was interested in how, in their eighth and ninth decades of life, these women and men pieced together the stories of their lives which had been guided by a constant principle for more than half a century. But East Germany presented me with an altogether different opportunity. What happens, I wondered, to political commitment when the structures informing the ideology change irrevocably? How is new information incorporated into already existing belief structures?

It is often said that only in retrospect does one come to realise the extraordinary nature of events which one has lived through. This was not the case with the autumn of 1989. One could not help but realise, even as events were unfolding, that these were exceptional times. The maps of Eastern and Central Europe would never look the same. When nations change, I wondered, what happens to the stories people tell about themselves in relation to their country which is no longer? It was this question which led me to East Germany.

The project which I originally designed focused primarily on the founding members of *Neus Forum*, a group of thirty people who gathered at a home in the outskirts of Berlin one weekend in September 1989, and which only two months later had attracted half a million signatures for its petition to the government. My attraction to this group was not only based on the fact that it had been the largest of the groups created in September 1989. I was fascinated by the language of the founding statement of the group: the combination of the failure of its leading members to dissociate themselves from socialism while at the same time repudiating the socialist state. The first meeting of the group happened in the home of Katja Havemann, the widow of Robert Havemann, symbol of East German resistance whose persistent criticism of the state was offered, in his words, 'Not as one disappointed in the socialist idea but as its confirmed partisan' (Allen 1991: 62). Havemann spent the last few years of his life under house arrest, and it was at this very home, in Grunheide, that eight years later *Neus Forum* was founded. However, as I began conducting my research I came to feel that much of the mass support which *Neus Forum* had garnered was based on a negative identification; many people signed the *Neus Forum* appeal because they saw this group as challenging the existing state, not because they identified with the group's political platform.

Therefore, very soon after beginning my data collection I decided to expand my investigation to include other internal critics of East Germany, who were not necessarily affiliated with *Neus Forum*. In keeping with earlier research which I had conducted, I decided to conduct in-depth interviews with leading internal critics of East Germany, a portion of whom were founding members of *Neus Forum*. Of the approximately twenty-five questions contained in the interview schedule which I developed, only one specifically addressed the role of *Neus Forum*, and this was pitched at a very general level ('Can you describe the role of *Neus Forum* in contributing to the major changes – *"die Wende"* – which have occurred since autumn 1989?'). For those individuals who were associated with *Neus Forum*, there was an additional portion of the interview schedule which probed for information on this group. Later, however, I came to feel that the enhanced focus on members of *Neus Forum*, simply because they were members of the group, was inappropriate, given the breadth of the questions which guided me in my research.

CONSTRUCTING/CONSTRUCTED AUDIENCE

It is clear that as people tell me the stories of the lives they lived in East Germany they are producing them not only in a particular historical context, but also that they are telling them to a particular audience. Ostow states that 'by early 1992, there was reason to suspect that citizens of the former German Democratic Republic had become the world's most interviewed population' (Ostow 1993: 1). Elsewhere she refers to the 'carnival of interviewing and biographical publications' which followed the revolutionary changes of 1989, stating that 'Being interviewed played a part in the reconstruction of the self that informed every GDR citizen's *Wende* (or turnaround)' (1993: 3–4). I was constantly questioning who these individuals perceived me to be, and reflected on how this might impact upon the stories which they told me.

One never knows exactly how one is viewed by one's interviewees, but on many levels I was an outsider to those I interviewed. For some, this was a bonus. Several people told me explicitly that the interview had been a useful experience for them, providing them with an opportunity for a 'strangers on a train' encounter. However, in a small number of cases, the fact that I was not only from the West, but specifically from the USA, produced an overtly hostile reaction.

My meeting with Christian Fuhrer, the pastor of the Nikolai Church in Leipzig, the site of the Monday night candle-lit vigils which had become the sign of the changing times, was an example of this. I was staying at the squat of a young woman who had agreed to act as my translator for a number of interviews which she had helped to arrange in Leipzig. (In recent years, I have come across her by-line several times in international publications.) One of these interviews was with Fuhrer, and I had anticipated this meeting with great interest. When we arrived, and he realised that I was an American, he became clearly agitated. He spoke one sentence to her in German, and she, without a moment's pause, turned to me and, translating his sentence, she announced: 'He said "not another fucking American"'. There was a moment of real tension which followed this. He was both appalled and surprised that she had related his comment to me. I asked if perhaps he would prefer not to go ahead with the interview, giving my assurance that I understood the basis for his frustration and apologised for contributing to it. Somewhat embarrassed, he said he wished to continue. Of all the things I learned from that meeting, the one which has stayed with me longest was the raw emotion which he spontaneously displayed when he learned where I was from.

Fortunately, while none of the other interviews reached that overt level of tension, there were moments when it was clear that a similar dynamic was in motion. In chapter 2 I described a tension-filled moment in my interview with Bärbel Bohley in which she passionately criticises the questions I have posed to her, and the assumptions upon which she feels they are based. Researchers like me from the West come to ask questions of others, without posing questions to ourselves. This interview format does not allow for genuine discussion; indeed, in her words, it is 'meaningless'. This was important feedback for me. Before we began the interview, we had had coffee and had discussed my personal background and my reasons for interest in this subject. Similar to my experiences in other research settings, I felt that I had been interviewed for the job of interviewer, and that approval had been granted. Correctly, she placed me in the category of 'people from the West', but I was clear that part of what had driven me so to go to East Germany when I did was to challenge some of my own political beliefs, which formed a core part of myself. Had the format of the interview itself, with me guiding the questions to learn more about her understanding of her own life and times, introduced a one-sidedness which I had not intended?

Encounters like this caused me to reflect deeply on the cultural specificity of standard research practice. How is it that we come to know and understand the meaning-making system of other people? What criteria do we apply when we assess the quality of the interpretations we make of other people's lives? Is there such a thing as getting an interpretation right? Or wrong? What is it that we base our judgements on? And how do we see ourselves as feeding into the process we are documenting? These questions would stay with me long after I had finished collecting my data in East Germany.

And yet, outsider though I was, people opened their doors to me, time and time again. I had arrived in East Germany not knowing a single person who might participate in my research (though of course I had some contact leads). Almost without exception, people were welcoming and generous with their time, despite the fact that many had been asked to 'tell their stories' by others before me. Yes, I was an outsider, but maybe this was how outsiders were to be treated in East Germany: trusted, despite experiences of being betrayed; welcomed, despite experiences of being exploited.

OPPOSITIONAL ACTIVISTS AND INTERNAL CRITICS IN THE GDR

Although I had begun my research by describing my focus as 'the politics of opposition', I soon came to appreciate the complexity of using the term 'opposition' in the East German context. Torpey reports that in his research with long-time independent political activists of East Germany, many felt the term 'opposition' was 'a label pinned on them by the "bourgeois" media of the West' (1995: 9). They felt that their audience was not the West, but rather their fellow citizens. Many people perceived their political positions as being critical of the system, but not in opposition to it. They wished to reform really existing socialism, but not to do away with it altogether. They believed that change could happen within their country, leaving the nation-state in action. On the very day that the Wall was opened, leaders of the main opposition groups issued a public appeal called 'For Our Country', reflecting a fidelity to the principles of socialism: 'We ask of you, remain in your homeland, stay here by us ... Help us to construct a truly democratic socialism. It is no dream, if you work with us to prevent it from again being strangled at birth. We need you' (Borneman 1991: 34–35).

The balance between being in opposition to the state, and wishing to enter into dialogue with it, was a very fine one. Having quickly realised this, I decided that a discussion of the terminology itself would be a useful starting point for the interviews, and so I began these with a question about the meaning of the term 'opposition' and its relationship to internal criticism. Through these many conversations, I came to a better appreciation of the complex nature of criticism, theoretical and actual, as it functioned in the one-party state of East Germany. Bärbel Bohley describes the transformation in her own political consciousness in the following way:

> The premise of oppositionists in the GDR had always been: 'We want reforms. We want to reform the existing society. We are not really an opposition.' [Later, through forced exile, she came to feel that] opposition is an integral part of a normally functioning society, and that a political opposition plays an important democratic role. *(Philipsen 1993: 294)*

There is no word or phrase which easily encapsulates the spirit of the critical movement in East Germany which had existed since the mid-1970s; many East Germans identify the expulsion of the popular singer Wolf Biermann, in November 1976, as a critical moment in the awakening of their political consciousness. As I listened to a range of descriptions of the impact of this event, I envisioned Bob Dylan, at the height of his career, being stripped of his US citizenship on the grounds of his provocative lyrics, and imagined the rippling effect this would have had across the country. Biermann's expulsion alienated many East Germans, and from this time forward there existed a small, but significant, critical movement which was forced to operate underground.

The activists who fought against the abuses of the state did not see themselves as trying to bring down the government, much less the state, but rather as citizens of East Germany, trying to build a better East Germany. This sentiment is precisely that encapsulated by Bertolt Brecht's statement: 'Let others speak of their shame, I shall speak of mine' (Woods 1986: 200), an example of Walzer's 'connected critic' discussed in chapter 4. The paradox of this position, embodying both a sense of identification with, as well as a critical stance apart from, the object of its scrutiny, was evident throughout my interviews. Leading internal critic Werner Fischer explains 'we never questioned this system as such ... we did believe in the reformability of the system, particularly after '85, during the post-Gorbachev era. [We wanted] to adapt socialism to a more human face, as it was known to us since ... Dubček coined this phrase in '68'. However, after the crushing defeat of the Prague Spring in August 1968 (ten months into Dubček's liberalisation), the critical intelligentsia of East Germany were unique among dissidents in the Soviet Bloc in their conviction that socialism could be reformed from within.

In the mid-1980s, East German dissidents found cause for hope in the leadership of Mikhail Gorbachev, who in 1985 introduced his policy of '*glasnost*' (or 'openness') which was to lay the foundations for *perestroika*, his plan for the economic, political, and social restructuring of the Soviet Union, announced at the Twenty-Seventh Party Congress in 1986. Because of East Germany's uniquely close ties with Moscow, East German internal critics hoped that Gorbachev's vision would have a particular relevance for their country. However, when it became clear that Honecker had no intention of following Gorbachev's lead – and, indeed, only increased the rigidity of the system – hopes for the reformation of socialism died.

When I look back on the early stages of this research, I see that in some ways I was trying to save, if not socialism as it was practised, then at least its founding principles. This is not surprising given my preoccupations of the previous years and my own political leanings. I found solace in terms like 'really existing socialism' which, from my perspective, mediated the blows for the principles of socialism. Following the events of 1989, Frida, who I had originally met through my project on lifetime socialist activists in Britain, wrote to me:

> Can you imagine turning your back on the Ninth Symphony just because it has been badly performed? Well, I can't! What is great and good and beautiful does not turn out to be paltry and rotten because the wrong people got hold of it and misinterpreted it.

I had some sympathy with this view, and one of the questions I included on the interview schedule, for instance, reflects this: 'Various people have commented that because of the reality of existing socialism, the left is now deprived of a language. If the language of socialism has been tainted, is that also true about all of its principles?' As I re-read this question now, it seems to communicate a sense of yearning and loss on my part, especially evident in the word 'all' contained in the phrase 'all of its principles'. For myself, I wanted to know what of socialism, if anything, they felt there was worth salvaging. Of course the responses which I received varied considerably, but most agreed on this: socialism had died, not in 1989, but probably some decades earlier, when the leaders of the country lost their own beliefs and decided that if socialism were to survive it would have to be imposed from above rather than organically nurtured.

It was not that I wanted to resurrect socialism in an unfettered way, however. If I did not want to accept, unquestioningly, the triumphalist interpretation of the reasons for the demise of socialist states, neither could I simply dismiss all critiques of socialism as originating from that position. I knew that by going to East Germany and speaking with the people who had spearheaded these changes, I would be confronted with stories and perspectives that were otherwise not available to me. And so it was that I did everything I could do to make it possible to go to East Germany, finally arriving in Berlin in February 1992.

In the course of the following six months, I conducted in-depth interviews with forty women and men – including Jens Reich – all of whom had been closely involved in the changes which occurred in autumn 1989. Some respondents had been part of the (underground) citizens' movement for a long time, others were involved in the arts and had helped to organise the 4 November demonstration – which many identify as the harbinger to the opening of the Wall five days later – some were affiliated with the church (which had played a critical role in negotiations between the citizens' groups and the state), and some were lifetime members of the Communist Party who had expressed their criticism of the state from within this powerful organisation. Two of the forty had been official employees of the Stasi who, at the time of our interviews, were forming an 'insiders' committee', as they called it, gathering together persons like themselves who had worked for the Stasi, who wished to discuss and analyse the past. The interviews were primarily in East Berlin, with about one-quarter of them taking place in Leipzig.

Looking back nearly fifteen years later on the research that I conducted in East Germany, four themes emerge from the data I gathered: (1) the difficulty of recounting and evaluating life experiences in a dramatically altered context to the one in which the experiences were lived; (2) the impact of generation on engagement with and perception of political changes; (3) the relationship between the physical Wall and the Wall 'inside the head'; and (4) the presumed importance of, and complexity surrounding, the negotiation of forgiveness.

Before turning to any of these, it is important to emphasise the political and historical context in which I was operating. In the spring and summer of 1992, when I conducted my interviews, East Germany was already a place of the past, but for many East Germans the pace and the extent of the changes which had taken place since the fall of the Wall two and a half years earlier had presented ongoing challenges.

As human beings, we are always rewriting our pasts in light of new circumstances in the present. Certain events which once seemed crucial to who we are later appear devoid of significance, while other experiences are recalled with a new-found importance. The situation for East Germans in the early 1990s represented an acute form of this everyday challenge, as people re-thought and re-crafted the lives they had lived under state socialism.

Nowhere was this challenge more dramatically illustrated than in the plight of East German historians, most of whom lost their jobs after 1989, and virtually all of whom publicly revised arguments which they had put forth in publications written prior to 1989 (Berger 2003). Some of these historians later published autobiographically based histories, such as Günter Benser, who wrote that 'I was surprised to see how closely the different phases of my own life corresponded with the evolution and passing away of the GDR' (cited in Berger 2003: 74). The role of East German historians is significant, as it is they who will, or will not, contribute to the way in which the 'story of the GDR' is ultimately written. East German historians have tended to argue against reducing the forty years of the history of the country to its 'inglorious end' (Berger 2003: 75). What occurred in 1989 was not inevitable, but rather was the outcome of not taking opportunities which presented themselves. 'There had been alternatives and turning-points at which, in A. J. P. Taylor's famous phrase, history failed to turn' (Berger 2003: 75). But these same historians, who provide rather different accounts of the downfall of their country to those offered by their western counterparts, have been marginalised. 'At worst they are completely ignored by the "official historical discourse" in the FRG [West Germany].' At best they are perceived as espousing a "half-hearted revisionism"' (Berger 2003: 81). Their perspective on, and retrospective accounts of, the critical historical events in the forty years of East Germany are an important contribution to the writing of their country's history. Yet, whether these accounts will be written into the official national narrative of East Germany remains to be seen.

THE SEARCH FOR A NARRATABLE PAST

There has been a longstanding debate within the social sciences regarding the veracity of accounts which individuals provide about the details of their own lives. When those who engage in life history research try to collect personal accounts of people's lives, how can we assess veracity? There are a number of angles from which to answer this question. First, we might ask ourselves: how do we ever know if what we are told is true? Sometimes there are resources which are available to assist us in our attempts to determine the factual basis of the stories we hear. But, very often, the accounts are so deeply rooted in the biographical that external fact-finding is difficult, and possibly irrelevant.

Perhaps a more interesting question, and one which is relevant to our considerations here, is: what does 'truthfulness' in the context of life history research actually mean? When people tell us about their lives, they are always doing so from a particular moment in time – the present – and the meaning of previous life experiences is forever changing in light of new circumstances. Thus it is that our understandings, of our selves and of our past experiences, are always subject to review over time. Moreover, not only are we are always audience to our own tales about who we are, and who we have been, but we also tell our stories to others, and our perceptions of who they are undoubtedly colours what we tell them.

In the months and years following unification, there was a widespread pressure to tell a particular kind of story about one's experiences under state socialism. Nowhere was this more explicitly reflected than in the remit of East Germany's truth commission, the *Enquete Kommission Aufarbeitung von Geschichte und Folgen der SED-Diktatur in Deutschland* ('The Study Commission for the Assessment of History and Consequences for the Socialist Unity Party (SED) Dictatorship in Germany'). In contrast to other truth commissions, such as that of South Africa, the *Enquete Kommission* was almost wholly unconcerned with personal testimony about the conditions of life under state socialism. Indeed, only 327 individuals were invited to give personal testimony, and most were the 'unsung victims of SED rule' (McAdams 2001: 91). The first *Enquete Kommission* was followed by a second, established in May 1995. Here, the explicit purpose was to investigate, in the words of Rainer Eppelman, Chair of both the first and second Commissions and himself a former dissident of East Germany, 'the thousands of people ... who did not permit themselves to succumb to the criminality or immorality ... of the SED dictatorship, who complained, stood firm, and achieved some kind of protest' (as quoted in Yoder 1999: 73–74).

The two *Enquete Kommissions* thus identify two kinds of narratable pasts: that of the victims, and that of the unsung heroes. Most East Germans, however, were neither heroes nor victims, but rather did what they felt they needed to do in order to achieve a particular quality of life for themselves and their families. Even small resistance came at a very high price – for instance, the compromising of educational opportunities for one's children. There have been numerous accounts of reading Stasi files since they were opened; the more nuanced of these refuses the stark portrayal of good and evil which such files might suggest. As Timothy Garton Ash writes:

> What you find here, in the files, is how deep our conduct is influenced by our circumstances ... What you find is less malice than human weakness ... And when you talk to those involved, what you find is less deliberate dishonesty than our almost infinite capacity for self-deception ... If only I had met ... a single clearly evil person. But they were all just weak, shaped by circumstances, self-deceiving; human, all too human. Yet the sum of all their actions was a great evil. *(Garton Ash 1997: 223–224)*

Still, the trend has been to categorise the 16 million East Germans in dichotomous terms: they were either good or bad. As Monteath (1997) comments: 'It remains to be seen whether history will remember that group of people who neither engaged in persecution nor offered resistance, but simply conformed to the daily pressures of life in the GDR, living unheroically within the restrictions imposed by

an authoritarian regime' (1997: 284). Moreover, the assumption underlying East Germany's truth commission is that the categories of victims and perpetrators were distinct. In one of my meetings with
Wolfgang Ullmann, one of the architects of the Commission, he said
to me: 'if you look into Stasi files you see there are spies and there are
those who are spied on: there is a very clear borderline between those'.
However, not everyone I spoke with agreed that the borderline
between these categories was indeed so clear, as we will see later in
this chapter.

When the Wall came down, East Germany was flooded with oral
historians from around the world (myself included), most of them
from the West. With hearts and minds captured by the images which
they encountered through the media, most of these researchers were
in search of a particular kind of story (not necessarily the same story,
of course). In the months following the fall of the Wall, there was
much talk about the anticipated 'liberation of memory' which it was
thought would follow from the collapse of the Iron Curtain. But what
they found when they turned on their tape recorders was often different to that which they had expected. The different stories which
respondents had to offer were taken to be a sign of speechlessness,
epitomised by the claim, widely held among western academics, that
'East Germany's harsh political structures had led to a general speechlessness: to a popular memory full of blank spaces' (Thompson
1990: 20). (For a discussion of this, see Andrews 2000.)

Virtually none of the East Germans with whom I spoke gave any
evidence of seeing themselves as newly liberated, in memory or in
anything else. Only months after the Wall came down, Jens Reich
posed the question: 'So, are we happy that this unloved and deformed
creature of the cold-war period is now at last dying?' His response
reflects the ambivalent emotions experienced by many of the East
Germans with whom I spoke:

> Strange to say, I am not happy and neither are others around me.
> Now that the state is decaying, people begin to yearn for some of its

more sympathetic traits. In a peculiar way, many of us feel homesick for that inefficient and lazy society which is so remote from the tough and competitive society into which we are now thrown ... So we say farewell, but with an oppressive sense of uneasiness.

(Reich 1990: 97)

In the months that I was there, daily life for those around me was in acute transition. One example which epitomised for me the special characteristics of this transitional moment concerned the physical remapping of Berlin. After unification, many street names in East Berlin had been changed to reflect the ideals of the newly formed country. However, Berlin maps available at that time did not show the correct names of the streets. In some cases this was not a problem, as new labels were placed above the old (and were considerably larger), but more often the new labels simply stood alone. In effect what this meant was that people living in the eastern part of the city, what had so recently been East Berlin, could not tell you how to get from one place to another. East Berliners could of course travel themselves to places which they knew, but they could not direct others, like myself, who were new to their neighbourhoods; on the other hand, those who knew the new names could not supply the insider knowledge, such as descriptions of tell-tale landmarks along the way, which customarily accompany the giving of street directions.

IDENTITY, IMAGINATION, AND THE WALL
But if the renaming of the streets of East Berlin serves as a metaphor for the confusion of many of its habitants, the psychological challenges posed by the disbanding of the Wall were far more widespread and enduring. For many years, and for many people, the Berlin Wall was representative of the captivity of a people, not just in Germany, but around the world. Jens Reich describes the 'Wall-sickness' which afflicted East Germans:

'Wall-sickness' was the eternal, lamenting analysis of our life blighted and circumscribed by *Die Mauer*. It came from being in a cage in the centre of Europe. Wall-sickness was boredom. We felt condemned to utter, excruciating dullness, sealed off from everything that happened in the world around us. Wall-sickness was loneliness, the feeling that you were condemned to die without having ever seen Naples, or Venice, or Paris, or London.

(Reich 1990: 76)

The Berlin Wall has been the source of countless books, art works, poetry and music. To say that it has captured the imagination of millions of people is not an exaggeration. Indeed, typing the phrase 'Berlin Wall' into Google results in just under 30 million hits.

While the Berlin Wall had a very real effect on the lives of East Germans from the time it was built, in 1961, until the time it 'fell' (and was eventually dismantled), in 1989, the force of its existence is still in evidence. I asked each of the forty people I interviewed about their reactions to the opening of the Wall on 9 November 1989. The responses which I heard were deeply moving, and revealed to me the complexity of the relationship which my respondents had to the demise of their country (Andrews 2003b).

A powerful example of this is the account given to me by Reinhard Weißhuhn, an East German who had been part of the small underground opposition in his country for more than twenty years, beginning in the 1970s. The interview takes place in the front room of his flat, which is situated 200 m from the border between East and West Germany. Here he describes how he experienced the opening of the Wall, and the psychological challenges this posed for him:

On the way home [at about 10.30 p.m.] I noticed many people all running into the same direction ... they were all running to the end of the world ... the street was full of cars and one could hardly walk at all ... I then walked with the stream and got to the border crossing, Bonholmer Strasse ... which was the first crossing to be opened. Two hundred metres from here. It was so crammed full with people you couldn't move. And everybody was pushing through the crossing. The policemen were just standing around, they didn't know what to do and were completely puzzled. I asked a few people ... what was happening. Of course, I know, I could see, but I didn't actually, I didn't understand. And I stood there for about a half hour in this crowd and then went home and switched the television on. Then I watched everything on television, transmissions from everywhere, Ku-damm and all other border crossings. And I could see that people were coming over, that is as seen from the west .... I was totally paralysed ... all this continued for the next few days and it took me a whole week before I went across, Potsdamer Str. It is difficult to describe ... this was such a very elementary transformation of one's existence, of ... the whole world in a way.

Weißhuhn's description of how he learned of the opening of the Wall is interesting for several reasons. First, it is clear that although he was active in the opposition movement, he, like others, was surprised by what he encountered as he returned home that November evening. While in retrospect it is possible to identify the signs of imminent demise that now seem so clear, it is important to remember that only ten months before the fall of the Wall, in January 1989, Honecker defiantly pronounced 'The Wall will still stand in fifty and also in a hundred years', and on 7 October of that same year, the date marking the fortieth anniversary of the creation of the country, he again expressed his belief in the future of the country, even in the face of evident growing disquiet. 'Socialism will be halted in its course neither by ox, nor ass' he proclaimed. It was only one month later that Weißhuhn encountered so many people running 'to the end of the world' – that is to say, to the world that lay on the other side of the Wall. In Weißhuhn's account, he first followed the flow of the people, until he arrived at the border crossing, the Wall. There he stood for a half hour, trying to take in what he observed. The policemen stood around, not knowing what to do, and Weißhuhn himself struggled to make sense of what he saw but could not understand. Ultimately, he returned to his own home, and watched the events through the lens of West German television. From this mirrored perspective, the crowds poured in, rather than rushed out.

But the effect of witnessing these events, even from the once-removed position which Weißhuhn tried to adopt, is paralytic for him. He cannot join the crowds, but neither can he resist travelling across the border. Weißhuhn then elaborates on his response to the opening of the Wall. Here one can see that his explanation is framed by his perception of me as someone from outside of the two Germanies. He describes to me in detail the geography of the corner of Berlin upon which his psychological transformation was played out:

> I'll try to explain. I have lived, I have been in Berlin since '73 and I have always lived two hundred metres from the Wall. And this Wall, to me, has become a symbol of captivity in every respect, also in a metaphoric, symbolic sense. And this is what I have been ramming my head against for the last twenty years. And I had, as a way of survival, I had resolved to ignore this Wall as far as I could ... And I tried to do the same throughout the week, when the Wall had gone. I did not only try to suppress the fact that the Wall had been there previously, but I also tried to suppress the fact that it had gone. And it didn't work. When I went across the Wall for the first time, I did so at Potsdamer Platz, where there hadn't been a crossing, they had only torn a hole, simply torn a hole into the Wall, yes. And that's where I wanted to go through, precisely there. I walked through like a sleepwalker. I could not conceive of the idea up to the moment when I was through, that that was possible. Well, and then I stood for a very long time over at the other side in no-man's land, and could not move forward or backwards. And then I cried, I was totally overwhelmed.

For Weißhuhn, it was important that he cross the border not where there was a clear opening, such as Bonholmer Strasse where he had seen the masses cross on the night of 9 November, but rather at Potsdamer Platz, where a hole had been torn into the Wall. Somehow this hole contained within it more evidence of the struggle which had led to these events. A number of respondents with whom I spoke mentioned to me the difficulty of accepting that the Wall, which had symbolised the strength of the repression of the people, could be disbanded so suddenly and so totally. To what extent had its strength merely existed in the eyes of those whose lives it restrained?

Actress Ruth Reinecke was one of the organisers of the now famous demonstration in Alexanderplatz in the heart of East Berlin, on 4 November, which attracted more than half a million people, who chanted '*Wir sind das volk*' – 'We are the people'. Looking back with hindsight, many now identify this moment as a critical event which contributed to the opening of the Wall five days later. But for those who lived this experience, there was no such sense of inevitably. Indeed, when, on the night of 9 November, Reinecke watched the television and heard the news, she simply did not believe it, and went to bed. '*Ganz normale*' she told me, 'totally normal'. It was not until the following day that she realised what had happened. What was her reaction? I asked. 'I was not happy, not happy. The Wall, the Wall was something very special. It was in all of our heads. That it had come down, this had to be a positive thing of course … Maybe somehow I felt in advance that what we had stood up so vehemently for on November 4th was giving way to this new thing.' What exactly 'this new thing' would turn out to be, no one could have known. But that a fundamental change had happened was unmistakeable. Reinecke expands on her feelings at that time:

> When the Wall was opened, suddenly another world existed which I did not know, which I would have to live in, whether I wanted it or not. There was of course a great curiosity to explore the world. This still exists. On the other hand … there was some fear that I could not stay any more the same person I had been so far. At that time, this was a problem for me.

As a repertory member of the Maxim Gorki Theatre, a theatre of international repute, Reinecke had travelled many times to the West. Perhaps for this reason, it held less of a mystical appeal for her. She explains:

> Because I worked in a theatre, I had the privilege to go to the West … When I went to this other Germany, I knew I could have

nothing to do with this other Germany. My home and my roots are in the GDR. The question which was always posed to me was why I had not left this country for the West. I always answered that I belong to this country.

Reinecke's repeated use of the phrase 'this other Germany' reveals the distance which she observes between herself and the West. Elsewhere in our interview, she tells me that when people ask her where she is from, three years after the demise of East Germany, she responds: 'I am from the GDR. Here. I am from here. Where is the West?' Would she still respond in this way today, fifteen years after unification? It is difficult to know, but in our interview she speculates on this: 'The GDR citizen inside myself will always accompany the movements which will take place in my life. You can't say, "well on Sunday I will deal with the past". It's going on and on. And it is a good thing that it functions this way.' For her, and others with whom I spoke, one of the greatest challenges facing them, in the first few years following uni-fication, was to re-evaluate their sense of national belonging. Reinecke, in her late thirties at the time of our interview, had grown up for her entire life in the GDR. But this country, her home, no longer existed. What then happened to this sense of belonging? Michael Ignatieff states that 'belonging … means being recognised and under-stood' (1994: 7). This is precisely what many East Germans were searching for after the loss of their country.

A QUESTION OF GENERATIONS

All East Germans lost their country, but clearly people experienced this loss in very different ways. One of the most important factors influencing this experience was that that of age: how old was a parti-cular person at the time of critical events in the country's history? Mannheim's (1952) work on the sociology of generations, discussed in chapter 3, hypothesises that when someone is born is highly influential in how they regard history, and that those events which occur during an individual's youth exercise a particularly powerful influence. John Bodnar reformulates this equation slightly, arguing that 'generational memory is formed in the passage of time, not simply born in pivotal decades and events' (1996: 636). Bodnar asserts that while individuals' basic narratives may be moulded from memories of their formative years, these memories are not static but rather are themselves under constant reconstruction. Thus, experiences of youth are both internalised and used as a central framework of identity, even while they are revisited and reinterpreted throughout an individual's life in light of new circumstances and knowledge. Henning Schaller, the head of set designs at the Maxim Gorki Theatre at the time of our interview, echoes this sentiment when he tells me: 'Identity is related to the consciousness of history.' One's consciousness of history, in turn, is influenced by one's standpoint in relation to historical events.

There are three key dates in my East Germans interviewees' biographies which have helped to shape their reactions to the demise of their country (Andrews 2003a): 7 October 1949, the founding of the country; 13 August 1961, commencement of the building of the Berlin Wall; and 9 November 1989, the opening of the Berlin Wall. The age of the respondents in my East German project ranged over about fifty years, from the young Steffen Steinbach who, as a key grassroots member of *Neus Forum*, was responsible for answering the telephone in Bärbel Bohley's home in the 'heady days' of autumn 1989, to Ursula Herzberg, who was in her early seventies at the time of our interview. Virtually all of the women and men with whom I spoke indicated to me the impact of the timing of historical events on their own biography.

The salience of generational consciousness among my interviewees manifested itself not only in the content of stories people told, but also in what stories were regarded as tell-able. Ulrike Poppe, for instance, describes growing up near to the forest, 'and through this forest, the Wall was built. I remember my parents always reminding us not to go too deep into the forest because there were soldiers with guns ... We heard the shooting day and night'. As she was only eight years old when the Wall began to be built, she and her friends made up a game, 'the frontier game':

> One was a solider, and the others smugglers, and we smuggled 'leaflets' and the leaflets were the leaves from the trees. I remember once being very proud because no one found my leaflets because I had swallowed them. The smugglers were always the good guys, and the soldiers were the evil ones.

In this story, one is transported into the experience of looking onto to the building of the Wall, from the perspective of a child. The Wall is something to be overcome; and this is achieved by making it a feature of the game. There are other potential stories which are more difficult to articulate than this one, because they are marked by inaction and silence; they are defined by their absence of story, the course of events which did not happen. Wolfgang Herzberg, the first oral historian in East Germany, says that a primary reason why the founding generation was left unchecked for so many decades was because his own generation, those born roughly at the same time of the nation, had 'too much respect for anti-fascism'. It was not until these 'GDR babies' themselves had children that this spell would be undone. Their children, the grandchildren of the founding generation, would be the ones to say that the emperor had no clothes.

My interview with Ruth Reinecke was particularly marked by the theme of generations, which emerged time and again throughout our conversation. For instance, when Reinecke describes the enormity of the challenge that the opening of the Wall presented for her, she completes this discussion by contrasting her own experience with that of her then nine-year-old daughter: 'For my daughter it is completely different. She is growing up in a different, a wider world, a more colourful world.' Reinecke's daughter was only six at the time of unification, and though Reinecke recalls her daughter telling her 'I am afraid. I am afraid', in fact the transition for her has not been too tumultuous. The experience of Reinecke's mother, a Jew who survived the Holocaust, is very different. She, and those of her generation, helped to build East Germany out of the ruins of the Second World War. For them, East Germany was both a place and an idea. For this East German cohort, the demise of the country, coupled with the apparent moral bankruptcy of the ideology upon which it was built, was paralytic. Reinecke describes the devastating effects of the recent changes on her mother's generation:

> Of course it is much better and much nicer if in the end you can say you have worked for something which has brought happiness to people. And now nothing, absolutely nothing, has remained ... My mother ... shares part of the responsibility, myself as well. She helped to construct this country, she worked for this country. And now when she realises what the country was really like, she became ill ... She is unable to say anything at all.

Reinecke is compassionate towards this generation, regarding them as both 'the most responsible and the most punished' regarding the demise of the country. She describes this generation as:

> very bitter now; they will be silent for the rest of their years. Their youth, their thoughts, their creativity has been invested in a life which is now nothing. And this is a very bitter knowledge ... therefore I have a lot of sympathy with this generation.

But not all of Reinecke's generation share her sympathy. Annette Simon, born three years before Reinecke, is a psychologist, and the daughter of the East German novelist Christa Wolf. The older generation, she says,

> feel very much betrayed, and they are very much still identified with East Germany. To me this is very strange. I don't feel like this. It's typical this attitude of the elderly, but it also makes me angry. I can't understand this attitude. There is so little working through for them, but of course it is understandable because this means questioning your whole life ... With the vanishing of the state, their own identity becomes lost. I cannot prevent being sour with this generation. It is a combination of pity with anger.

For people of Reinecke and Simon's generation, there is a pronounced sense of a generational divide, especially between them and the generation of their parents. Reinecke is noticeably more sympathetic with the plight of her mother and others like her than Simon, but the two women share a sense that this older generation is deeply responsible for socialism as it was practised ('really existing socialism') in East Germany.

My interviews with Ursula Herzberg were among the most emotionally challenging for me, personally, in this regard. At the time of our meetings, I had already conducted many interviews with older people who were engaged with their own life review, particularly in relation to my project on sustained socialist commitment in Britain. Never before, however, had I encountered someone who genuinely felt that they had wasted their life. As a young Jew living in Germany, Ursula had been sent on the *kindertransport* to England. Her family stayed behind, and there they were murdered by the Nazis. At the end of the war Herzberg, who had by this time become involved in left-wing politics in England, was persuaded to return to help build the new Germany. This decision was 'not easy' for her. She explains:

> I knew what had happened in Germany ... I was Jewish and I knew my mother would probably be missing and not be there any more. I had had some experience with the Nazis until I was seventeen ... I found it very very difficult emotionally to return to that country voluntarily. But on the other hand we were told by our comrades 'who else would be there to reshape Germany and rebuild Germany if it's not these few anti-fascists who survived or came out of concentration camps?' because a majority of the Germans had been with Hitler and supported him ... and for that reason I thought it was my duty to return to this country. So I returned.

Herzberg had read the book I had written on the British socialist activists. She was intrigued by this study, and said to me several times that had she not been persuaded to move back to Germany, to rebuild a new nation from the ashes that remained, she could have been one of the people in my study. I was struck by a powerful sense of Robert Frost's 'the road not taken'; our conversations were marked by her acute awareness of the life she might have had.

She was a woman of ideals, who had lived and fought for what she thought was right, but in retrospect her assessment of her life is that she 'spent fifty years of my life on the wrong horse … [socialism] doesn't work the way I thought it would work, you see, it doesn't work, that's why I say I put myself on the wrong horse'. Herzberg is painfully aware of the implications of the decisions she made long ago, and knows how she and the others of the founding generation of East Germany, are regarded by younger generations, represented by Reinecke and Simon. She is brutally honest with herself, and with me, and it is my challenge not to try to sweeten what she tells me:

> Bitterness was for a long time my feeling. I was absolutely bitter after these changes. Usually, I thought to myself, my God, you have wasted, absolutely wasted your whole life, fifty years of your life you could have done all sorts of things … I would never have returned to Germany from England if I had known what was going to happen forty or fifty years later. I certainly would not have returned. I think I could have been a progressive person and worked for progress, wherever, in England or wherever … I certainly wouldn't have gone back to Germany.

The sentiments Herzberg expresses here are not so unusual, though the implications of them in her own life are more dramatic than they are for most. The meaning of events and actions in our lives, and those of others, are most often only apparent in retrospect. We make decisions based on information we have at a particular moment in time, but this information is always incomplete, and our decision-making abilities are invariably flawed by our temporally partial vision. Freeman (2003) states that:

> Oftentimes, human beings are only able to recognize and understand the meaning(s) of experience after it has occurred. This

phenomenon is especially evident in the moral domain: the morality (or immorality) of an action (or inaction) is often gauged only
after the action has been completed. As such, we are often, and
tragically, too late in our arrival on the moral scene.   *(2003: 54)*

In Herzberg's story, we see a living embodiment of this 'tragedy'. For
her, the importance of her age is critical for two reasons: (1) because of
the length of time she dedicated to what she would later regard as 'the
wrong horse', and (2) because she is old, and most of her years are
behind her. 'I'm glad I'm old now, I wouldn't like to be young again …
Enough is enough' she tells me. She is tired. Still, she tells me 'now,
now I have some ideas', but the repetition of the word now indicates
the unsaid part of that thought: 'I have some ideas now, *but it is too
late.*' It is time for others to play their role in the making of history.
'It's easier for the young ones', she tells me. They have time on their
side, they can adjust to the new changes, and find their own way. As
for herself, what does Herzberg see in her own future? 'I can't see a role
for myself much really.'

The intersection between history and biography is evident
throughout the conversations I had in East Germany. For some, the
possibilities for the future were both exciting and frightening, represented by the 'more colourful world' of Ruth Reinecke's daughter. But
for some of those of the older generation, the judgement which has
been cast upon their life's work has been harsh indeed, and this has
rendered them silent and without hope.

FORGIVENESS AND REWORKING THE PAST

I did not go to East Germany with the intention of exploring the
meaning of forgiveness; yet, it is this topic more than any other
which my research there led me to contemplate. I have already
described the importance of the timing of my interviews in East
Germany, in relation to the opening of the Stasi files. If I thought
about forgiveness at all at that time, it was in a rather straightforward way: how, if at all, could those who had been spied upon

bring themselves to forgive those who had betrayed them? Was forgiveness a desirable goal and, if so, what could contribute to its
possibility?

It was in my interview with Katja Havemann that the complexity
of this term was made clear to me. She recalls that initially she had
'imagined that they [people who worked for the Stasi] would feel
relieved when they finally were able to come out of this role ...
We hoped that they would readily say that 'yes, we were really wrong
about this one' – a perspective she describes in our interview as 'naïve'.
She, and others who had suffered at the hands of the Stasi were, she
says, ready to forgive them, and wanting to forgive them. But their
forgiveness was never sought. Instead, what she discovered was something very different:

> They [long pause] still can't forgive us, what they did to us, you
> know ... We are the living guilty conscience .... They can't forgive
> us for the things that they did to us ... but [pause] ... then there's
> also these documents [the Stasi files] ... I can't hate. But I can't
> forgive this. And I'm alive ... When history is written, it will come
> to this: It really did happen.

But who will write that history? And what will they include? What
will be left out? What 'really did happen', and why? The struggle to
participate in the construction of this narrative is precisely the battle
being fought between East and West German historians, referred to
earlier. I leave the conversation with Havemann very much impressed
by how disappointed she was not to have the forgiveness she was
willing to extend accepted by those whom she was prepared to forgive.
Not only did they not want it, indeed they could not forgive her for
reminding them of who they had been and what they had done. She
was, she said 'the living guilty conscience'. In East Germany, unlike in
some other dictatorships, most of the victims of the state survived.
Havemann emphasises this to me: 'we're still alive, we experienced it
all. We're still witnesses.' Here the word 'still' underscores the fact of
her survival; she has not been destroyed. Rather, she is a force to be

reckoned with, and she will not go away. Yet, why is it so important to Havemann, and to others like her who have been wronged, to forgive those who caused them suffering? And if forgiving the wrongdoers is of paramount importance, why don't they just forgive them? Does forgiveness require the participation of both the wrongdoer and the wronged?

Conversations such as the one with Havemann led me to realise the significance and the complexity of the process of forgiveness, something which was to become a recurrent theme in my interviews. Many people seemed to feel that only through forgiveness could they overcome the hurts of the past. But is the promise of healing, and thus of reduced suffering (for oneself, and/or others), sufficient reason to forgive? And if it is imperative to forgive, who should be forgiven, for what, and how? Elsewhere I identify a number of questions which lie at the heart of the meaning of forgiveness:

> Is the knowledge of a past wrong sufficient grounds for granting forgiveness, or rather are there conditions which, if not met, necessitate its withholding? Must forgiveness, once offered, always be accepted? What does it mean to forgive, and what does it mean to receive forgiveness? Must forgiver and forgiven share a construction of forgiveness? What implications, if any, are there if their constructions of this act are at variance? Do forgiver and forgiven need each other to engage in this process?
> *(Andrews 1999: 111–112)*

The more I thought about forgiveness, the more engaging I found these questions to be, both theoretically (Andrews 2000) and in relation to my own data (Andrews 1999). Hannah Arendt's *The Human Condition* provides one of the most thoughtful cases for pursuing the path of forgiveness. It is, she tells us, 'the only reaction which does not merely re-act but acts anew and unexpectedly, unconditioned by the act which provoked it and therefore freeing from its consequences both the one who forgives and the one who is forgiven' (1958: 241). Forgiveness is important, because it makes possible a new beginning.

But a new beginning for whom? Forgiveness depends upon developing an understanding of how a certain course of action came to be adopted, but it does not rationalise it. The road to forgiveness is one which requires the development of understanding of another party's framework of meaning, and it is for this reason that it is increasingly being considered within its wider political context. As Donald Shriver writes:

> the concept of forgiveness ... belongs at the heart of reflection about how groups of humans can move to repair the damages that they have suffered from their past conflicts with each other. Precisely because it attends at once to moral truth, history, and the human benefits that flow from the conquest of enmity, forgiveness is a word for a multidimensional process that is eminently political.
> *(Shriver 1995: ix–x)*

In East Germany, in the months immediately following the opening of the Stasi files, the air was filled with conversations about forgiveness; its possibility or impossibility; why it was important for the individual, and for society; and critically, who to forgive and what to forgive them for. Some people with whom I spoke described not only the struggle to forgive others, but the need to forgive themselves as well. These conversations caused me to contemplate the complexities of forgiveness, particularly as it transpires in politically charged and often public circumstances. Eventually, I developed a model of forgiveness (Andrews 2000), in which I argued for three vital pre-conditions for forgiveness: (1) confession, (2) ownership, and (3) repentance. Only when these conditions are met is there a possibility for a real and lasting forgiveness between injured party and perpetrator. Forgiveness, I argued, is something which happens between people, and is dependent upon a dialogue between them for its realisation. In the case of forgiving oneself, this dialogue is between a present and past self, as one looks back on actions which one did or didn't do, the turning of a blind eye, to that which they knew, or should have known.

Earlier in this chapter, I quoted Wolfgang Ullmann, pastor and architect of the East German truth commission, proclaiming that there was a clear distinction between victims and victimisers. If this premise is accepted as true, then questions of who should forgive whom are rather straightforward. But many with whom I spoke thought that this stark contrast was itself an impediment to examining one's own past, for there will always be those who were more implicated than oneself. Werner Fischer, one of the leading anti-state activists in the 1980s who was later placed in charge of disbanding the Stasi, comments to me:

> People are only too eager to point a finger at the other person, to the guilty one, 'that was him, the Stasi' in order to disguise their own shame of not having been able to – even only in a very minute way – show resistance. This simply must happen, but at present does not, that people ask themselves, 'how far have I contributed to make this system function, if only by my silence?'. This is an exceedingly difficult process.

Fischer then comments about this self-interrogation on a more personal level:

> I refuse to accept a polarisation of victim/victimiser, although I personally use these terms too in a careless way … I am very cautious with this categorisation. Do I know in how far I, as a so-called 'victim' who was in prison and so on, contributed in a certain way to a stabilisation of the system? Because the Stasi strengthened this apparatus, could only strengthen it by constant referral to the opposition. That is how the system legitimised itself. In that respect I belong to the criminals, who ensured that the Stasi found more and more reasons to expand. Who can judge this?

Lotte Templin, oppositional activist and wife of Wolfgang Templin, makes a similar comment, telling me that for her it is important to inspect her Stasi files, so she can decipher those parts of her past for which she must assume personal responsibility. Having been targeted for abuse by the state over a protracted period of time, it would have been easy for her to retreat into a position which abdicated any responsibility for the consequences of decisions she had made which affected her life, and those of her children. Jens Reich comments upon the tendency to hide behind the state:

> 'They' were guilty for anything that went wrong in your professional career. Indeed it is true that they stopped the development of hundreds of thousands of gifted people. But there also exist other reasons for professional failure. Yet the legitimate and the illegitimate reasons for failure could never be disentangled. As in your professional, so in your personal life. *(1990: 78)*

Individuals such as Reich, Templin, and Fischer struggled to realistically assess their own biographies, as they strongly promoted others to do as well. Their motivation to do so was primarily that identified by Arendt above, simply to create conditions for a new beginning. This was considered to be important not only for them personally, and interpersonally, but for the whole of the society. Equally, however, one could argue that the rigorous self-examination which these dissident activists advocate has less severe consequences for them than it might have for others who did not criticise the state. Moreover, the heavily politicised divisions between East and West which followed unification meant that the environment was not conducive to such self-exploration. As Fischer comments:

> Unfortunately, what I had expected from people did not happen, that they come clean about their actions. Of course they can only do so if they are without fear. And the atmosphere was and still is today not very conducive for that to happen … many people hope that their collaboration with the system will never be discovered. I think that this is tragic not only for their personal future development but for the inner peace of the country. In human terms, I find this reprehensible.

Fischer's comment here echoes the sentiments of Havemann, expressed above. One can hear the disappointment and disillusion with those who did not 'come clean', which for him marks not only a 'tragedy' for them personally, as it is a unique missed opportunity, but which compromises the possibility for 'the inner peace of the country'. Forgiveness, which has long been regarded as something which transpires between individuals, is here imbued with a much larger importance; with it rests the hope for the redemption of the society.

Looking back on the talk I heard Jens Reich deliver in 1990, I am struck by two things: first, the world at that time seems so very far away from the one in which we now live. Literally, the globe was different. But I am also struck by the timing of these momentous happenings in terms of my own biography. Having just concluded my study on lifetime socialist activists when I sat in Lady Mitchell Hall in Cambridge University, listening to Reich, somehow the groundwork had been laid for me to be captured by the tale which he told. The demise of East Germany, and the meaning of a newly unified Germany, have been the topics of countless publications, both within Germany and beyond. In these pages I have tried to present a different kind of narrative – an account of what I saw and how I understood it when I spoke with forty East Germans in the months following the opening of the Stasi files. These stories have stayed with me over the past fifteen years; as I return to re-examine the data, I wonder about the people I spoke with for my research. Where are they now, and how do they now regard the changes of 1989? And how will they look upon these changes twenty-five years from now? The story of East Germany is one which is still being rewritten, and doubtless the process will continue. Why and how the changes happened as they did is something which continues to be debated. There is and can be no ultimate writing of this story, as inevitably the version which is told reflects the placement of the teller and the moment of the telling.

In our interview, Bärbel Bohley tells me that 'the socialism that can be discussed does not exist any longer. But the people that lived through it do.' Although I was compelled to go to East Germany because of my interest in the fate of socialism, this focus soon became over-shadowed by my desire to know and understand how a small group of people who 'lived through it' made sense of the new society which they had helped to create. Their stories, individually and collectively, suggest a different framework for understanding East Germany's 'revolutionary moment' (Philipsen 1993: 22) and its powerful impact on the lives of East Germans.

6 South Africa: told and untold stories

Much has been written about personal narratives and the importance of storytelling in post-apartheid South Africa. Njabulo Ndebele (1998) comments that one of the major effects of the Truth and Reconciliation Commission (TRC) was 'the restoration of narrative. In few countries in the contemporary world do we have a living example of people reinventing themselves through narrative' (1998: 27). What is special about South Africa is not the re-invention of self through narrative, but rather that this has been carried out by the state, in a very conscious effort to remould national identity. (While states customarily recreate and maintain national identity through the recital of particular stories, which is ultimately read as history, rarely does this occur as an explicit project intended to engage the whole nation.) The first decade of 'the new South Africa' has been characterised by an extraordinary effort to remake national identity through gathering and weaving together individual stories. In South Africa, one can observe collective memory in the making.

For this reason, among others, it is perhaps not surprising that South Africa has ignited international passions in a way that few nations in recent history have managed. Its history of the twentieth century is a quintessential tale for our time, with images – ranging from the shootings in Soweto to Mandela's release from prison – which are indelibly marked on the conscience of the world. South Africa has become the repository for the political imagination, the stage of the allegorical morality play between good and evil.

Several years ago, on my first visit to South Africa, I went on a 'memorial' tour in the townships of Cape Town. The three guides, former combatant soldiers of *Umkhonto We Sizwe* (MK) – the military wing of the African National Congress (ANC) – escorted us from one location to another, all unmarked sites of apartheid's bloody struggle. The geography of this city drips with a history which might never be named, other than by those who experienced it.

Also on this trip was an affluent family from California, a twelve-year-old girl and her parents. The parents were explaining to their daughter that here in South Africa, white people lived separately from everyone else and that this was called apartheid. I was almost as interested in their conversation as I was in the 'tour' itself. For them, South Africa was the embodiment of the 'other' – an other which was riddled with racism and inequality, but also a place of miracles where, against all odds, good triumphed over evil. I wondered to myself if the experience of racial segregation was really as foreign to this twelve-year-old as this conversation might lead one to assume. The daughter and I began chatting; she described to me ways in which life at her private school in California were very different from the environment we were then travelling through. She was saddened to see the shards of so many destroyed lives. The tour concluded, and we dropped the family off at their five-star hotel on the waterfront. A tour such as this would not have been included on everyone's itinerary of Cape Town (for a range of reasons: some simply feel that Cape Town, and indeed South Africa, are places to be enjoyed, not to become depressed. Others regard such token forays as painfully voyeuristic). Clearly for this family, it was an important part of their trip to South Africa. But what did it represent to them? How, if at all, did they make sense of this experience in relation to their own daily lives?

My questioning of this family was only part of a larger, fuller questioning of myself. Why was this lens into the gaps of disparity important for me as a tourist, and yet almost wholly absent from my experience of growing up in Washington, DC? My visits to South Africa were haunted by that which I circumvent in my daily life, on my home territory. For me, as for others, South Africa was as much a psychological as a geographical location. There are good reasons why the transformation of South Africa has attracted intense interest from researchers around the world: in many ways the bold experiment that has been unfolding has implications for much of Africa, if not beyond. Yet, it is my inclination that many who come from abroad to write about this foreign land are as much engaged in a personal journey of exploration and discovery as they are in documenting the intricacies, the hopes, and the pains, of the birth of the new nation.

SOUTH AFRICA, BIOGRAPHY, AND THE POLITICAL IMAGINATION

I came to my research on South Africa through a rather roundabout route. South Africa for me, as for many of my generation, had long been a key site of political protest. At university in the late 1970s and early 1980s, we held weekly demonstrations on our campus, in the hope that such small actions around the globe would contribute to the possibility of freeing Nelson Mandela, who embodied for all of us the struggle of good against evil. I do not think that I was in any way unusual in the intensity of my feelings for a place which I had never visited, and thought likely that I would never see. It was perhaps this elusive quality of South Africa – the fact that it was both there but not there, quite literally a forbidden place for anyone who saw themselves as engaged in the anti-apartheid struggle – combined with the absolute clarity of the struggle there, that created for so many of us such a powerful and enduring attachment.

When Trevor Huddleston agreed to be part of my study of British lifetime socialist activists, I was both nervous and terribly excited. As the founder of the anti-apartheid movement, he had played a vital role in awakening the conscience of the world to the wrongs which we in the West had helped to create. I had not anticipated that what was scheduled as a one-off interview would develop into a friendship which lasted until he died, about ten years later. Father Trevor told me many, many stories about South Africa. He told me about his early days there, and how it did not seem to him an act of courage but rather of conscience to insist on living in the community which he was meant to serve, rather than in the whites-only area as had been expected. (Eventually this, and his other activities, led to him being recalled from his post in South Africa. He did not return for nearly forty years.) He told me of bringing books to the young Desmond Tutu, suffering from TB in a hospital, and of how he gave Hugh Masekela his first trumpet. All of this brought me that much closer to this place which had for so long inspired in me such political passion and imagination.

Still, my encounters with Bishop Trevor were primarily aimed at documenting his life story. It was in fact my work in East Germany which eventually led me back to South Africa. Being in East Germany at the time of the opening of the Stasi files and the establishment of the truth commission, I was witness to very raw conversations about the meaning of forgiveness, and living in the presence of a community as it wrestled with the deeper, social meanings of this term. This interest in narratives of forgiveness eventually led me back to South Africa, and with it came a sense of returning to this place which had represented so much in the early formation of my political conscious-ness. Of course, by this point the political landscape had changed so dramatically since my days in university – indeed, had changed in ways that none of us had ever truly believed would be possible. In terms of political narratives, the birth of the new South Africa was a story which had captured the imaginations of even the most apathetic political observers. And yet, the pain of that ruptured society did not cease with Mandela's release from prison. So many losses, so many unanswered questions, so much deep heartache could not be over-come by a change of regime, even one of this magnitude. The question which haunted South Africa, and continues to haunt her, is how to move from the past into the future. The official response from South Africa was that this transition must be rooted in memory, and that memory must be spoken. It is not through amnesia that deep pain becomes almost bearable, but rather through an acknowledgement of it. As Barbara Myerhoff writes about her work with survivors of the Holocaust: 'Any disaster becomes more bearable once it is named and conceptualised ... Without Re-membering we lose our histories and ourselves' (Myerhoff 1982: 107, 111). One of the people with whom

Myerhoff was working explained to her that 'the only pain worse than recollection was the pain of considering the possibility that the stories would be untold' (1982: 112). It was this principle which underlined the creation of South Africa's TRC.

The TRC was established in the Preamble of the Promotion of National Unity and Reconciliation Act (1995). Among the primary functions of this body was that it should establish 'as complete a picture as possible of the nature, causes and extent of gross violations of human rights' committed between 1960 (the year of the Sharpeville Massacre) and 1994 (the year of Mandela's inauguration). (The other two functions dealt with amnesty claims for perpetrators and reparations for victims.) Victims of gross violations of human rights would be allowed to 'report to the Nation' their painful stories. And so it was that, over two years, nearly 22,000 South Africans engaged in a national project of sharing their stories of pain with one another, while the rest of the country, and much of the world, listened. (While only 2,000 of the statements from victims were delivered in public hearings, the national news was dominated by personal accounts of trauma suffered during the apartheid years.) Town halls, community centres, and churches throughout the country became transformed both as places for the commission to operate, and as sites for the performance of pain.

South Africa, with other African nations, has a long history of storytelling, and perhaps it is for this reason that the TRC was, with all of its shortcomings notwithstanding, one of the most successful in achieving its stated aims. By the end of the twentieth century, truth commissions as a means for working through a traumatic national past had become if not common, not unusual. In the twenty years preceding the creation of South Africa's TRC, there had been truth commissions in fifteen other nations. Nonetheless, in South Africa the public performance of truth telling became more widespread and had more of a national focus than it had in any previous incarnation. One could even say that, in South Africa, a critical part of the national narrative as it was being constructed was that, through the TRC,

South Africans were collectively processing their past. The national story was about a nation storytelling.

Implicit in the South African truth commission model is a profound belief in the healing power of stories. It was widely believed that national truth telling would serve the purpose of national reconciliation, as the stories themselves would function as a bridge between past and present, between victim and victimiser. As Dullah Omar, former Minister of Justice, explained 'a commission is a necessary exercise to enable South Africans to come to terms with their past on a morally accepted basis and to advance the cause of reconciliation' (TRC Homepage, accessed 7 October 2004). But reconciliation cannot come about simply through a recital of pain. Person after person came before the commissioners to tell them that they could not begin to think of forgiving those who had tormented their loved ones until they knew the full story of what had occurred. These men and women could not move beyond the past because they could not narrate it. For the possibility of reconciliation, much less forgiveness to exist, many asserted that first they must learn who, what, where, when, and why.

Much of the research which has been conducted on the TRC has focused on the personal testimonies which were delivered before the commission. I, like many others, have spent countless hours reading this testimony, and reading about it. But the more engrossed I became in these painful personal accounts, the more I began to think about the larger stories of which these testimonies were but a part. While I retained my interest in the processes and materials generated by the TRC, my focus shifted from the content of individual tales to a consideration of the influences and assumptions which underlay the process of national storytelling.

This chapter will explore three different meta-narratives which were crucial to the knowledge production of the TRC. The first of these is the larger-than-life narrative of the Commission itself. The proceedings of the Commission received exceptionally widespread media attention nationally and internationally. What was this interest based upon? Why was the Commission so much more successful as a national export than it was in the hearts and minds of those who engaged with it directly? Which truth, or sets of truths, was it seeking to uncover? Is reconciliation a realisable goal for individuals whose lives have been shattered, or is this something which can be achieved only at the level of the nation as a whole?

The second meta-narrative concerns the assumed relationship between telling and healing. What correspondence, if any, is there between the healing of a nation and the healing of individuals who participate in truth commission mechanisms? What is the function of the stark categorisation of victim and perpetrator which underlies the design for the truth commission? Does this construal render some stories more tell-able than others? What impact does this have on the potential for collective healing? What of the potential for individual healing? Do individuals who offer their testimony to a truth commission do so in the expectation that they will be healed, or are their actions motivated otherwise?

Third, what role does individual memory play in the construction of collective memory in South Africa? Can the brutality of apartheid be reduced to its individual effects? How did the TRC's political agenda of giving birth to the new South Africa affect which stories were selected to be woven into the collective memory of the nation? The project of nation-building was used as an incentive to bring both injured and injurers alike before the Commission. How did this political mission of the TRC affect the process and content of its knowledge production?

THE 'MIRACLE' OF THE TRC

By the end of the twentieth century, truth commissions had become a standard mechanism for nations in transition to process their fragmented pasts, and this trend has only increased in the present time. (Hayner identified twenty-one truth commissions which had been established around the world, in addition to Indonesia, Colombia and Bosnia which were all considering establishing commissions at the time of her writing, Hayner 2001.) Why was the truth commission of South Africa considered to be so special, when so many others had gone virtually unnoticed, not only by the international community, but even in the environments in which they operated?

It is notable that the success of the TRC is far greater in the eyes of the world than it is domestically. Many South Africans feel that the promise of the commission surpassed anything that it ultimately delivered – a sentiment which is characteristic of truth commissions more generally (Hayner 2001). But, arguably, South Africa's truth commission was more ambitious than any which had preceded it, and this meant that the potential for disappointment was greater. Among the many aspects which set the TRC apart from previous commissions, five are outstanding: (1) the commission sought to engage an unusually large portion of the population, so that it could be, and could be seen to be, a genuinely national democratic project; (2) there was considerable media attention which was dedicated to covering the TRC throughout the weeks, months, and years of its existence; (3) the TRC was dedicated not only to documenting the truth of past injustices, but to an overt project of national reconciliation; (4) vast financial resources were put in place to support the TRC's activities; the budget was $18 million a year, a very considerable sum given the strains on South Africa's new economy, but an amount still judged to be insufficient by many observers (Hayner 2001: 223); and (5) the TRC had the power to grant individual amnesty for politically motivated crimes committed between 1960 and April 1994. In this chapter I shall deal only with the first three of these components, as a breakdown of the finances of the TRC (including the debates over reparation) and the highly controversial decision to grant amnesty for political crimes are very complex issues, and have less explicit implications for the analysis of post-apartheid meta-narratives. They are mentioned here, however, as the debates surrounding them undoubtedly contributed to the explosion of interest in the TRC, as compared to other commissions.

21,400 people gave testimony before the TRC (roughly 0.05 per cent of the total population of 40 million). This level of public engagement in the process of national truth telling compares favourably with other commissions. For instance, in East Germany, 327 people of the population of 16 million gave testimony to the truth commission, or approximately 0.002 per cent of the population (see Andrews 2003b). Despite the commission's attempt to attract widespread participation, it was nonetheless criticised for being overly oriented towards individuals. The violence of apartheid, it was argued, could not be reduced to a litany of the damage it had wrought on individual lives. As Albie Sachs, Justice of the Constitutional Court of South Africa, queried: 'Why focus on individual cases of torture, assassination and violence, when apartheid itself was a denial of humanity that involved dispossession of land, suppression of language, culture and personality?' (Sachs 2000: 95). Apartheid was directed at whole communities, as illustrated by legislation such as the Group Areas Act (1950), which resulted in the forced removal of 3.5 million people from their homes. Yet there were virtually no mechanisms within the operating systems of the TRC which were designed to document the extent and nature of this societal, as opposed to individual, damage. As Mamdani comments: 'By individualising victimhood [the TRC] surrendered the task of comprehending the social nature of dispossession' (2000: 19).

Not everyone who wanted to give testimony before the TRC was allowed to do so (usually on the grounds that their suffering had not stemmed from politically motivated crimes, or that it did not occur within the designated time-frame). Of those who did testify, only a small portion were used as indicative cases to illustrate particular phenomena in the Final Report. The individual accounts which were included were intended, in the words of the TRC Final Report, as 'windows on the experiences of many people'. But the process by which some stories were considered appropriate windows, and others not, was never transparent, and for many this raised critical issues which were never addressed. As Posel (2002) comments:

> It is never clear why some aspects of the broader picture are
> deemed relevant and not others; nor why some scholars and not

others are cited. But this raises the bigger question: how much
information was considered 'enough' and according to what
criteria of sufficiency?   *(2002: 160)*

By necessity, not all victims of apartheid were able to have their
experiences documented by the truth commission; however, the
lack of transparency of the criteria used for selection meant that
many South Africans came to feel that, for whatever reasons, their
story was not considered relevant to the purposes of the TRC.

The media attention on the TRC's proceedings, especially those
2,000 hearings which were open to the public, was exceptional by any
standard: a large array of newspapers gave prominent coverage to the
daily revelations, often carrying three or four stories in each issue, and
leading with the most sensational among them; four hours of radio
were broadcast live over national radio each day; there was a television
show called Truth and Reconciliation Special Report which aired on
Sunday evenings and which was the most widely viewed programme
in the country (Hayner 2001: 42). Effectively, this meant that the
drama of apartheid was played out again and again in locations
throughout the country, not only in the town halls where testimonies
were collected but in any place that had access to television, radio, or
newspaper.

But how, exactly, were these stories of apartheid gathered? Most
discussions of the TRC findings devote little or no attention to analysing the methodology which was employed. Significantly, however,
the stories which were gathered by the commission's researchers
were the product of a very blunt research tool, the statement protocol.
The protocol went through eight versions, growing from eight pages to
twenty. Bonner and Nieftagodien (2003) provide one of the most
detailed and critical descriptions of this form, arguing that it recorded
only that information which was relevant for the TRC's database.
When people came to tell their stories, they were strongly guided

> to offer only the skimpiest data on motivation, and [instead] to focus
> on the immediate antecedents of the act. The very structure of the

form and the direction in which it steered the statement-takers
precluded a consideration of the wider context.   *(2003: 178)*

In other words, the contours of the stories selected for public testimony
were heavily influenced by what the TRC considered to be relevant.
Witnesses were given clear instructions of where their 'stories' were to
begin, and were given no platform to contemplate the wider causes of
the event(s). An example of this can be seen in Version 4 of the protocol.
As Bonner and Nieftagodien comment:

> Deponents were guided by an inventory of the points their state-
> ment was expected to cover: ... 'briefly describe what happened to
> you or the person you are telling us about, please tell us what
> happened? Who got hurt, killed or kidnapped? When did it happen?
> Who did it?'   *(2003: 177)*

There are only one and a half pages, or forty lines, provided for
the response to these questions, although additional pages were made
available. When the form asked questions pertaining to the political
context of the event being described, respondents are advised to focus
exclusively on the day of the occurrence (for instance, a political rally).
Again one sees here a powerful determination of the nature of the
stories which were ultimately collected. Thus the democratic basis of
the TRC was limited not only by the finite number of individuals who
could testify, but equally by a very restrictive sense of what would
constitute relevant information.

Another reason contributing to the raised public expectations of
South Africa's truth commission was its very name. With the exception of Chile, the truth commissions which preceded it did not have
reconciliation as part of their explicit remit. (A review of the names
of these commissions makes for an interesting read. Some names
reflected the specific focus on investigations into the disappeared,
while the report of Argentina's truth commission, *Nunca Mas*
('Never Again'), carries a particularly weighty moral overtone. Only
more recently, following the example of Chile and South Africa, have

truth commissions – Peru, Sierra Leone, East Timor, and Ghana – begun to incorporate the language of reconciliation not only into their titles, but into their missions.)

Priscilla Hayner (2001) argues that a strength of a truth commission is its capacity to advance national or political reconciliation by means such as clearing up high-profile cases and establishing a consensus on basic points of fact. This, however, is very different from reconciliation at an interpersonal level. Moreover, the assumed relationship between truth and reconciliation – at the level of the individual and the nation – is not supported by evidence. More truth does not necessarily lead to higher levels of reconciliation. Hayner cites a national poll conducted by Market Research Africa showing that 'two-thirds of the public believed that revelations resulting from the truth commission process had made South Africans angrier and led to a deterioration in relations between races' (2001: 156).

With that said, the TRC itself was partially responsible for the widespread expectation of personal reconciliation. For instance, one of the posters encouraging South Africans to participate in the TRC proceedings read: 'Let's speak out to each other. By telling the truth. By telling our stories of the past, so that we can walk the road to reconciliation' (cited in Hayner 2001: 156). Here, the implicit equation was clear: the more stories, the more truth, the more reconciliation. This was not, however, the experience of many who did agree to participate. As one witness asked a commissioner: 'Have you come here to hurt us? Just tell me, have you come here to open our scars?' She told the commissioner she had 'put grass over the past' – using a Xhosian expression. 'And now you want us to remember? Is this going to bring back my son?' (Gobodo-Madikizela 2003: 87–88).
Kaizer Nyatsumba (2000) writes that:

> The sad truth is that, for a host of reasons, South Africans are not any more reconciled now, especially across the racial divides of old, than they were before the inception of the Commission. We

> have had wonderful and very moving examples of reconciliation
> taking place between victim and perpetrator or a victim's family
> and a perpetrator after the truth had been told. However, such
> reconciliation as has taken place has not found resonance across
> the country. *(2000: 90–91)*

However, there are others who regard this evaluation of reconciliation
as being too much focused on the individual and giving insufficient
attention to the reconciliation of the nation as a whole. Sachs, for
instance, argues that:

> Reconciliation doesn't need each victim to forgive each perpetrator,
> and for the perpetrator to apologize, and for the parties to embrace.
> That is asking too much, and it is inappropriate ... Reconciliation
> means the nation, and the world, acknowledging that these terrible
> things happened. *(2000: 96–7)*

Sachs turns to the overall, lasting effects of the TRC to evaluate
whether or not it has furthered national reconciliation. From his
perspective as a magistrate, the TRC has wielded great influence in
determining what tales are tell-able, as well as that which cannot be
denied. 'The process has created such a powerful and intense moral
climate', he writes

> that it wipes out any possibility of denial. Even the most right-wing
> newspapers always start the editorials by saying that we have to
> acknowledge that terrible things were done in our name. Once that
> is done, it creates a climate which puts intense moral pressure on
> those who supported the system of apartheid to change, and to
> contribute towards change. *(2000: 96)*

The TRC can be judged to have facilitated the cause of national
reconciliation only at this macro level of analysis: it helped to create
a national narrative which, though contested by many, nonetheless
was able to produce a framework for the whole country to understand
and come to terms with the past.

THE 'TALKING CURE'?

There is an assumption that truth commissions perform a healing function for the nation (by documenting a traumatic history in order to move beyond that past) as well as for the individuals who participate in them. As Hayner states: 'It is often asserted that following a period of massive political violence and enforced silence, simply giving victims and witnesses a chance to tell their stories to an official commission ... can help them regain their dignity and begin to recover' (2001: 134). A key function of truth commissions, then, is to provide a forum for victims of human rights abuses to tell their story, and there is a strong belief that this telling is an important first step towards healing. This idea that talking about trauma helps people to overcome it is one of the cornerstones of modern psychology – and yet there are very important differences between a therapeutic setting and that of a truth commission. Perhaps the most critical difference is that of purpose: what motivates the speaker to recount their pain?

While clients usually enter therapy with the hope and expectation that some kind of personal healing will ensue, those who participate in truth commissions may do so for a wider range of reasons. As Hayner comments:

> It is not always clear what motivates victims and witnesses to come forward ... some deponents have expected that a commission would take legal action against known perpetrators, and others have hoped the commission would grant them compensation for their suffering. *(2001: 136)*

It appears that many people who chose to testify before the TRC did so less to be healed than to be heard. It is commonly said of truth commissions that one of the most important functions which they can perform is that of transforming knowledge into acknowledgement: '[acknowledgement] is what happens and can only happen to knowledge when it becomes officially sanctioned, when it is made part of the public cognitive scene' (Nagel cited in Weschler 1990: 4). A truth commission, as an officially recognised body of a post-traumatic state, is thus empowered with a legitimacy which is difficult to find elsewhere. Maier (2000) identifies two forms of acknowledgement: the first concerns one party appreciating the pain another has endured, while the other involves an identification of one version of the facts as authoritative. Both types of acknowledgement are possible with truth commissions, which function as a forum for a conversation between a state and its injured people. Through the thousands of testimonies which it collects, and ultimately weaves into a national narrative, it communicates to its wounded citizens a sense of belief in them and the tales that they tell. Although this may have a healing affect (just as the reverse – a denial of those stories – is psychologically detrimental) there is no evidence to suggest that this is a key motivating factor for most people who testify.

The narrative of the 'healing' benefits of giving testimony is considered facile, if not altogether misleading, by many who operate close to the process. Healing is not something which can happen in a moment. There is no guarantee of 'tell and be healed'. Rather, as South African activist priest Michael Lapsley explains, 'It is naïve to think it takes five minutes to heal. We'll spend the next hundred years trying to heal from our history' (quoted in Hayner 2001: 142).

Far from healing, many of those who did give testimony to the TRC experienced some kind of re-traumatisation. The Trauma Centre for Victims of Violence and Torture in South Africa estimates that '50 to 60 per cent of those who gave testimony to the commission suffered difficulties after testifying, or expressed regret for having taken part' (quoted in Hayner 2001: 144) though this figure was based on the number of victims they worked with, rather than a study specifically designed to examine this issue.

Fiona Ross, in her study on the gendered dimensions of bearing witness, writes of the proclivity to equate 'the speaking self with the healed self [which] was anticipated to be effected through the linking of "voice" and "dignity" ' (2003: 78). This tendency is reflected not only in much of the analysis of the TRC but indeed in the rhetoric of some of the commissioners as well, who often referred to the healing power of stories. This is typified in the following statement made by Desmond Tutu:

> Storytelling is central, not only to many religious practices in this country, but also to the African tradition of which we are a part. Ellen Kuzwayo is quoted as saying: 'Africa is a place of storytelling.' We need more stories, never mind how painful the exercise may be. Stories help us to understand, to forgive and to see things through someone else's eyes. *(Quoted in Ross 2003: 78)*

Who is the 'we' referred to here? 'We the nation' may well need more stories, and indeed this might be one of the most effective ways for fragmented portions of the population to access each other's frameworks of meaning. In this sense, personal storytelling can be reasonably regarded as one mechanism for advancing the cause of national reconciliation. But what of those who offer up their stories in this public forum? What effect does it have on them?

Accounts offered by individuals who have testified before the commission reveal the intensity of this experience. For some, their participation in this process has exacted a high psychological cost, resulting in an unanticipated further destabilisation of their already shaken identity. Yazir Henri writes of his experience of testifying before the TRC. He explains that

> prior to testifying before the TRC in 1996 I spent six years not talking to anyone about what had happened to me; I re-invented my life … My past was too dangerous to remember but I still felt it. For six years I lived in a silence that excised me from my own memory and history. My body eventually gave in to the weight of this silence, with which my psyche could no longer cope – almost as if it could not hold the heaviness that came with my mind's consistent failure at forgetting itself … the TRC offered me the possibility of breaking this silence. The history I reclaimed in the process was one of dignity for those of my generation who had been destroyed … It was also for myself, whose life had not only been destroyed but officially had disappeared

> without a trace. My life existed somewhere in the liminal space
> between that which is recorded officially and that which remains
> officially off the record. I cannot begin to explain the pain of living
> a life with no record, where one breathes but there is no
> existence.
> *(Henri 2003: 269)*

Henri's account of his psychological journey of reclaiming his life that had 'disappeared without a trace' is full of pain, and courage. But it is not a simple or happy tale. Although testifying before the TRC gave him 'the possibility of breaking this silence' it did not end his suffering, but rather added to it. 'It took me almost a complete year to recover psychologically from my testimony and the form it took publicly after having testified ... I went to the hearings with a broken body and a fractured mind. I left those confines with my body more broken and my mind more fractured' (Henri 2003: 264–265). Despite the devastating effects, both physical and psychological, that giving testimony had on Henri, he nonetheless

> drew immense strength from this process. The acknowledgement
> of my existence as a member of its [the ANC's] former military
> wing at the highest political level has been crucial to me establish-
> ing within myself the honour, dignity and self-respect for having
> committed my youth to the liberation struggle in South
> Africa.
> *(Henri 2003: 265–266)*

Clearly, establishing a public record of the facts is itself a critical step toward regaining personal dignity; it is a rewriting of the self into existence.

We can see in Henri's account that establishing a clear record of the facts, and thus vindicating himself from unsubstantiated rumours, was for him the benefit of giving testimony. He did not go there to be healed, and nor was he, but through this process he was able to begin filling in the silent spaces that had come to define him.

In therapy, traumatised individuals may take months or even years to bring themselves to speak of their experiences. Successful therapy is an unfolding over a period of time which is specified by the needs of the client. In this way, the persons who offer the account experiences themselves as being supported, not only at the moment of their telling, but before, and most critically, after doing so. This critical dimension of the therapeutic relationship, which is in fact what makes it work and why people who engage in it often do experience a long-term healing effect, is precisely what is missing from the context of the truth commission. Victims and witnesses who testified before the TRC typically spent one hour providing the details of the trauma they endured. 'The interview is focused on recording specific details of events witnessed or experienced, going to the heart of the deponent's most painful memories' (Hayner 2001: 139–140). The South African truth commission was somewhat unusual in that it did attempt to establish a referral service to follow up on persons who had given testimony, but this system 'never functioned well and was not widely used' (Hayner 2001: 140). Michael Lapsley describes the experience of many of the townspeople who gave testimony in the following way: 'The circus comes to town and the circus leaves – and then what?' (Hayner 2001: 142). Truth commissioner Pumla Gobodo-Madikizela echoes a similar concern: 'I felt like a messenger who travels around villages bringing bad news, breaking people's hearts, without staying to pick up the pieces' (2003: 88).

Another issue which clearly divides the therapeutic setting from that of the truth commission is the role of audience. When individuals tell their stories of pain and suffering, who do they construct as their listener(s)? What skills and training does that audience bring to this demanding task? Clearly one who serves as a truth commissioner, or even a statement-taker for the truth commission, will not have received the same kind of training as one who works in a therapeutic setting. Yet, they are expected to listen in a way which demands a great deal of practice. A number of the commissioners have written accounts of their experiences of listening to these tales of horror (e.g. Boraine 2000; Gobodo-Madikizela 2003; Tutu 1999), and all have commented upon the personal difficulty that this responsibility posed for them.

Desmond Tutu reflects that he

> thought of God's sorrow many times as we listened to harrowing
> tales of the kind of things we are capable of doing to one another.
> Awful things that seemed to beggar description and called into
> question our right to be considered fit to be regarded as human
> at all.   *(1999: 94)*

Tutu concludes his account with the observation that while he feels privileged to have engaged 'in the work of helping to heal our nation ... it has been a costly privilege for those of us in the commission ... we were effective only to the extent that we were, in Henri Nouwen's celebrated phrase, "wounded healers"' (1999: 233). The South African poet Ingrid de Kok, in her poem 'Bandaged', communicates the intensity of speaking and being a witness to severe trauma:

> Cut down as flowers,
> chopped up like wood
> burned in a blaze of fire.
>
> Bones unfleshed.
> Throat choked.
> Cheek charred
> in the cave of the mouth.
> Ear burst. Eye torn.
>
> Gravel. Grave in sand.
>
> O listen, let us not turn away
> from seeing and hearing
> the witness speak with bowed neck.   *(Cited in Ross 2003: 4)*

One of the most challenging aspects of listening is the ability to suspend the expected tale, and leave oneself open to hearing a new kind of story. The TRC, by its very design, had very clear cut criteria for the stories it sought to document. Central to this was the stark categorisation between victims and perpetrators of human rights abuses. This polarisation, however, comes with a cost. Njabulo Ndebele, Vice Chancellor of the University of the North in South Africa, comments that the TRC hearings, by their very design,

> may confirm the image of blacks as helpless victims, suffering complainants before whites who claim to understand their plight and declare themselves to be willing to help. In this way blacks will always be the numerical majority weighed down by the psychology of suffering minorities. They will be the eagle that grew among the chickens and is no longer able to fly. *(1998: 27)*

Many who came to give testimony did not see themselves as victims, and indeed had dedicated themselves to resisting this characterisation of themselves and those around them. As Yazir Henri writes: 'I have had to avert the downward spiral of victimhood and the entrapment of the TRC's victim box to find my own humanity' (Henri 2003: 270). In its hearings on Human Rights Violations, the TRC operated from an implicit framework which was intended to follow an ideal progression: a 'victim' appears before the commission, recounts their traumatic experience, and in so doing experiences some degree of personal healing, all the while contributing to the project of national reconciliation. Throughout this process, the commissioners strongly encourage those storylines which suggest the possibility of forgiveness, as these can later be used as exemplars for rebuilding bridges between fragmented parties. Stories which are elicited as a strategy to further a clearly specified agenda, such as that which formed the basis of the TRC, will most probably be subject to a very selective listening.

Yazir Henri recalls his experience of giving testimony before the TRC. Before Henri had finished, Archbishop Tutu said:

> he had listened to my story with reverence and that he understood what I had been through. My head fell against the witness table and

my knees would not carry me from his gaze. I felt the weight of his
words tearing my heart from my body and my mind shouted, 'How
can you say what you cannot know? ... But I am not finished! ...
There is more!'   *(Henri 2003: 270)*

The potential for healing is truncated when individuals are not given
the space to recount their experiences and emotions in the way which
they perceive them. Henri's question 'How can you say what you
cannot know?' is a question for all of us. How could Tutu have understood what Henri had been through? The cries 'But I am not finished!
There is more!' are cautionary words for all who strive for clear beginnings and endings. For even while Henri had told his tale, it was still
not finished.

Veena Das (1990) writes that 'Death may be considered at one
level as essentially marked by its non-narratability, by its rupture of
language' (1990: 346). Here she recalls the words of a group of survivors
of large-scale human tragedy in India, spoken to a professor of the
Indian Institute of Technology: 'It is our work to cry, and your work
to listen' (1990: 346). It was Henri's work to cry, and Tutu's work – and
our work – to listen. But the deep act of listening is the very challenge
which many involved in the documentation of personal narratives
struggle with, as it demands that we suspend, in our hearts and our
minds, the stories we expect to hear, and open ourselves to the
accounts as they are told to us.

Fiona Ross (2003) suggests that research and writing 'may offer
a form of witness ... [meaning] the general sense of recognising and
acknowledging suffering. Witnessing requires attentiveness' (2003: 3).
Citing the work of Felman and Laub with testimonies of Holocaust
survivors, she argues that witnessing 'is a social process that rests on
careful attention, "listening" '. Felman and Laub highlight the dialogic
nature of giving testimony: 'Testimonies are not monologues; they
cannot take place in solitude ... The absence of an empathic listener,
or more radically, the absence of an addressable other, an other who
can hear the anguish of one's memories and thus affirm and recognise

their realness, annihilates the story' (Laub 1992: 68–71). Returning to the painful encounter between Yazir Henri and Desmond Tutu, does Tutu's presence (and that of the other commissioners) make the articulation of Henri's story possible? However unfinished, it seemed that Henri's testimony was something which could only have been constructed in the presence of others. Henri was left speechless, a living embodiment of the non-narratability of trauma while, in his words, 'the Archbishop had completed my testimony for me' (2003: 270).

And how do we as researchers embark on that deep act of listening? Dominick LaCapra uses the term 'empathic unsettlement' to indicate 'a kind of virtual experience through which one puts oneself in another's position while recognising the difference of that position, hence not taking the other's place' (cited in Ross 2003: 3). Ross comments on the delicate balance which is indicated by this term: 'It is potentially dangerous: too close an identification may usurp the position of the other, too great a distance may represent others negatively' (2003: 4). This is the balance which we as researchers must strive to achieve; not only is it the most ethically defensible, but it is also the one most likely to assist us in our attempts to understand that which we cannot know.

Although many qualitative researchers have argued that their work 'gives a voice' to those who are marginalised, as discussed in chapter 2, in the examples cited here, we can see the reverse effect. Yazir Henri writes 'The dispossession of my voice through a continuous recycling of my by now unmoored testimony was compounded by the superimposition of other voices and narratives onto my own' (2003: 268–269). It seems that as researchers we must re-train ourselves; how can we improve our ability to really listen, to entertain the idea that there is, just possibly, a story that we haven't anticipated, maybe even one that contradicts our expectations? Our work demands that we develop greater sensitivity to the presence of our own voice. This requires a self-awareness, even humility at times, which we might not always have.

PERSONAL AND HISTORICAL NARRATIVES: THE MAKING
OF COLLECTIVE MEMORY

There has been much made of the fact that the TRC's focus on eliciting personal narratives was very compatible with the African cultural tradition of storytelling. Christopher Colvin's research with the Khulumani Western Cape Support Group, a victim support and advocacy group, however, complicates 'the "natural history" of storytelling that celebrates storytelling as idyllically "cultural" (evoking romantic images of the "traditional" black, rural experience)' (2002: 242), and argues instead for the analysis of a political economy of storytelling, which 'in a post-apartheid context is also about the creation and exchange of new kinds of valued objects (stories of victims and perpetrators ...) and about the creation of new kinds of subjects (healed victims, repentant perpetrators)' (2002: 242). Both the process and product of storytelling in South Africa has been altered by the imposition of the highly politicised context of the TRC. These observations notwithstanding, however, public performance of storytelling for the purposes of establishing and disseminating historical narratives is not new in South Africa in the post-apartheid era. Isabel Hofmeyr (1993), in *'We Spend our Years as a Tale that is Told': Oral Historical Narrative in a South African Chiefdom*, summarises the central role of historical narratives and their ability to both reflect the past while addressing current concerns:

> Not only do historical narratives refer to the past and mediate an understanding of the past through their form, the stories and their tellers also pass through time and are shaped by its often precipitously changing circumstances. Stories, then, comment on the passing of time and times past; they also enfold fragments of the past in themselves while they simultaneously transmute under the pressures of a changing social climate.   *(1993: xi)*

The emphasis here is on the spoken story as a vehicle for transmitting culture, through the identification of an historical plotline which is passed from generation to generation, sensitive to 'the pressures of a changing social climate'. The storytelling which occurred under the auspices of the TRC did have some resemblance, in both form and function, to the cultural storytelling of which Hofmeyr and others write. Overall, the TRC functioned well as a conduit for the making of collective memory, from its very inception. Although there was some public discourse about the healing nature of storytelling for individuals, in fact its real purpose for being was to assist the nation in moving beyond a traumatised past. Critical to this project was establishing a common collective identity, something which Jose Zalaquett, of Chile's Rettig Commission, says is written into being by truth commissions (cited in Wilson 1996: 14). However, as Mark Osiel comments,

> the fashioning of national identity through the cultivation of collective memory is almost inevitably conflictual. Historians remind us that when memory is invoked we should be asking ourselves: by whom ... against what. *(Osiel 1997: 255)*

Which stories are to be included in this new South African narrative? What is the relationship between the experiences of individuals and the fate of the nation?

We have already seen that only 0.05 per cent of South Africa's population actually gave statements to the TRC, and a far smaller percentage will have had their stories detailed in the Final Report. However, these relatively small numbers notwithstanding, as a means for constructing historical narratives of South Africa's apartheid past, it was very effective:

> the historical exercise was primarily to narrate a moral truth about wrongdoing, conflict and injustice, and it was one which could be represented effectively by a relatively small number of carefully selected individual cases that exemplified collective 'truths'. *(Posel 2002: 152)*

The process of national storytelling under the auspices of the TRC, then, functioned in ways not dissimilar to that described by Hofmeyr above: an historical narrative is woven through the practice of oral storytelling which is performed in a public forum. 'The symbolic impact of truth commissions', Richard Wilson argues,

> lies in how they codify the history of a period. Popular memory of an authoritarian past is often fluid, unfixed and fragmentary and it is impossible to investigate all the cases brought to a commission, so truth commissions fix upon particular cases and events in order to create 'the global truth' of an abusive period. *(1996: 17)*

What emerges, then, is the macro-question: what is the global truth or truths of South Africa's abusive past? The ways in which the TRC framed the boundaries of the stories which it collected, and thus the range of possible answers to this macro-question, can be understood only by placing the purpose of the commission into its appropriate historical context. The goal of the TRC, its very founding purpose, was to advance national reconciliation. As André Du Toit comments: 'If truth commissions address fundamental moral questions – of justice and truth, violence and violation, accountability and reparation – they do so ... as eminently political projects' (2000: 122).

The political project of the TRC was to help pave the way for the birth of the new South Africa. This mission, more than any other theme, is evidenced throughout the proceedings of the commission. First and foremost, the truth commission of South Africa was intended as a bridge from the past to the future, a key lynchpin in healing the wounds of a deeply divided nation. In the Foreword to the Final Report, Desmond Tutu appeals to fellow South Africans to use the report not to attack others, but rather as an instrument that can contribute to 'the process that will lead to national unity through truth and reconciliation' (Tutu 1998: 4). The importance to the nation of looking forward is echoed by Nelson Mandela, in the handover ceremony of the Truth and Reconciliation Report in October 1998, when he comments upon the country's 'hope and confidence in the future' and refers to the report as 'the property of our nation [which] should be a call to all of us to celebrate and to strengthen what we have done as a nation' (BBC Online network http://www.monitor.bbc.co.uk).

The transcripts of the proceedings of the TRC are peppered with the phrase 'the new South Africa'. The thousands of pages are awash with sentiments like the following:

> We hope that as we listen to those who are not statistics but human beings of flesh and blood, that you and I will be filled with a new commitment, a new resolve that our country will be a country where violations of this kind will not happen, that the context will be inhospitable for those who seek to treat others as if they were nothing.
>
> *(TRC 1998, 5: 411)*

Victims of horrendous crimes are thanked for having given their testimony, as their special contribution to building this new country, and the entire endeavour is seen as an important aspect of the overriding goal to achieve national unity and reconciliation. As Christopher Colvin writes: 'Part psychotherapy, part legal testimony and part historiography, "telling your story" has become a powerful, if ambivalent, way to contribute to a new history of the old South Africa' (2002: 234). While there are many in South Africa who support this nation-building function of the TRC, there are some who regard it as part of specifically ANC vision. As one spokesperson for the far right Freedom Front phrased it:

> The ANC wants to build one nation out of a large variety of people's [*sic*] and tribes ... We ... oppose the concept of one-nation; we don't believe in it, one nation does not exist in the multiracial country ... The TRC not only seeks to give the people a common memory; they want to rewrite history ... We will not accept their version of history.
>
> *(Quoted in Christie 2000: 109)*

The Freedom Front are not alone in their cynicism about nation-building, and indeed the project has been the target of some controversy within South Africa. As one observer describes it: 'what the ANC meant by national liberation as their goal, while appearing inclusive of all groups, is not shared by all groups' (Christie 2000: 113). While most countries have some degree of diversity within their populations, South Africa is perhaps unusual in that there are approximately 160 different ethnic groups (Christie 2000: 116); perhaps not surprisingly, then, 'there are multiple visions, perspectives and solutions to what constitutes South Africa and in turn these have consequences for what it means to be engaged in a nation-building project' (Christie 2000: 98). Effectively, the TRC was building a grand narrative of a country which most agree never existed. As Christie comments: 'South Africa has never really been a nation in the classical sense of what constitutes nationhood ... A South African nation has yet to be born' (2000: 106).[1]

Critical to that project, then, is building a national memory which can function as the basis for a collective identity: 'A common memory in theory is one of the first steps toward a more unified nation and nation-building' (Christie 2000: 117). But what does it mean to share a common memory? Does it mean that there is a consensus on what constitutes critical events in the nation's history? Or, further, does it mean that a people must share an interpretation of the causes and consequences of those events? If this were the meaning of collective memory, which lies at the heart of national identity, it is hard to imagine a context where this level of homogeneity would exist, not only in South Africa, but anywhere. Charles Maier, Director for the Center for European Studies at Harvard University, writes of the historian's challenge to create a contrapuntal narrative:

[1] Reprinted by permission of Sage Publications Ltd from Andrews, 'Grand national narratives and the project of truth commissions: a comparative analysis' in *Media, Culture & Society* 25(1) pp. 45–65, © Sage Publications 2003.

the historian must create a narrative that allows for contending voices, that reveals the aspirations of all actors, the hitherto repressed and the hitherto privileged. Perpetrators have a history as well as victims, but in what sense do they share a narrative? In fact, their narratives intertwine just as all adversarial histories must ... To resort to a musical analogy: written history must be contrapuntal, not harmonic. That is, it must allow the particular histories of national groups to be woven together linearly alongside each other so that the careful listener can follow them distinctly but simultaneously, hearing the whole together with the parts.   *(Maier 2000: 274–275)*

Returning to Mark Osiel's comment, cited earlier, members of a society which have suffered an administrative massacre may seek to establish a shared understanding of what went wrong. However, this may be an unrealisable goal. In the case of South Africa, there is not much evidence to suggest that there is a version of its national history which is shared across the population. But, through the TRC, there has been a forum for gathering individual narratives which are intended to represent certain collective truths, and in the telling and retelling of these accounts (on television, in newspapers, on the internet, in popular books and research publications) there is a dawning of a collective, albeit fragmented, national identity.

In this chapter, I have discussed a number of macro-narratives which were influential in directing stories which were told, and those which were absent, in the TRC's documentation of the official history of South Africa: the 'miracle' of the Commission itself; the talking-as-healing narrative; and the making of collective memory in the new South Africa. Within each of these larger themes there are many issues to consider, and I have only touched upon them here. What contributed to these tales being told in the way in which they were? What were the expectations of the tellers? Of the audience? What is my responsibility as a second-, or third-hand audience? What, ultimately, were these stories about? How do they function in the creation of a national historical narrative? My purpose in this chapter has been rather modest: to shift the lens away from the use of 'unmoored testimony' of individuals towards an exploration of the dominant macro-narratives which help to determine the contours of the say-able. In these collective political narratives we can observe the history of South Africa's troubled past in the making, which in turn will impact upon how South Africans approach the future.

7 Questions and endings

Not long ago, I was asked to present a paper to a group of doctoral students. I thought for a long time about what I wanted my message to be. Intuitively, I felt that I did not want to talk to them about my research as such, but rather about the process of my research and how I saw the work I had been engaged with since the time I, too, was a PhD student. I decided to talk to them about listening, about uncertainty, about the questions we ask and the answers we hear and those we do not hear. The title of my talk was 'As if I didn't already know'; for me, these words encapsulated the place that is so often abandoned by those of us in pursuit of our projects. At the end of this talk, one student raised his hand, and very thoughtfully asked me where all of this would lead to: 'Do you only ever arrive at more questions, or are there some answers in the work that you do?' I have thought about this question quite a bit in writing this book. There are some answers, small answers or answers of a provisional kind, but these invariably are incomplete, always begging for further exploration. I think that the portraits of lives and times contained in these chapters are accurate depictions of particular aspects of historical moments. But, ironically, my reaction to his question is not so much an answer, as a question: why is it, I wonder, that we are always looking for answers, and what would an answer into an investigation about how lives shape and are shaped by historical times actually look like? My work has always led me on to more and more questions. I have never had the sensation that I had 'arrived' at a definitive answer – nor even that there was such an answer to be arrived at – but this, I believe, is a consequence of the nature of the work itself, focused as it is on uncovering layers of meaning, rather than identifying solutions to any given problem.

Here in this final chapter I shall explore a small number of common themes which have appeared in the four case studies. I will begin with a re-evaluation of the story model as it applies to political narratives. How illuminating might it be to explore these four case studies as morality plays, marked by unambiguous plot and caricatures? What is obscured by such a stark construction?

Second, I shall consider the importance of boundaries to political narratives. If one regards these cases as stories, or even as parts of stories, or even collections of stories, then where do they begin and where do they end? Some of the cases discussed in these pages depend upon a construction of definitive beginnings and endings, memory fault-lines which definitely separate the past and present. Precise moments of beginning and ending lend clarity to storylines, but do they assist in our attempt to arrive at a deeper understanding of the historical moments in which we live?

Third, I shall explore the ways in which each of the four case studies deals implicitly with how individuals frame their identity in relation to the nation-state. How is this identity project negotiated and sustained in these different contexts? Based on these case studies, is there anything which one can say more generally about the relationship between nation-building and the process by which individuals and groups create and sustain meaning in their lives? How are individual and collective political narratives woven into the fabric of the nation?

The final set of issues I shall explore in this chapter is the relationship between age, aging, and political narratives. I shall address this from two different angles. First, I shall examine the potential of political narratives to function as a primary source of generational cohesion: what are the stories which we inherit from those who came before us, and how do we reformulate them in order to inhabit them, to make them ours? The age range both within and across the four case studies is considerable. How does movement through the life cycle – aging – affect the political stories of individuals and groups? Is there any meaningful sense in which we can say that social movements age, or is this a property only of individuals? In this discussion, I explore the impact of my own aging on the interpretive lenses which I have employed in my research, investigating not only my positioning with regard to my research, but my re-positioning (and re-positioning again) throughout the decades in which I have carried out these projects.

YEARNING FOR MORALITY PLAYS

There is something timeless and deeply compelling about morality plays, which helps to explain why they have endured as a genre for over six hundred years. We are never in any doubt as to who is good, and who is bad, and what constitutes the conflict between these opposing forces, and how it should be resolved. The general format of morality plays, or 'morall playes' as they were known in Middle English, is a battle over the soul of 'Humanum Genus', generically translated as Humankind. The central character functions as a battle-ground between vice and virtue, and other key characters have names like Beauty, Kindred, Worldly Goods and Good Deeds, Lust-liking, Flesh and Pleasure, and Covetous[ness]. While morality plays have their origins in religious teaching, their potential as a medium for communicating historical events was not lost on playwrights in the Middle Ages and later, including Shakespeare. It is an art form which has not lost its appeal. Indeed, in the case studies included in this book there is strong evidence to suggest that the morality play has re-emerged in the late twentieth and early twenty-first centuries, no longer in the theatre (though productions of Everyman, for instance, are still performed) but rather in the realm of politics.

The application of the morality play model is most apposite in the USA, particularly in the post-9/11 era. The language which has been employed throughout the Presidency of George W. Bush is clearly intended to divide the world into heroes and villains. Following the attacks of September 11, he stated unequivocally 'either you are for us, or you are against us'. Four months later he delivered a State of the Union Address in which he began by saying that 'the civilized world faces unprecedented dangers'. He reaffirms for the American people that 'our cause is just', but the enemy still lingers. Laying the groundwork for the military invasion that was already in preparation at that time, Bush describes 'states like Iraq' as constituting 'an axis of evil'. While September 11 heralded a new type of war, with a new type of enemy, Bush was supremely confident in his construction of the events at that time as being a conflict between the forces of good and evil. The enemy may hide in the caves of foreign lands, but ultimately they would be 'smoked out'; they would be defeated.

But as is evident in the case study I carried out in Colorado Springs in the early 1990s, the absolute language of morality plays was not heralded in with the events of 9/11. Rather, the groundwork had already been laid by Bush Senior for the programme his son would later pursue with such rigour. As reported in chapter 4, President Bush, Sr. was himself a man who clearly was driven by a vision of a world divided into good and evil. This stark categorisation applied, also, to the domestic domain in which Americans were either good (meaning supportive of governmental policies at home and abroad) or bad (those who openly protested against such policies). It is this very questioning of the morality play plotline which motivated anti-war activists in Colorado Springs to display a flag at their anti-war vigil.

It was noticeable to me that when participants in my research on lifetime socialist activists spoke of the political causes to which they had dedicated their lives, their description of the interwar years, the time during which most of them had become radicalised, was one in which the forces of good and evil were in direct combat. The impact of the Russian Revolution was felt around the world, and – before the abuses of communism became known – inspired many with a deep sense of hope for a world which had lost its bearings. Christopher's comment that 'everything seemed to add up and everything seemed to cut the same way' echoes the feelings of many of his generation who became politically engaged during the interwar period.

Nowhere was this conflict played out more dramatically than in the Spanish Civil War; on the one side, the fascist triumvirate of Franco, Mussolini, and Hitler; on the other side, the workers of the world, symbolised by the International Brigade. In July 1938, Dolores Ibarruri, 'La Pasionaria', told the defeated volunteer soldiers from around the globe: 'You can go proudly. You are history. You are the heroic example of democracy's solidarity and universality. We shall not forget you, and when the olive tree of peace puts forth its leaves again, mingles with the laurels of the Spanish Republic's victory – come back' (cited in Andrews 1991: 111). The greatness in these words was worthy of a Greek tragedy. It would be forty years before democracy returned to Spain. But when it did, the two respondents from my British study who had been engaged in the original conflict did indeed return to celebrate the eventual fall of fascism.

In July 1988, fifty years after the end of the Spanish Civil War, I helped to organise an event to bring together some of the people who had been involved in the anti-fascist struggle in that country. Frida, who by that time was not only a participant in my study but also a good friend and neighbour, had driven an ambulance in Spain during the Civil War. Together, we organised a party which would become the site of tremendous re-connecting between people who had not seen one another in half a century, but for whom this battle continued to hold a deep significance in their lives. Seven years after this gathering, Frida died; some of her ashes were sprinkled in Spain, so important had that moment in her life continued to be.

But the certainty which had characterised the interwar years for many of these respondents did not stay with them for the rest of their lives – although their general political commitment and engagement did. For instance, Christopher, who is quoted above praising the Communist Party and its role in his initial politicisation, describes how he later felt very limited by the inflexible dictates of the party; he describes his experience of party membership in the 1930s as 'walking on one leg without using the other'. While Christopher would continue to regard his life as one which was dedicated to combating the wrongs of the world as he perceived them, the structure of the morality play, as it were, would become more flexible, less severe, enabling it to better accommodate the complexity of long-term commitment.

When I arrived in East Germany in 1992, it was a place in which villains and heroes loomed large. In chapter 5, I describe the judgemental atmosphere in which so many were trying to carve new identities for the selves they had been under state socialism. Small acts of resistance were celebrated as defining moments, the expression of an authentic self which had, by force of circumstances, kept a low profile. East German sociologist Marianne Schulz's comment to me that all East Germans had come to identify themselves as both resistance fighters and victims, is very telling. In the years immediately following the opening of the Berlin Wall, the language of victimhood became the common medium for discussing the forty years of the GDR. Even the well-publicised confrontations at symbolically pregnant sites such as Checkpoint Charlie were known as the 'tater/opfer', or victim/victimiser talks. In my forty interviews with East Germans, I asked them what they felt about this stark characterisation: was it really as clear cut as such terms imply, or were there shades of grey, did people shift in their positioning depending on the particular issue, time, and space being discussed? I heard a wide range of responses to my question: clearly the applicability of the morality play analogy was imbued with powerful political implications.

Actress Ruth Reinecke summarises this when she explains to me that 'this relationship between victims and victimisers is used for ideological purposes ... this is too little to reduce the whole thing to victims and victimisers'. Werner Fischer, long-time dissident and the person responsible for the disbanding of the Stasi and a man whose own mother reported on him to the Stasi, has an ambivalent relationship to this binary construction. He tells me that he refuses to accept a polarisation of victim and victimiser: 'This divides the society of the former GDR into goodies and baddies, and that just won't work.' Fischer then proceeds to list a number of complicated scenarios in which the categories of victim and victimiser become rather confused. 'I am not able to draw a very clear line', he tells me.

Jens Reich, scientist and founding member of *Neus Forum*, also questions the widespread use of these absolute categories. He says that despite the current binary construction between victims and victim-isers, there was only a very small portion of society 'who are in a deep sense really victims. Crushed, destroyed, physically or psychologi-cally.' He describes these people: 'They haven't a voice and still have no sufficient voice ... but 99% of the population are neither real victims; they are perpetrators of misdeeds in the sense that they waited too long. I think everybody has this guilt, including myself'.

One of the participants in this research felt very differently, however. Wolfgang Ullmann, one of the key architects of the East German Enquete Kommission, the truth commission, is dismayed by the tendency to blur what is for him a very clear distinction between 'the spies ... and the people who were spied on. I'm very sharply against any attempt to mingle up these groups.' Ullmann's position contrasts with that of Reich; he does not feel that 'everybody has guilt' but rather, that it is important for the moral order of society that individuals are held accountable for their past actions and it is right that they are judged accordingly.

The viewpoint which Ullmann articulates here is also that enshrined in the structure of the East German *Enquete Kommission*, as discussed in chapter 5. The function of that commission was to ease the transition into reunification, and the means for doing this was to critically evaluate the forty years of the existence of the GDR. Ullmann insists on the morality play structure as its blunt clarity facilitates the political resolution at hand: those who have committed sins must be seen to have done so and punished accordingly.

The function of the East German truth commission was clearly different from that of South Africa's TRC. The former was set up as a means for concluding the history of the country. Through documen-tation (759 academic papers, in addition to148 research reports) the *Enquete Kommission* was established in order to produce 'a judgement of Communism and its methods' (Kamali 2001: 117). The TRC, in contrast, was established as a means for travelling from a traumatic past towards a future marked by reconciliation and unity. Here, the morality tale was of a very different nature – the villains were the rulers of the past, the heroes those of the present. Critically, the morality tale structure rests on clear temporal separation. Mark Osiel (1997) remarks on the propensity of truth commissions to function as morality plays, whereby forces of good and evil come into open conflict, and those who have inflicted harm must be held accountable for the suffering they have caused. The media fascination with the hearings of the TRC contributed to the impression of high drama between forces of good and evil.

Yet, Osiel also identifies the limitations in the morality play model: 'the weakness of the morality play as genre for social drama and mnemonic didactics is relatively clear. It lies in the polarity of the conclusion: the unequivocal triumph of the unflinchingly good over the unregenerately evil' (Osiel 1997: 286). Specifically, there is not room for the complexity of truth which can emerge in such settings. The observations of Janet Cherry, Researcher on the TRC, lend credence to this statement:

> All liberation struggles have their saints, their martyrs and their heroes – and the corresponding villains. It has been said that history is always written by the victors. Yet the writing of history such as it emerged in the TRC hearings can sometimes destroy this hagiography: the valiant youth who defied the police becomes merely a drunken thug; the brave freedom fighter is revealed as a traitor. The villain can even be revealed as a 'decent man' who had little room in which to move.   *(Cherry 2000: 140–141)*

Examples of this abound in the proceedings of the TRC. A contrast between the testimonies of Winnie Madikizela-Mandela and Eugene de Kock is instrumental here. For many years, Madikizela-Mandela had been held in great national and international esteem, not only as the spouse of her jailed husband, but as one who symbolised bravery in the face of great adversity, who had played a prominent role in the Women's League of the ANC, and in the anti-apartheid struggle more generally. When her name became associated with the kidnapping, torture, and murder of Stompie Seipei, and the severe mistreatment of several others, the news was received by the international community with shock. She as much as any other person living outside of prison had come to symbolise the anti-apartheid struggle. It was unthinkable that such a character could fall so far. It was in this context that her testimony was delivered. Desmond Tutu, acting in his capacity not only as the Chairman of the TRC, but also as a long-standing personal friend and neighbour of the Mandela family, begged Madikizela-Mandela to apologise and to ask for forgiveness. This, she could not bring herself to do, other than to acknowledge 'it is true. Things went horribly wrong' (Tutu 1999: 135). Her fate as the anti-heroine was forever sealed by this incomplete confession, which would be long remembered for what she did not, and perhaps could not bring herself to, say.

In contrast was the case of Eugene de Kock, known as 'Prime Evil', commander of the South African death squads, a man who was personally responsible for the murder of thousands of black and white anti-apartheid activists. Despite the horror of the deeds he had done, his willingness to cooperate with the proceedings of the TRC went a very long way towards rehabilitating him in the eyes of the world. He knew what he had done, he accepted responsibility for these horrendous deeds, and he was deeply, deeply sorry for his actions. Pumla Gobodo-Madikizela, a South African clinical psychologist who served on the Human Rights Violations Committee of the TRC, interviewed de Kock several times about his former activities. She describes her feelings towards him: 'I felt nothing but pity, the kind one feels when a friend is in pain over an event that has deeply troubled him. [I wanted] to offer him some respite from the tortured emotions that seemed to be coursing through his brain and body' (Gobodo-Madikizela 2003: 114–115). De Kock's testimony became one of the most memorable exchanges in the entire proceedings of the TRC. Pearl Faku, the widow of one of the men murdered in the 1989 Motherwell bombing – for which de Kock was responsible – became the embodiment of forgiveness with her response to de Kock's public and sincere apology: 'I hope that when he sees our tears, he knows that they are not only tears for our husbands, but tears for him as well ... I would like to hold him by the hand, and show him that there is a future, and that he can still change' (Godobo-Madikizela 2003: 94). The journey which de Kock appeared to have travelled, as well as the way in which his apology was received, created the possibility of his moral redemption. In these contrasting two stories, each very painful in its own way, one can see evidence for Cherry's argument. That the 'mother of the nation' would one day be virtually disowned by the ANC, while the confirmed mass murderer moved the family of his victims to tears, reveals the limitations of the simple morality tale as a way of making sense of the truth commission hearings.

Cherry (2000) argues that most people are unable or unwilling to grapple with the nuances of truth or truths as they may emerge in truth commission hearings. People become invested in the positions which they occupy and in their associated perspectives on the trauma that has defined their lives. Shifting this narrative to one which allows for a more diffuse sharing of responsibility or culpability is something which may threaten the well-established identity they have created for themselves. As Michael Ignatieff comments: 'People ... do not easily or readily surrender the premises upon which their lives are based' (cited in Adam and Adam 2000: 44).

Truth commissions such as that in South Africa may well confirm factual truths but they usually fail at establishing 'a common interpretive truth. This moral truth of why something happened and who is responsible for it, is always heavily contested. Divided memories prevail because truth is tied to institutional and collective identity' (Adam and Adam in James and Van De Vijver 2000: 44). The truth, then, of truth commissions lends itself more to factual than moral scrutiny, as the question of whose memory is to define the past continues to be a site of important historical contestation.

In this discussion, we have seen that each of the four case studies presented in this book contains at its centre the potential ingredients for a morality play. Yet, on closer scrutiny, this model is insufficiently complex to allow for the nuances of the tales which were presented. Each of these settings provides a backdrop for a conflict between opposing forces: Americans debating what it means to be a 'good American'; the birth of communism and the international fight against fascism in England in the interwar years; the spies and the spied upon in East Germany; and repentant murderers and hubristic anti-apartheid activists in South Africa. The metaphor of the morality play invites the listener into the story, but the moral boundaries of life as it is lived and recounted are rarely so definitively and immutably drawn.

BEGINNINGS AND ENDINGS

In order for a story to function properly, it needs to have a beginning and an ending. Even young children know this, and one can sense their frustration if either of these are incomplete or not identifiable. However, from the perspective of the story's author, which beginning to begin with, and which ending to end with, are dependent upon what tale one wishes to tell. This simple lesson lies at the heart of our exploration into political narratives.

Throughout the case studies presented in these pages there have been a number of examples where political events were presented as if they stood alone in time, with no antecedent and nothing to follow. While there is, of course, a temporal basis to all narratives – this is one of their defining features – real-life narratives are unique in that they have no beginning and no ending, other than that which is artificially attributed to them. Here, as in fictional stories (of which personal narratives may be regarded as a close cousin) the choice of beginning and ending is a strategic one.

Much recent political discourse has been dominated by the language of endings, and there is a plethora of books whose titles reflect this fascination, with Daniel Bell's *End of Ideology* having recently been reprinted forty years after its publication in 1960. Bell's original argument, constructed only fifteen years after the conclusion of the Second World War, was that, in the West at least, 'the old passions are spent … In the search for a "cause" there is a deep, desperate, almost pathetic anger' (1960: 374). Interestingly, in the new Introduction of this book, Bell (2000) has amended his argument to account for the revitalisation of passion in politics that accompanied the momentous changes of 1989. One of the key texts which seemed to epitomise the western construction of the events of 1989 was Francis Fukuyama's *The End of History* which first appeared, with the same title followed by a question mark, in *The National Interest* in the summer of 1989. Fukuyama summarised his argument in the following statement:

> What we are witnessing is not just the end of the Cold War, or a passing of a particular period of postwar history, but the end of history as such: that is, the end point of mankind's ideological evolution and the universalization of Western liberal democracy as the final form of human government.   *(Cited in Fukuyama 1992: xi)*

These two books, written by a liberal and a conservative, both reveal a proclivity, verging on desire, to interpret the times in which one is living as an endpoint, the historical moment when the purpose and direction of the journey is revealed. Fukuyama's article was immediately the focus of great debate, which engaged many of the most renowned intellectuals of the day. Among other things, Fukuyama's argument epitomised the modern tendency to regard the times in which we are living as definitive moments which are historically unprecedented. While the books of Bell and Fukuyama are probably the most relevant to the discussion here, it is not incidental that titles of books in other fields mirror this tendency: *The End of Science* (Horgan 1997); *The End of Nature* (McKibben 2003); *The End of Faith* (Harris 2004); *The End of Certainty* (Prigogine 1997); even *The End of Time* (Thompson 1996). Each of these books was published in the years immediately preceding or following the millennium, and we could argue that such datelines might encourage intellectual explorations of this kind. However, I do not believe that their appearance can be attributed to this alone. Rather, these titles reveal an inclination to cast ourselves as living characters in stories which are approaching, or have arrived at, their final conclusion.

Dienstag comments on the dangers of constructing political narratives as entities with clear endings. While, generally, narratives are sequentially constituted stories with beginnings, middles, and endings, applying a definitive ending to a political narrative effectively threatens the wider political sphere, which is defined by the ongoing mediation of competing claims:

> A narrative that ends is without a future. However satisfying the tying up of all plotlines and the fade-to-black may be at the close of a film, in politics, the idea of a final end point can be a dangerous one. To imagine a political narrative that ends may be to imagine a too-perfect satisfaction with the present and therefore an end to politics as the realm of conflict, change, and growth.   *(1997: 18–19)*

The lifeblood of politics demands constant movement; the narrative must always be unfolding, a perpetual process of renegotiation, reconstruction, and retelling.

Usually these demarcations of endings follow times in which something is perceived to have been in abundance, be it ideology, or science, or religion, as the titles listed above indicate. One wonders if the current explosion of interest in narrative will be followed by a similar proclamation, announcing the end of stories. In some situations, this seems appropriate, when the story form cannot hold all that there is to communicate. For instance, in Henry Greenspan's very thoughtful work about Holocaust survivors, one of his interviewees comments that survivors 'make stories' out of what is 'not a story'. Greenspan then comments 'But, along with their particular content, these stories are also stories about the death of stories, a death often re-created within them. And even that death is itself only the most provisional analogy for a vastly more encompassing end of creations'

(Greenspan 1998: 14–15). The phrase 'end of creations' carries within it not only the end of beginnings (creations) but, by implication, the end of endings as well.

The political stories we construct about the times in which we live are replete not only with endings, but also (sometimes) beginnings. In chapter 4, I examined the implications of beginning the story of 9/11, as it were, on September 11, 2001. President George W. Bush clearly adopted this strategy, which is one of the reasons he was able to provide the 'reasons' for the attacks on the symbols of American life in the way in which he did. Bush did not regard the attacks as being a response to any prior activities of the USA, 'blowback' in the terminology of Chalmers Johnson (2000). Rather, the attacks came, like the planes themselves, out of the clear blue sky. The official reaction of the USA to the attacks was constructed around a very restricted narrative, one which did not allow for an acknowledgement of historical forces which contributed to the events of that day.

In contrast, I have been suggesting that all beginnings and endings of the political narratives which we recount and which we live are ones we select, and the choices we make are significant and strategic. Had George W. Bush, for instance, identified the causes of 9/11 not in the jealous disposition of others, but in events which had occurred in his own lifetime, his response, and that of the country, would have had to be different. Had the narrative opened with the activists who camped out in the cold winter of 1992 protesting US involvement in the Gulf War, it would have been very difficult to construct the story-line of national greatness combined with innocence which became so prevalent in the post-9/11 era.

The study of lifetime socialist activists which I conducted in England was not one which was largely characterised by definitive beginnings and endings, other than those imposed by the life history method itself, which encourages a narration of the self over time, beginning with the early years and moving up into late adulthood. Still, it was interesting for me that at the time that the interviews took place, in the mid-1980s, many of the respondents regarded the most significant challenge to socialism as 1956, the year of Khrushchev's Twentieth Party Congress, in which he acknowledged the crimes of Stalinism, and also 1968, the year of the Prague Spring, for many the time when the hopes and dreams of a socialist future were extinguished by the weight of the misdeeds of the socialist past. It was not until the events of 1989 that I returned to my transcripts and realised the import of some of the narratives which I had heard, rich descriptions of those times in which their political commitment had been tested, but had endured.

The East German study presents a different picture altogether. Few dates in the twentieth century were as historically pregnant as that of 9 November 1989, the day the Berlin Wall was opened. For many around the world, this was regarded as a time of a great new beginning. Yet, for many with whom I spoke, this night marked the end of possibilities. Sebastian Pflugbeil, leading environmentalist and founding member of *Neus Forum*, a participant of Round Table talks – the multi-party political forum which followed the fall of the Wall, created to determine the future direction of the country – and member of the *Volkskammer*, says:

> I had the very same physical reaction [to hearing the news about the Wall being open] as I had at the moment when I heard that the Wall was being constructed in '61. I knew then immediately that … this would not end well … the entire citizens' movement collapsed from one day to the next.

Tarifa and Weinstein comment that 'the revolutions of 1989–1990 have introduced a "new calendar" in the lives of the central and eastern European nations' (1995/1996: 73). Indeed, in my research in East Germany, there was much evidence to suggest that the tumultuous events had resulted not only in political change, but in a more private restructuring of individual identity. As a society undergoes acute social and political upheaval, members of the community are presented with a challenge of rearranging their own identities, a challenge of recasting their pasts in a way that makes sense from the perspective of the present. The stories which people told to themselves and to others about the lives they had led under state socialism were no longer viable. Actions which had been carried out in secret were suddenly transformed into salient indicators of identity, while the minutiae of daily living, with all of the large and small compromises which that entailed, were no longer considered a part of oneself. Within five years of unification, the pendulum would swing again, this time towards the birth of a new, revitalisation of East German identity (see Andrews 2003b).

The 'new calendar' referred to above was assumed by many western onlookers to represent a new freedom. They believed that citizens who had lived for so many years under the microscope of an authoritarian state would embrace the opportunity to share thoughts and experiences which had been hitherto hidden from public view, epitomised by titles such as *À l'est la mémoire retrouvée* (Brossat *et al.* 1990), whose cover is decorated with a photograph of a smashed statue of Lenin. Many researchers who gravitated towards Central and Eastern Europe at this time saw endless potential for the excavation of the previously silenced or repressed. In fact, the reality proved to be rather different. One speechlessness – that imposed by state censorship – was replaced with another, as only those (very few) individuals who had been active in the underground oppositional movement felt at liberty to talk freely about their former lives. Others, those who had led ordinary, non-heroic, mostly compliant lives felt that self-disclosure left them vulnerable to the judgemental gaze of the rest of the world.

East German author Christa Wolf describes the effect of these pressures on the self-narrations which followed in the wake of the political upheavals:

> I have the impression that many former GDR citizens, experiencing a new alienation and finding that if they are candid with others their openness is used against them, are employing this experience as a

pretext to avoid any critical self-questioning and are even revising their life histories. I am sometimes amazed to hear normal, well-adjusted acquaintances of mine reveal what brave resistance fighters they have been all along. I know how hard it is to work yourself out of feelings of injury, hurt, helpless rage, depression, and paralyzing guilt and soberly to confront the events or phases in your life when you would prefer to have been braver, more intelligent, more honest.   *(1997: 301)*

Wolf summarises the chasm between the reality as she and others have experienced it, and the expectation by others of an enhanced new freedom. 'I and many people I know do not at all have the feeling that we have "thrown the old baggage overboard and are standing at a new beginning". Quite to the contrary, our baggage is getting heavier and we are prevented from making a new start' (Wolf 1997:119). The assumption of the liberating effects of the new beginning do not resonate with the accounts of many who have struggled with the challenging task of rewriting one's identity.

Although the changes of 1989 may not have delivered the hoped-for new beginning to citizens of East Germany, the *Enquete Kommission*, as argued earlier in this chapter, did in fact mark an official ending. The 15,000 pages of testimony and expertise (McAdams 2001: 90) which it collected simply functioned as a vehicle for concluding the affairs of a country which was no longer in existence, even at the time that the data were collected. The writing of the history of the forty years of East Germany, which includes the work of its truth commission, is a clear example of Dienstag's claim that a narrative with an ending has no future. And yet, as discussed earlier, the demise of the country has been accompanied by a resurgence of claiming East German identity. The political narrative of the state may have ended, but the same cannot be said for that of its people.

In South Africa, the memory fault-lines were made explicit under the remit of the TRC: the history relevant to human rights abuses which would be reviewed began with the Sharpeville Massacre of 1960, and concluded with the end of apartheid in 1994. While it is undeniable that during these thirty-four years the practices of apartheid were particularly aggressive and authoritarian, characterised by a systematic violation of human rights, in fact the horrors of Sharpeville were but an extension of an already existing policy of abuse. As Colin Bundy, Vice Chancellor of the University of the Witwatersrand, comments:

> to treat this period as 'the history with which we have to come to terms' effectively frees us of the obligation to arrive at a similar reckoning with any other history. The high noon of human rights violations was preceded by a long dawn – a pre-history of dispossession, denial and subordination ... What the TRC threatens to do is to uncouple these histories: to define three decades of the past in terms of perpetrators and victims and tightly defined categories of wrong, and to suggest that this is 'the beast of the past'.
>
> *(Bundy 2000: 17)*

Bundy's argument is very powerful. While it is necessary for truth commissions to identify specific time-frames as the focus for their investigations (the *Enquete Kommission* in fact covered the whole of the forty years of the existence of the GDR), this logistical strategy should not be misinterpreted as a statement of historical discontinuity. For apartheid to be uprooted, not just legally but from the moral fibre of the society, the conditions under which it was created and allowed to flourish must be identified and addressed. The 'beast of the past', as Bundy calls it, is not so readily contained.

I have argued in chapter 6 that one of the most crucial functions of South Africa's truth commission was to create a decisive rupture with its traumatic past, and thus to christen the birth of the new South Africa. Clearly the demarcation of a 'new beginning' was imperative for the nation. In this sense, the function of South Africa's truth commission was the reverse of that of East Germany. The *Enquete Kommission* had served to conclude the affairs of the former country, to try to make some sense of the forty years of state socialism; the

TRC, in contrast, was created with the clear intention of building national unity and reconciliation between divided people and communities, to breathe new vitality into the country in order that it might process, and ultimately move beyond, its blood-drenched history. Paul Connerton remarks upon the importance for new regimes to distance themselves from that which preceded them:

> A barrier is to be erected against future transgression. The present is to be separated from what preceded it by an act of unequivocal demarcation. The trial by fiat of a successor regime is like the construction of a Wall, unmistakable and permanent, between the new beginnings and the old tyranny. To pass judgment on the practices of the old regime is the constitutive act of the new order. *(1989: 7)*

Truth commissions are very effective at erecting such a barrier; South Africa's TRC, for all of its problems, is heralded across the globe as a symbol of the new 'rainbow nation', full of the hope that comes with new beginnings.

INDIVIDUAL IDENTITIES AND IMAGINED COMMUNITIES

Benedict Anderson, in his now classic *Imagined Communities: Reflections on the Origin and Spread of Nationalism* (1983), defines a nation as 'an imagined political community'. Yuval-Davis (2006) provides an important critique of this overly abstract national imagination, arguing instead for recognition of 'active and situated imagination' (2006: 203):

> The different situated imaginations that construct ... national imagined communities with different boundaries depend on people's social locations, people's experiences and definitions of self, but probably even more important on their values. [This involves] ... deciding whether [others] stand inside or outside the imaginary boundary line of the nation and/or other communities of belonging, whether they are 'us' or 'them'. *(2006: 203)*

These questions are central to each of the case studies presented in this book, as they explore how national identity is negotiated by individuals living through times of heightened political change. What does it mean to be an American, in a world dominated by one superpower? What does it mean to be English in the post-colonial world? What does it mean to be East German, when there is no longer an East Germany? Or South African, as this country tries to recreate itself as a nation, a unity which was never experienced by its disparate groups of people? How do the people whose voices we have heard throughout this book position themselves with regard to their country?

Here it is important to distinguish between the sense of a formal national identity, as it is promulgated by the state and enshrined in public institutions, and that which individuals experience more privately. The process by which a formal national identity becomes internalised – that is to say, 'owned' by an individual in such a way that it becomes part of their self-definition – is complex. The collective identity of a nation-state can be accessed through the stories it tells about its own history, symbolised for instance in its national monuments which indicate those people and events which are to be remembered and commemorated. What do these stories reflect about the nation? What and who are absent from these stories? Finally, how do individuals make sense of these stories in relation to their own lives, and to their own sense of self? Herbert Kelman describes national identity as something which

> typically contains within it beliefs and values pertaining to the meaning of human existence, the nature of social institutions, the conduct of human relationships, and the definition of the ideal personality. These are rooted in the group's historical experiences, and are reflected and elaborated in its documents, traditions, and institutional form.
> *(1997: 172)*

National identity, in its formal sense, is present from birth; we are, from the moment we enter this world, a member of a particular nation, and we ingest the norms of our community with our mothers' milk. It is simply part of human life. However, as we develop cognitively and emotionally, we also develop the capacity to evaluate the communities into which we have been born. Here begins the journey by which we acquire, internally, our sense of who we are in relation to the country of our birth. The process of early childhood socialisation lays the groundwork for sympathetic reception to national myths, but as we mature we must find a role for ourselves in the meaning of those stories.

Kelman (1997) argues that that the incorporation of the national identity into a personal sense of self involves a combination of 'knowledge, affect, and action' (1975: 173). 'If national identity is to become an integral part of an authentic personal identity', he writes,

> Individuals must acquire some substantive knowledge of the historical and cultural context of its beliefs and values; they must see these beliefs and values as personally meaningful to them; and they must somehow translate them into concrete practice in their daily lives. *(1997: 173)*

In addition, Kelman argues, incorporation of national identity into an integral sense of self requires a certain level of personal orientation towards the nation itself: How important is it for the individual to be a member of this particular nation? How strong is their sense of belonging? As Yuval-Davis comments 'Belonging tends to be naturalized, and becomes articulated and politicized only when it is threatened in some way. The politics of belonging comprises specific political projects' (2006: 196), a claim which has been illustrated throughout these pages.

The research projects which I carried out in the USA and East Germany grapple most directly with the questions of national identity raised here. In both cases, participants in my research are motivated in their actions by a sense of critical loyalty, which Staub (1997) describes as

> commitment to the group's ultimate welfare, and/or to universal human ideals and values, rather than to a policy or course of action

> adopted by the group at any particular time. It also means the will-
> ingness and capacity to deviate from – not support but resist and
> attempt to change – the current direction of one's group. *(1997: 222)*

This concept of critical loyalty allows for the possibility that individuals may perceive the basic values of the group (in this case, the
nation) as 'stand[ing] in conflict with current practice' (1997: 222).
Staub, like Michael Walzer (1987), argues that critical loyalty and
critical consciousness do not jeopardise group membership, but rather
lend it an increased legitimacy.

In the USA, anti-war activists flew an American flag at the site of
their vigil precisely because they regarded expression of dissent as not
only a right, but as a duty in a democratic society. As Bruce says: 'If I
didn't care … why would I even bother?' Bruce regards his activism as
a sign of his commitment to a larger good. One of the key national
narratives of the USA is that it is a country which gave birth to itself
when its civil liberties were jeopardised – a narrative epitomised in the
famous words of Patrick Henry: 'Give me liberty, or give me death.'
Citizens of the USA who openly contest the policies of their government, thereby exercising their constitutional right to the freedom of
speech, often believe they are motivated in their actions by a love for
their country.

This position is for me, personally, one with which I have much
sympathy, as I have already discussed in these pages. The construction
of 'good' and 'bad' Americans, epitomised not only in the McCarthy
era fifty years ago, but so dominant in our own times, is one which
effectively silences potentially critical voices of the population, as
individuals may become understandably concerned about the effect
that their public expression of criticism may have on their personal
and professional lives.

The concept of critical loyalty also encapsulates the feelings of
many East Germans with whom I spoke. One of the questions which
I asked each of the participants in my research concerned the terminology they would use to describe themselves politically. While many
researchers writing about political activists in East Germany refer to

them as 'the opposition' in fact this is a term which was used only very guardedly by those with whom I spoke. Political activists in East Germany were unusual among Soviet Bloc dissidents, in that they perceived themselves as fighting for better socialism for many years after the Prague Spring, a date which elsewhere is associated with the demise of socialist idealism. In East Germany, however, this was not true. Standing at the podium at the famous demonstration of half a million people in Alexanderplatz, East German author and internal critic Christoph Hein asked the crowds to 'imagine a socialism where nobody ran away'.

These activists in 1989 were following in the footsteps of the previous generation of critics, epitomised by Robert Havemann, a man who had spent time in a Nazi concentration camp with Honecker but who later became one of the latter's most pronounced critics. Havemann once described himself 'not as one disappointed in the socialist idea but as its confirmed partisan' (Allen 1991: 62). He, and others like him, saw themselves as patriots, and wanted to defend their country against those who were running it. Those who chose to stay and fight for a better socialism in East Germany were not taking an option exercised by many of their compatriots, namely to leave. In 1989, 343,854 emigrants left for the West (Naimark 1992: 86). Three days before the opening of the Berlin Wall, Bärbel Bohley described those who had stayed behind: 'The consensus is: we want to stay here, we want reforms here, we don't want to introduce capitalism' (*East European Reporter*, Winter 1989/90: 17). Werner Fischer summarises his feelings towards the state:

> my roots were here [in the GDR], … I had become firmly rooted to this soil, where was the friction that sparked controversy. I did not want to see the GDR disappear. This is how many opposition members express it today: 'better to have a stormy relationship than none at all'.

In chapter 5, I described the intensity with which some people spoke about their East German identity. Here, I think it is important to emphasise that this sense of belonging was quite distinct from the official East German identity propagated by the state. Indeed, the project of national-identity-building was high on the agenda of the socialist state, and there were a wide variety of programmes – for instance, the Free German Youth (FDJ) and the Young Pioneers – in which individuals were virtually required to participate, whose explicit purpose was to instil and promote a very particular concept of the duties of citizenship among its populace. Perhaps because of this, rather than despite it, many East Germans appeared to have 'a fundamental ambivalence towards the manifest successes and failures of the East German state' (Jarausch *et al.* 1997: 41).

This, however, was distinct from the sense of an internalised national identity which was apparent in many of my interviews. Interestingly, an internalised East German identity has been allowed to flourish once it was cut adrift from the state's imposition of practices intended to enhance national identity; thus East German identity has experienced a revitalisation in the post-unification era (Andrews 2003b; Yoder 1999). One of Yoder's (1999) research participants describes what she means by 'East German identity': it means simply having had 'a common history, experiences, life relationships, upbringing, schooling, work world ... and these have formed people in a special way' (1999: 135); for another, it indicates '[e]xperience under the Wall and a particular socialisation pattern' (1999: 136). Yoder states that 'the most common identification may be summed up as "East Germans in a united Germany"' – an identity which some interviewees referred to as 'the eastern biography' (Yoder 1999: 136). All with whom I spoke mentioned the impact of the citizens' movement of 1989 on individuals' experience of their national identity. Michael Passauer, East German pastor, describes this to me:

> In Autumn '89 ... the GDR citizen for the first time identified himself very closely ('skinclose') with the GDR ... 'We are the people'. This we had for about half a year, and this we, I

> experienced ... we had this strong self-confidence, we were
> able to break down totalitarian systems.

As Passauer speaks, one can feel his passion for, and his connection with the citizens' movement. Here, his use of pronouns is revealing. He begins with the abstract 'GDR citizen' and from there moves to 'we', then 'I', and then back to 'we'. This shift in language can be read as an indicator of the strength of his own very personal engagement with the events he describes, both as an individual and as one who is consciously part of a larger collective.

One of the questions I asked in my interviews was: 'When you are asked where are you from, what do you say?' Most interview participants paused over their response, but eventually gave some form of the answer 'the GDR' – in the present tense, with comments such as 'throughout my life I will remain a citizen of the GDR'. The personal manifestation of East German national identity did not, then, disappear along with the state. Rather, the experiences of having lived in the GDR, this shared history with others, has been incorporated into the self as an enduring source of identity. Here the attachment is literally to an 'imagined community', as the country continues to exist only in history books and the memories of individuals.

The importance of national identity did not emerge as a very strong theme in the study on lifetime socialist activists. One reason for this might be that this was not an area which I had specifically targeted for exploration, and it is possible that I was not attuned to messages which would have given me insight into this aspect of my respondents' self-perceptions. One exception to this, however, was Jack, who began his first interview with the proud claim that he was born 'on our national day, St George's Day, and the anniversary of the birth of Shakespeare', 23 April 1907. He saw his life's work as a dedication to the interests of the working people of his country, and as such it was only fitting that he, along with the Bard, should be born 'on our national day'. Many times in our conversations together he described himself as 'a patriot for my class'.

In the intervening twenty years since conducting that research, the question of what constitutes English and British identity has attained a new prominence. Tests have been devised which persons applying for British citizenship will have to pass, posing questions on topics ranging from the price of a television licence to the terms given to particular regional accents. Perhaps had my interviews with the lifetime socialist activists been carried out now, rather than two decades ago, respondents would have spoken more about what being British meant to them. English identity, too, has had a new lease of life. Although the flag of St George, the patron saint of England, was in little evidence before the new millennium, that is no longer true. In June 2006, the month of the World Cup, it was estimated that that the imagery of the flag of St George brought in close to $2 billion of retail sales, plastered on everything from underwear to portable refrigerators (*The Washington Post*, June 20, 2006).

Discussions about the meaning of 'Englishness' have entered into common political discourse, with some distancing themselves from this terminology (preferring to locate themselves as Europeans) while others place it at the heart of their political party platform. The 2006 electoral success of the British National Party (BNP) can be seen as an example of the latter. One of the key effects of the attacks in London in the summer of 2005 has been a national re-examination of the meaning of 'Britishness'. As devastating as the events themselves were, the real national shock came days later, when it became clear that three of the four men who had been responsible for the bombs had been born and raised in Britain. Norman Tebbit, renowned cabinet minister of Margaret Thatcher, claimed that these events were a vindication of his 'cricket test' comment made fifteen years earlier: 'A large proportion of Britain's Asian population fail to pass the cricket test. Which side do they cheer for? … Are you still harking back to where you came from or where you are?' Although his comments had long been widely dismissed as racist, following the attacks he commented: 'Had my comments been acted on those attacks would have been less likely … What I was saying about the so-called "cricket test"

QUESTIONS AND ENDINGS 203

is that it was a test of whether a community has integrated' (Tebbit 2005). Multiculturalism, he argued, was undermining British society; the attacks were proof that 'a multicultural society is an impossibility' (Tebbit 2005).

Several months later the Chancellor of the Exchequer, Gordon Brown, suggested the establishment of a 'Patriotism Day', an equivalent to the Fourth of July in the USA. (Some might argue that this is a belated replacement for Empire Day, which was celebrated annually from 1901 to 1958, on 24 May, Queen Victoria's birthday.) British citizens are being forced to re-examine the meaning of their national identity in the context of a multicultural Britain, and it is most probable that this topic would have been a part of the conversations with the group of socialist activists had they been conducted in the current political context.

The project of national identity-building in the new South Africa was the context which motivated many to offer their testimony to the TRC. As Osiel (1997) comments:

> When a society suffers trauma on a [large] scale, its members will often seek to reconstruct its institutions on the basis of a shared understanding of what went wrong. To that end, they conduct surveys, write monographs, compose memoirs, and draft legislation. But mostly, they tell stories. The 'telling and retelling' of a people's central stories constitute its collective identity. *(1997: 76)*

As discussed in chapter 6, many people felt it was their civic duty to relate the painful details of their personal suffering and loss, as a critical component of coming to terms with the past and, in so doing, creating possibilities for a different kind of future. The experience of testifying was, for many, so painful that their willingness to expose themselves, to relive their trauma, can be regarded as a personal sacrifice which they made as an offering to the birth of the nation, as they were told time and again that through the national endeavour of sharing of stories they would travel, as a wounded but determined people, the long road to reconciliation. And the 22,000 South Africans who did testify in front of the TRC could see their accounts as pieces to be woven into a national narrative. The new collective identity which they helped to create was one which was built upon a fundamental premise of discontinuity with a past which is 'not a past of pride, but of abuse' (Wilson 1996: 18).

Customarily, national identities function as way of distinguishing one nation from all others. (The psychological construction of 'us and them' is, in fact, central to all identity formation; the term 'self' or 'selves' becomes meaningless in the absence of an 'other' or 'others'.) However, unusually, 'The most significant site of otherness for the new South Africa has not been other nations, it has been itself' (Wilson 1996: 18). And one of the most effective means of creating that critical break with the past is through the mechanism of truth commissions. As Wilson comments, most people within the ANC, the leading political party, felt that there was a direct correlation between truth telling and nation-building: 'Let's have the truth and use the truth to build a nation' (1996: 14). The fact that reconciliation has proven to be a far more elusive project than many had thought does not detract from the general argument that the desire to be part of the project of nation-building was, for many, a vital motivation behind their willingness to publicly recount the trauma which they had endured.

POLITICAL NARRATIVES OVER TIME

The stories which have filled these pages are clearly snapshots of particular historical moments, as recounted to me by people who lived through these times. Together, the four case studies cover some of the most critical political events of our times, including the attacks of 9/11, the collapse of state socialism in Eastern and Central Europe, and the rebuilding of South Africa in the post-apartheid era. The pictures presented here are both larger and smaller than the individuals who contributed to my research projects. They are smaller, because an interview is always and only a situated event.

No longitudinal study can overcome the fact that, inevitably, it will always be limited in time, regardless of how extensive the period covered is. One who has been interviewed can always respond to the researcher that their project only portrays their feelings, insights, understandings, and misgivings of a particular day, or moment in their lives. (As researchers we must accept that sometimes our work does not even accomplish this.) In this sense, the stories give us only partial insight into the lives of those with whom we have spoken.

At the same time, however, the stories collected here function as windows onto political movements and times which are not reducible to individual human beings. They derive their very meaning from being part of a larger whole, and without this dual perspective it is difficult, if not impossible, to access the meaning of what is being said. Although the focus in my presentation of the four case studies has been on individual accounts of living through times of political turmoil and change, throughout my discussion I have emphasised the social character of these selves. As Tim Keegan comments: 'in the narratives of ordinary people's lives, we begin to see some of the major forces of history at work, large social forces that are arguably the real key to understanding the past' (1988: 168). We can make sense of their words only if we consider the conditions of their lives, who they are, when and where they are living, and what constitute the primary historical events – and the debates over the meaning of such events – of their times. As many have argued, we are never just individuals, and the research presented here offers evidence of the futility of compartmentalising discussions about individuals and societies. We cannot meaningfully explore one without the other. But just as individuals develop in the course of their lives, so do the societies which they inhabit. As social communities, we become occupied with different ideas, and reconstruct our collective identity in alignment with our changing preoccupations.

Invariably, we are born into particular communities which are dominated by certain political narratives. In a sense, they are our inheritance. As we grow in our social consciousness we then learn to inhabit these narratives, to make them our own. Our political identity is expressed in our response to the political events of our times. According to Karl Mannheim (1952), times of accelerated social and political upheaval tend to produce a generational consciousness: that is, an awareness of oneself as being part of a larger collective of people living through – being shaped by and helping to shape – larger historical events and movements. This consciousness in turn increases the likelihood of engaging in political action, which has the knock-on effect of contributing to social change. Barbara Myerhoff describes this symbiotic dynamic in the following way:

> Sometimes conditions conspire to make a generational cohort acutely self-conscious and then they become active participants in their own history and provide their own sharp, insistent definitions of themselves and explanations for their destiny, past and future.   *(1982: 100)*

This book is about people who have become 'active participants in their own history', people who have consciously engaged with the key political movements of their day and who have tried to help shape the future of the societies in which they live. But their starting point is always with the political narratives they have inherited, those stories which underpin the identity of their communities.

We can see concrete examples of this in each of the four case studies. In the USA, anti-war activists framed their protest around the discourse of 'support for the troops'. The legacy of Vietnam played a key role in the way in which arguments were constructed, both for and against military engagement in the Gulf. Protestors who lived at the vigil offered an active resistance to the portrayal of themselves as disloyal citizens. Recasting political protest and dissent as evidence of civic engagement, these activists offered a reformulation of the narrative of responsible citizenship.

The British lifetime socialist activists demonstrated throughout their long lives a very acute appreciation of the political times in which they lived. If one of the key dominant political narratives of the twentieth century revolves around the cult of individualism, then through their collective example they offer an antidote to this. While pursuing different political projects, each of them resisted the urge to become increasingly oriented towards the needs of the individual self. Indeed, as they aged, they became even more outward-looking. Through their lives' work, they challenged the dominant political narrative of rugged individualism.

In East Germany, the women and men who spearheaded the political changes which eventually led to the downfall of state socialism were themselves of a particular political generation. While the bulk of people who left the GDR in the months leading up to the opening of the Wall in 1989 were young, those who stayed behind to 'fight for a better socialism' were the daughters and sons of the founding generation of East Germany. Elsewhere I have referred to this group as 'GDR babies', born at approximately the same time as the country was formed. They occupied a pivotal position in the history of their country, between their parents who established the country, and their children, who fled it. One interviewee, himself a 'GDR baby' who had lost much of the previous generation of his family to the Holocaust, describes his generation as having had 'too much respect for anti-fascists'. His argument was this: had he and others of his generation not been so acutely aware of the circumstances of their parents' lives prior to the founding of the country, they might have launched a more concerted and effective challenge to the mismanagement and corruption which came to define their society. Honecker's status as one who had defied the Nazis and had served time inside a prisoner camp made him, in the eyes of many, immune to criticisms of being a dictator. Eventually, however, it was this generation of 'GDR babies' who reclaimed the right to determine the meaning of citizenship in East Germany, with the national identity re-appropriation epitomised by the flagship phrase 'we are the people'.

Finally, in South Africa, those women and men who chose to participate in the proceedings of the TRC were, among other things, assisting in the rewriting of the national narrative. The effect of confronting and challenging those who had been engaged in systematic human rights abuses, and insisting that they be answerable for their actions, was to shift the framework of national identity. The narrative of the rebirth of South Africa is saturated with generational consciousness. In the speech which Nelson Mandela made on the day he was released from twenty-seven years of prison, 11 February 1990, he pays tribute to 'the endless heroism of youth, you, the young lions. You, the young lions, have energised our entire struggle.' In the fifteen years since his release, he has continued to prioritise intergenerational dialogue, recognising that the nation's future success demands that the frustrations of the youth be channelled into meaningful political action. Mandela's political rhetoric is built upon a deep historical consciousness, one which identifies the strength of the movement not only from its broad current appeal but also from its historical underpinnings. Here one can see that the political narrative of the rebirth of the nation is thus infused with another narrative, that of intergenerational solidarity.

Mandela's explicit anchoring of the anti-apartheid movement in an historical context invites a question regarding the aging of social movements. Customarily, aging is understood to be a property of individuals, and sometimes of cultures. As a society, we are oriented towards the precise anniversary of birth dates of individuals, and chronological age is imbued with a broad range of meanings. Indeed, chronological age is one of the most dominant paradigms we use to distinguish one group of individuals from another. Sometimes, though less often, societies are discussed in terms of how long they have existed. Here again, longevity is understood to carry a certain symbolic meaning. Interestingly, however, social and political movements tend not to be analysed in this way, despite the fact that much of their underlying strength is built upon their ability to pass from one generation to the next. As mentioned earlier, individuals inherit the larger political narratives of their communities, which they then reshape and reform to fit the circumstances of the day.

This transformation of political narratives over time, characterised by a blend of continuity and change, is one of the defining features of an enduring social movement.

In *The Sociological Imagination*, C. Wright Mills implores his reader to:

> continually work out and revise your views of the problems of history, the problems of biography, and the problems of social structure in which biography and history intersect. Keep your eyes open to the varieties of individuality, and to the modes of epochal change.
> *(Mills 1959: 225)*

This has been my challenge in the preceding pages; that the stories presented here might help us to better understand the times in which we live, and at the same time that we may gain a deeper appreciation of individuals' lives by exploring the broader social and political frameworks which lend them meaning. For it is, ultimately, the dynamic tension between biography and history which stimulates the heartbeat of political narratives.

Bibliography

Adam, H. and K. Adam (2000). 'The Politics of Memory in Divided Societies', in W. James and L. Van De Vijver, eds., *After the TRC: Reflections on Truth and Reconciliation in South Africa*. Cape Town: David Philip Publishers

Ali, T. (2002). 'A Political Solution is Required: September 17, 2001', in K. Heuvel, ed., *A Just Response: The Nation on Terrorism, Democracy and September 11, 2001*. New York: Thunder's Mouth Press

Allen, B. (1991). *Germany East: Dissent and Opposition*, rev. edn. New York: Black Rose Books

Anderson, B. (1983). *Imagined Communities: Reflections on the Origin and Spread of Nationalism*. London: Verso

Andrews, M. (1991). *Lifetimes of Commitment: Aging, Politics, Psychology*. Cambridge: Cambridge University Press

(1995). 'Against Good Advice: Reflections on Conducting Research in a Country Where You Don't Speak the Language', *Oral History Review* 20/1: 75–86

(1998). 'One Hundred Miles of Lives: The Stasi Files as a People's History of East Germany', *Oral History* 26/1: 24–31

(1999). 'Truth-telling, Justice, and Forgiveness: A Study of East Germany's "Truth Commission"', *International Journal of Politics, Culture and Society* 13/1: 103–120

(2000). 'Forgiveness in Context', *Journal of Moral Education* 29/1: 75–86

(2002). 'Feminist Research with Non-feminist and Anti-feminist Women: Meeting the Challenge', *Feminism and Psychology* 12/1: 55–78

(2003a). 'Generational Consciousness, Dialogue, and Political Engagement', in June Edmunds and Bryan Turner, eds., *Generational Consciousness, Narrative and Politics*. Boulder, CO: Rowman & Littlefield

(2003b). 'Continuity and Discontinuity of East German Identity Following the Fall of the Berlin Wall: A Case Study', in Paul Gready, ed., *Cultures of Political Transition: Memory, Identity and Voice*. London: Pluto Press

(2004). 'Memories of Mother: Counter-narratives of Early Maternal Influence', in M. Bamberg and M. Andrews, eds., *Considering Counter-narratives: Narration and Resistance*. Amsterdam: John Benjamins (forthcoming). 'Never the Last Word', in M. Andrews, C. Squire, and M. Tamboukou, eds., *Doing Narrative Research in the Social Sciences*. London: Sage

Andrews, M., S.D. Sclater, M. Rustin, C. Squire, and A. Treacher (2000). 'Introduction', in M. Andrews, S.D. Sclater, C. Squire, and A. Treacher, eds., *Lines of Narrative: Psychosocial Perspectives*. London: Routledge

Apfelbaum, E. (2001). 'The Dread: An Essay on Communication across Cultural Boundaries', *International Journal of Critical Psychology* 4: 19–35

(2002). 'Restoring Lives Shattered by Collective Violence: The Role of Official Public Narratives in the Process of Memorialising', Proceedings of the Conference on Narrative, Trauma and Memory: Working through the SA Armed Conflicts of the Twentieth Century. University of Cape Town, South Africa

Arendt, H. (1958). *The Human Condition*. Chicago: University of Chicago Press

Bauman, Z. (1992). *Intimations of Postmodernity*. London: Routledge

Bell, D. (1960). *The End of Ideology: On the Exhaustion of Political Ideas in the Fifties*. Glencoe, IL: Free Press

(2000). *The End of Ideology: On the Exhaustion of Political Ideas in the Fifties: With 'The Resumption of History in the New Century'*. Cambridge, MA: Harvard University Press

Berger, S. (2003). 'Former GDR Historians in the Reunified Germany: An Alternative Historical Culture and its Attempts to Come to Terms with the GDR Past', *Journal of Contemporary History* 38/1: 63–83

Bhabha, H.K., ed., (1990). *Nation and Narration*. London: Routledge

Bhavnani, K.K. (1990). 'What's Power Got to do with it?: Empowerment and Social Research', in I. Parker and J. Shotter, eds., *Deconstructing Social Psychology*. London: Routledge

Bodnar, J. (1996). *Bonds of Affection: Americans Define their Patriotism*. Princeton, NJ: Princeton University Press

Bonner, Philip and Noor Nieftagodien (2003). 'The Truth and Reconciliation Commission and the Pursuit of "Social Truth". The Case of Kathorus', in D. Posel and G. Simpson, eds., *Commissioning the Past: Understanding South Africa's Truth and Reconciliation Commission*. Johannesburg: Witwatersrand University Press

Boraine, A. (2000). *A Country Unmasked: Inside South Africa's Truth and Reconciliation Commission*. Oxford: Oxford University Press

Bornat, Joanna, Prue Chamberlayne, and Tom Wengraf, eds., (2000). *The Turn to Biographical Methods in Social Science: Comparative Issues and Examples*. London: Routledge

Borneman, J. (1991) *After the Wall: East Meets West in the New Berlin*. New York: Basic Books

Braungart, M. and R. Braungart (1986). 'Life-course and Generational Politics', *Annual Review of Sociology* 12: 205–231

Brison, S. (2002). *Aftermath: Violence and the Remaking of a Self.* Princeton, NJ: Princeton University Press

Brossat, A., S. Combe, J.-Y. Potel, and J.-C. Szurek (1990). *À l'est la mémoire retrouvée.* Paris: Editions la Découverte

Bruner, Jerome (1987). 'Life as Narrative', *Social Research* 54/1: 12–32

Bundy, C. (2000). 'The Beast of the Past: History and the TRC', in W. James and L. Van De Vijver, eds., *After the TRC: Reflections on Truth and Reconciliation in South Africa.* Cape Town: David Philip Publishers

Butler, R. N. (1963). 'Recall and Retrospection', *Journal of the American Geriatrics Society* 11, 523–529

Camus, A. (1960). *Resistance, Rebellion and Death.* New York: Modern Library

Cavell, S. (1997). 'Comments on Veena Das's Essay "Language and Body: Transactions in the Construction of Pain"', in A. Kleinman, V. Das, and M. Lock, eds., *Social Suffering.* London: University of California Press

Chang, N. (2002). *Silencing Political Dissent: How post-September 11 Anti-terrorism Measures Threaten our Civil Liberties.* New York: Seven Stories Press

Charen, M. (1991). 'They Can Protest but they Aren't Patriotic', *Gazette Telegraph.* Colorado Springs, CO, February 6: B11

Charles, R. (1972). 'America, the Beautiful', on album 'A Message from the People', http://www.sing365.com/music/lyric.nsf/America-The-Beautiful-lyrics-Ray-Charles/C12412B331C5297E48256C24000E44FD, accessed 12 June 2006

(2006). http://www.cnn.com/2004/SHOWBIZ/Music/06/10/obit.charles, accessed 12 June 2006

Cherry, J. (2000). 'Historical Truth: Something to Fight for', in C. Villa-Vicencio and W. Verwoerd, eds., *Looking Back, Reaching Forward: Reflections on the Truth and Reconciliation Commission of South Africa.* London: Zed Books

Chilton, P. A. and C. Schaffner (2002). *Politics as Text and Talk: Analytic Approaches to Political Discourse.* Philadelphia: John Benjamins Publishing Co.

Chomsky, N. (2002) 'September 11th and the Aftermath: Where is the World Heading?: November 3, 2001', in K. V. Heuvel, ed., *A Just Response: The Nation on Terrorism, Democracy and September 11, 2001.* New York: Thunder's Mouth Press

Christie, K. (2000). *The South African Truth Commission.* London: Palgrave

Cockburn, A. and J. St Clair (2001). 'Counterpunch', November 12, http://www.bushwatch.com/patriotism.htm, accessed 12 June 2006

Collins, J. and R. Glover, eds., (2002). *Collateral Language: A User's Guide to America's New War*. New York: New York University Press

Colvin, C. (2002). 'Limiting Memory: The Roots and Routes of Storytelling in Post-apartheid, Post-TRC South Africa', in Proceedings of the Conference on Narrative, Trauma and Memory: Working through the SA Armed Conflicts of the Twentieth Century. University of Cape Town, South Africa

Connerton, P. (1989). *How Societies Remember*. Cambridge: Cambridge University Press

Craige, B. J. (1996). *American Patriotism in a Global Society*. Albany, NY: State University of New York Press

Das, V. (1990). 'Our Work to Cry: Your Work to Listen', in V. Das, ed., *Mirrors of Violence: Communities, Riots and Survivors in South Asia*. Oxford: Oxford University Press

(1997). 'Language and the Body: Transactions in the Construction of Pain', in A. Kleinman, V. Das, and M. Lock, eds., *Social Suffering*. London: University of California Press

deGruchy, J. (2000). 'The TRC and the Building of a Moral Culture', in W. James and L. Van De Vijver, eds., (2000). *After the TRC: Reflections on Truth and Reconciliation in South Africa*. Cape Town: David Philip Publishers

Denzin, N. (1989). *Interpretive Biography*. London: Sage

Dienstag, J. F. (1997). *'Dancing in Chains': Narrative and Memory in Political Theory*. Stanford, CA: Stanford University Press

Du Toit, A. (2000). 'Truth as Acknowledgement and Justice as Recognition', in R. Rotberg and D. Thompson, eds., *Truth v. Justice: The Morality of Truth Commissions*. Princeton, NJ: Princeton University Press

East European Reporter (1989/90). 4/1

Falk, R. (2002). 'A Just Response: September 19, 2001', in K. V. Heuvel, ed., *A Just Response: The Nation on Terrorism, Democracy and September 11, 2001*. New York: Thunder's Mouth Press

(2003). *The Great Terror War*. New York: Olive Branch Press

Flones, A. (2001). 'Empty Patriotism: Ideologues at the Gate', http://www.bushwatch.com/patriotism.htm accessed, accessed 12 June 2006

Freeman, M. (2003). 'Too Late: The Temporality of Memory and the Challenge of Moral Life', *Journal für Psychologie* 11/1: 54–74

Fukuyama, F. (1992). *The End of History and the Last Man*. New York: Free Press

Garton Ash, T. (1997). *The File: A Personal History*. London: HarperCollins

Gitlin, T. (2003). 'Varieties of Patriotic Experience', in George Packer, ed., *The Fight is for Democracy: Winning the War of Ideas in America and the World*. New York: Perennial

Gobodo-Madikizela, P. (2003). *A Human Being Died that Night*. Boston: Houghton Mifflin

Greenspan, H. (1998). *On Listening to Holocaust Survivors: Recounting and Life History*. London: Praeger

Hammersley, M. (1992). 'On Feminist Methodology', *Sociology* 26/2: 187–206

Harris, S. (2004). *The End of Faith*. New York: W. W. Norton

Hayner, Priscilla (2001). *Unspeakable Truths: Confronting State Terror and Atrocity*. London: Routledge

Hendrix, J. (2006). http://www.popstarsplus.com/music_jimihendrix.htm, accessed 18 July 2006

Henri, Y. (2003) 'Reconciling Reconciliation: A Personal and Public Journey of Testifying before the South African Truth and Reconciliation Commission', in P. Gready, ed., *Political Transition: Politics and Cultures*. London: Pluto Press

Hershberg, E. and K. Moore (2002). 'Introduction: Place, Perspective and Power – Interpreting September 11', in E. Hershberg and K. Moore, eds., *Critical Views of September 11: Analyses from Around the World*. New York: The New Press

Heuvel, K. V., ed., (2002). *A Just Response: The Nation on Terrorism, Democracy and September 11, 2001*. New York: Thunder's Mouth Press

Hofmeyr, I. (1993). *'We Spend our Years as a Tale that is Told': Oral Historical Narrative in a South African Chiefdom*. Portsmouth, NH: Heinemann

Horgan, J. (1997). *The End of Science*. Boston: Little Brown

Hughes, L. (1938) 'Let America Be America Again' International Worker Order Pamphlet A New Song.

Huntingdon, S. (2004). *Who are We? America's Great Debate*. London: Free Press

Ignatieff, M. (1994). *Blood and Belonging*. London: Vintage

James, W. and L.Van De Vijver, eds., (2000). *After the TRC: Reflections on Truth and Reconciliation in South Africa*. Cape Town: David Philip Publishers

Jarausch, K., H. Seeba, and D. Conradt (1997). 'The Presence of the Past: Culture, Opinion, and Identity in Germany', in Konrad Jarausch, ed., *After Unity: Reconfiguring German Identities*. Oxford: Berghahn

Johnson, C. (2000). *Blowback: The Costs and Consequences of American Empire*. New York: Henry Holt & Co.

Kamali, M. (2001). 'Accountability for Human Rights Violations: A Comparison of Transitional Justice in East Germany and South Africa', *Columbia Journal of Transnational Law* 40/1: 89–142

Keegan, T. (1988). *Facing the Storm: Portraits of Black Lives in Rural South Africa*. Cape Town: David Philip Publishers

Kelman, H. (1997). 'Nationalism, Patriotism, and National Identity: Social–psychological Dimensions', in E. Staub and D. Bar Tal, eds., *Patriotism in the Life of Individuals and Nations.* Chicago: Nelson Hall

Kenniston, K. (1968). *Young Radicals.* New York: Harcourt Brace

Kingsolver, B. (2001) 'And our Flag was still there', http://www.bushwatch.com/patriotism.htm, accessed 12 June 2006

Langellier, K. M. (2001). "You're Marked": Breast Cancer, Tattoo and the Narrative Performance of Identity', in J. Brockmeier and D. Carbaugh, eds., *Narrative and Identity: Studies in Autobiography, Self, and Culture.* Amsterdam and Philadelphia: John Benjamins Publishing Co.

Lather, Patti (1988). 'Feminist Perspectives on Empowering Research Methodologies', *Women's Studies International Forum* 11: 569–581

Laub, D. (1992). 'Bearing Witness or the Vicissitudes of Listening', in S. Felman and D. Laub, eds., *Testimony: Crises of Witnessing in Literature, Psychoanalysis and History.* New York: Routledge

Lieven, A. (2004). *America Right or Wrong: An Anatomy of American Nationalism.* London: Harper Perennial

Maier, C. (2000). 'Doing History, Doing Justice: The Narrative of the Historian and of the Truth Commission', in R. Rotberg and D. Thompson, eds., *Truth v. Justice: The Morality of Truth Commissions.* Princeton, NJ: Princeton University Press

Mamdani, M. (2000). 'A Diminished Truth', in W. James and L. Van De Vijver, eds., *After the TRC: Reflections on Truth and Reconciliation in South Africa.* Cape Town: David Philip Publishers

Mannheim, K. (1952) 'The Problem of Generations', in P. Kecskemet, ed., *Essays on the Sociology of Knowledge.* London: Routledge & Kegan Paul

Massig, M. (2002). 'October 17, 2001', in K. V. Heuvel, ed., *A Just Response: The Nation on Terrorism, Democracy and September 11, 2001.* New York: Thunder's Mouth Press

McAdams, A. J. (2001) *Judging the Past in Unified Germany.* Cambridge: Cambridge University Press

McKibben, B. (2003). *The End of Nature.* London: Bloomsbury

Meredith, M. (1999). *Coming to Terms: South Africa's Search for Truth.* New York: Public Affairs

Miliband, R. (1979). 'John Saville: A Presentation', in D. E. Martin and D. Rubenstein, eds., *Ideology and the Labour Movement: Essays Presented to John Saville.* London: Croom Helm

Mills, C. W. (1959). *The Sociological Imagination.* New York: Grove Press

Monteath, P. (1997). 'Jena and the End of History', in R. Alter and P. Monteath, eds., *Rewriting the German Past: History and Identity in the New Germany*. New Jersey: Humanities Press

Murrow, E. (1953). *Ford Fiftieth Anniversary Show*, CBS and NBC, June

Myerhoff, B. (1982). 'Life History among the Elderly: Performance, Visibility, and Re-membering', in J. Ruby, ed., *A Crack in the Mirror: Reflexive Perspectives in Anthropology*. Philadelphia: University of Pennsylvania Press

Naimark, N. (1992). ' "Ich will hier raus": Emigration and the Collapse of the German Democratic Republic', in I. Banac, ed., *Eastern Europe in Revolution*. Ithaca, NY: Cornell University Press

Ndebele, N. (1998). 'Memory, Metaphor, and the Triumph of Narrative', in S. Nuttall and C. Coetzee, eds., *Negotiating the Past: The Making of Memory in South Africa*. Cape Town: Oxford University Press

Nuttall, S. and C. Coetzee, eds., (1998). *Negotiating the Past: The Making of Memory in South Africa*. Cape Town: Oxford University Press

Nyatsumba, K. (2000). 'Neither Dull nor Tiresome', in W. James and L. Van De Vijver, eds., *After the TRC: Reflections on Truth and Reconciliation in South Africa*. Cape Town: David Philip Publishers

Osiel, M. (1997). *Mass Atrocity, Collective Memory and the Law*. New Brunswick, NJ: Transaction Publishers

Ostow, Robin (1993). 'Restructuring Our Lives: National Unification and German Biographies', *Oral History Review* 21/2: 1–8

Packer, G., ed., (2003). *The Fight is for Democracy: Winning the War of Ideas in America and the World*. New York: Perennial

Parker, T. (1996). *Studs Terkel: A Life in Words*. London: HarperCollins

Philipsen, D. (1993). *We were the People: Voices from East Germany's Revolutionary Autumn of 1989*. Durham, NC: Duke University Press

Plummer, K. (2001). *Documents of Life 2: An Invitation to a Critical Humanism*. London: Sage

Polletta, F. (2002). 'Plotting Protest: Mobilizing Stories in the 1960 Student Sit-ins', in J. Davis, ed., *Stories of Change: Narrative and Social Movements*. Albany, NY: SUNY Press

  (2006). *It was Like a Fever: Storytelling in Protest and Politics*. Chicago: University of Chicago Press

Posel, D. (2002). 'The TRC Report: What Kind of History? What Kind of Truth?', in D. Posel and G. Simpson, eds., *Commissioning the Past: Understanding South Africa's Truth and Reconciliation Commission*. Johannesburg: Witwatersrand University Press

Prigogine, I. (1997). *The End of Certainty*. New York: Free Press

Reich, J. (1990). 'Reflections on Becoming an East German Dissident, on Losing the Wall and a Country', in G. Prins, ed., *Spring in Winter: The 1989 Revolutions*. Manchester: Manchester University Press

Renan, E. (1882/1990) 'What is a Nation?', in H. K. Bhabha, ed., *Nation and Narration*. London: Routledge

Rice, J. S. (2002). ' "Getting our Histories Straight": Culture, Narrative, and Identity in the Self-help Movement', in J. Davis, ed., *Stories of Change: Narrative and Social Movements*. Albany, NY: SUNY Press

Ricoeur, P. (1984, 1985, 1988). *Time and Narrative*, 1–3. Chicago: University of Chicago Press

Rieder, J. (2003). 'Into the Unknown: Unity and Conflict after September 11, 2001', in J. Rieder and S. Steinlight, eds., *The Fractious Nation? Unity and Division in Contemporary American Life*. Berkeley: University of California Press

Rieder, J. and S. Steinlight, eds., (2003). *The Fractious Nation? Unity and Division in Contemporary American Life*. Berkeley: University of California Press

Riessman, C. (2004). 'Accidental Cases: Extending the Concept of Positioning in Narrative Studies', in M. Bamberg and M. Andrews, eds., *Considering Counter-narratives: Narrating, Resisting, Making Sense*. Amsterdam: John Benjamins Publishing Co.

(2005). 'Exporting Ethics: A Narrative about Narrative Research in South India', *Health* 9/4: 473–490

Rokeach, M. (1960). *The Open and Closed Mind*. New York: Basic Books

Rosenberg, T. (1999a). 'Afterword', in M. Meredith, *Coming to Terms: South Africa's Search for Truth*. New York: Public Affairs

(1999b). 'Foreword', in M. Meredith, *Coming to Terms: South Africa's Search for Truth*. New York: Public Affairs.

Ross, F. (2003). *Bearing Witness: Women and the Truth and Reconciliation Commission in South Africa*. London: Pluto Press

Rotberg, R. and D. Thompson, eds., (2000). *Truth v. Justice: The Morality of Truth Commissions*. Princeton, NJ: Princeton University Press

Sachs, A. (2000). 'His Name was Henry', in W. James and L. Van De Vijver, eds., *After the TRC: Reflections on Truth and Reconciliation in South Africa*. Cape Town: David Philip Publishers

Scheer, R. (2001). 'Commentary: A True Patriot Can Pose Hard Questions', October 23, http://www.bushwatch.com/patriotism.htm, accessed 12 June 2006

Scheub, H. (1996). *The Tongue is Fire: South African Storytellers and Apartheid*. Madison, WI: University of Wisconsin Press

(1998). *Story*. Madison, WI: University of Wisconsin Press

Shriver, D. (1995). *An Ethic for Enemies: Forgiveness in Politics*. Oxford: Oxford University Press

Staub, E. (1997). 'Blind versus Constructive Patriotism: Moving from Embeddedness in the Group to Critical Loyalty and Action', in E. Staub and D. Bar Tal, eds., *Patriotism in the Life of Individuals and Nations*. Chicago: Nelson Hall

Stoddard, E. W. and G. H. Cornwell (2002). 'Unity', in J. Collins and R. Glover, eds., *Collateral Language: A User's Guide to America's New War*. New York: New York University Press

Szymborska, W. (1996). 'The Poet and the World', Nobel Lecture, 7 December 1996, http://nobelprize.org/literature/laureates/1996/szymborska-lecture.html, accessed 13 June 2005

Tarifa, F. and J. Weinstein (1995/1996). 'Overcoming the Past: De-communization and Reconstruction of Post-Communist Societies', *Studies in Comparative International Development* 30/4: 63–77

Tebbit, N. (2005). ' "Cricket Test could have Stopped Bombings" ', 19 August, ePolitix.com http://www.epolitix.com/EN/News/200508/072d2cc0-3f3a-494f-8590-3e51127e853b.htm, accessed 20 July 2006

Thompson, D. (1996). *The End of Time*. London: Sinclair-Stevenson

Thompson, E. P. (1963). *The Making of the English Working Class*. London: Victor Gollancz

Thompson, P. (1978). *The Voice of the Past: Oral History*. Oxford: Oxford University Press

(1990). 'News from Abroad: Europe', *Oral History* 18/1: 18–20

Thornton, P. M. and T. F. Thornton (2002). 'Blowback', in J. Collins and R. Glover, eds., *Collateral Language: A User's Guide to America's New War*. New York: New York University Press

Tilly, C. (2002). *Stories, Identities and Political Change*. New York: Rowman & Littlefield

Torpey, J. (1995). *Intellectuals, Socialism and Dissent: East German Opposition and its Legacy*. Minneapolis, MN: University of Minnesota Press

Truth and Reconciliation Commission (1998). *Truth and Reconciliation Commission of South Africa Report*, 5. Cape Town: Truth and Reconciliation Commission

Tutu, Desmond (1998). 'Chairperson's Foreword', in *Truth and Reconciliation Commission of South Africa Report*, 5. Cape Town: Truth and Reconciliation Commission

(1999). *No Future without Forgiveness*. London: Rider

Villa-Vicencio, C. and W. Verwoerd, eds., (2000). *Looking Back, Reaching Forward: Reflections on the Truth and Reconciliation Commission of South Africa*. London: Zed Books

Walkerdine, V. (2003). 'Video Diaries as Data and as Television', CNR Narrative Workshop VI: Visual Narratives, King's College Cambridge

Walzer, M. (1987). *Interpretation and Social Criticism*. Cambridge, MA: Harvard University Press

Wang, Q. and J. Brockmeir (2002). 'Autobiographical Remembering as Cultural Practice: Understanding the Interplay between Memory, Self and Culture', *Culture and Psychology* 8/1: 45–64

Washington Post (2006). http://www.washingtonpost.com/wp-dyn/content/article/2006/06/09/AR2006060901547_pf.html, accessed 20 June 2006

Weschler, L. (1990). *A Miracle, a Universe: Settling Accounts with Torturers*. New York: Pantheon

Whitebrook, M. (2001). *Identity, Narrative and Politics*. London: Routledge

Williams, P.J. (2002). 'Pax Americana: September 12, 2001', in K. V. Heuvel, ed., *A Just Response: The Nation on Terrorism, Democracy and September 11, 2001*. New York: Thunder's Mouth Press

Willis, E. (2002). 'Dreaming of War: September 26, 2001', in K. V. Heuvel, ed., *A Just Response: The Nation on Terrorism, Democracy and September 11, 2001*. New York: Thunder's Mouth Press

Wilson, R. (1996). 'The Sizwe Will not Go Away: The Truth and Reconciliation Commission, Human Rights and Nation-building in South Africa', *African Studies* 55/2: 1–20

Wolf, C. (1997). *Parting from Phantoms: Selected Writings, 1990–1994*. Chicago: University of Chicago Press

Woods, R. (1986). *Opposition in the GDR under Honecker 1971–85*. New York: St Martin's Press

Yevtushenko, Y. (2002) 'Babi Yar in Manhattan: September 26, 2001', in K. V. Heuvel, ed., *A Just Response: The Nation on Terrorism, Democracy and September 11, 2001*. New York: Thunder's Mouth Press

Yoder, J. (1999). 'Truth without Reconciliation: An Appraisal of the Enquete Commission on the SED Dictatorship in Germany', *German Politics* 8/3: 59–80

Yuval-Davis, N. (2006). 'Belonging and the Politics of Belonging', *Patterns of Prejudice* 40/3: 196–213

Index